Historically Black Colleges and Universities

CONTEMPORARY EDUCATION ISSUES

Historically Black Colleges and Universities

❧ A REFERENCE HANDBOOK

Cynthia L. Jackson
and Eleanor F. Nunn

A B C ⬤ C L I O

Santa Barbara, California • Denver, Colorado • Oxford, England

Library of Congress Cataloging-in-Publication Data

Jackson, Cynthia L.
  Historically black colleges and universities: a reference handbook /
Cynthia L. Jackson and Eleanor F. Nunn.
          p. c. — (Contemporary education issues)
Includes index.
    ISBN 1-85109-422-9 (harcover: alk. paper) ISBN 1-85109-427-X (e-book)
1. African American universities and colleges—Handbooks, manuals, etc.
2. African American universities and colleges—History   I. Nunn, Eleanor F.
II. Title. III. Series.
  LC2781.J26 2003
  378.73'08996073—dc22

                                                    2003016814

07   06   05   04   03   10   9   8   7   6   5   4   3   2   1

ABC-CLIO, Inc.
130 Cremona Drive, P.O. Box 1911
Santa Barbara, California 93116-1911

This book is printed on acid-free paper.
Manufactured in the United States of America

⊷ Contents

❧ Series Editor's Preface

The Contemporary Education Issues series is dedicated to providing readers with an up-to-date exploration of the central issues in education today. Books in the series will examine such controversial topics as home schooling, charter schools, privatization of public schools, Native American education, African American education, literacy, curriculum development, and many others. The series is national in scope and is intended to encourage research by anyone interested in the field.

Because education is undergoing radical if not revolutionary change, the series is particularly concerned with how contemporary controversies in education affect both the organization of schools and the content and delivery of curriculum. Authors will endeavor to provide a balanced understanding of the issues and their effects on teachers, students, parents, administrators, and policymakers. The aim of the Contemporary Education Issues series is to publish excellent research on today's educational concerns by some of the finest scholar/practitioners in the field while pointing to new directions. The series promises to offer important analyses of some of the most controversial issues facing society today.

Danny Weil

❧ Preface

This book is unlike other sources that discuss historically black colleges and universities—HBCUs—for four reasons. First, it focuses specifically on HBCUs, whether public or private, two-year or four-year, and graduate and professional levels. Second, it provides information on the contemporary circumstances of HBCUs and their concerns in the twenty-first century. Third, it describes how HBCUs influence and shape the personal and professional lives of black individuals and black communities. Finally, as a reference handbook it is the only repository on essential resources about HBCUs for enlightenment and study.

The book was written for those interested in learning about HBCUs and, equally important, for those conducting research on HBCUs. A broad range of HBCU attributes is examined. The book is designed to provide readers and researchers with an understanding of the history of HBCUs with a specific focus on their continued need, potential, role, and circumstances in twenty-first-century U.S. higher education. Readers and researchers will find an examination of how HBCUs continue to provide avenues of higher education for blacks. Most important, readers and researchers will realize the extent of social, legal, political, and economic issues and events concerning the existence of HBCUs. Suggestions of further research on HBCUs also are included for those inclined to undertake the task.

It is not possible to give a detailed history of each of the 103 HBCUs given the focused purpose of the book. Where appropriate, specific HBCUs are highlighted as examples to enhance discussions and analyses. As graduates of HBCUs who have worked with HBCUs, we endeavor to provide a full picture of HBCUs. As such we present the strengths of HBCUs as well as their external and internal challenges.

The discussions and analyses in the book are based on research about HBCUs, governmental and other organizational reports and data, conversations with knowledgeable individuals, and our own experiential insights from our work with HBCUs. All of the references are available to the general public.

Chapter 1 gives an overview of HBCUs for the past 164 years, with special attention given to the decades from 1930 to the present. The roles these institutions play in the educational, intellectual, political, social, and economic progress of African Americans and, in turn, the nation and the world, are examined. HBCU leadership and the unique external and internal forces that can enhance and/or hinder the leaders and the institutions are also examined. Chapter 2 provides a chronology of historical and current events that necessitate HBCUs in the advancement of black people. The historical and legal implications of *United States v. Fordice* and other important legal decisions related to HBCUs are detailed in Chapter 3. Chapter 4 explains the role of philanthropy and government relations in perpetuating HBCUs. A collaborative model among HBCUs, state government, and a private corporation is described in Chapter 5. Chapter 6 outlines a suggested research agenda, and Chapter 7 contains a listing of the organizations, associations, and governmental and nongovernmental agencies that work specifically with HBCUs as well as accessible and creditable print resources that readers can access for more information. The appendixes contain listings of HBCUs and of their graduates.

The book is strengthened by the contributions of specific colleagues who willingly shared information and ideas with us. Patrick C. Coggins, the Jessie Ball duPont Endowed Chair Professor at Stetson University (Fla.), provided information from studies his research team conducted on HBCUs. Evelyn C. J. Carroll, retired chair of the Division of Education and the Department of Education at Spelman College (Ga.), contributed historical research on the relationship between HBCUs and philanthropic organizations. Norman Harris and Sylvia Hill both serve on the Union Institute and University (Ohio) Graduate College faculty as well as that of the former Clark Atlanta University (Ga.) and University of the District of Columbia, respectively. They contributed to the research questions in Chapter 6. The views expressed in this book are our own and do not necessarily reflect those of the organizations with which we are employed or affiliated.

Cynthia L. Jackson and Eleanor F. Nunn

Chapter One

⚬ Introduction

In *Back of the Big House: The Architecture of Plantation Slavery,* John Michael Vlach (1993) describes the ways black slaves saw and used opportunities to establish their influence on the plantation and to create a sense of belonging given their externally imposed status and condition. He describes how the slaves created a landscape within the larger landscape of the slave owner. Vlach writes:

> The creation of a slaves' landscape was a reactive expression, a response to the plans enacted by white landowners. To make their dominance over both nature and other men, planters acquired acreage, set out the boundaries of their holdings, had their fields cleared, selected building sites, and supervised the construction of dwellings and other structures. The design of a plantation estate was an expression of the owner's tastes, values and attributes. . . . The achievements of the planter class provided the social context that slaves would manipulate for their own ends. Ultimately, the slaveholders' world would become the raw material with which slaves would attempt to satisfy some of their own social aspirations. (3)

Vlach's description of, and explanation for, the reasons behind the "slaves' landscape" in relation to the "white landowners" plantation are similar to the historical and, in may ways, to the contemporary conditions and circumstances of historically black colleges and universities (HBCUs). HBCUs are a part of the higher education landscape of the United States. Their agendas are the hidden dimension of higher education.

"Slave owners set up the contexts of servitude, but they did not control those contexts absolutely" (Vlach 1993, 1). Arthur E. Thomas, former president of Central State University in Ohio, provides a similar explanation of the context for HBCUs. He states, "HBCUs were initially built not only to provide access to black youngsters through the minds of black people. In the minds of white people, they were built to contain and segregate black people" (Thomas and Green 2001, 139).

1

Twenty-four years before the U.S. Civil War began, the first institution of higher learning for people of African ancestry in the United States was established. The year was 1837. Richard Humphreys, a Quaker in Philadelphia, observed throughout his life the indignity afforded to blacks. In his will he bequeathed a portion of his estate for the education of blacks. In 1842 the school was named the Institute for Colored Youth and moved from its original site. Having undergone several name changes throughout its history, in the early 1980s the school's name was changed to Cheyney University of Pennsylvania and it became part of the State System of Higher Education of Pennsylvania. Its mission was and remains "to prepare and fit and qualify [blacks] to act as teachers." The school began as the equivalent of an elementary school and high school. Its curriculum was trades and agriculture. In 1931 it offered its first baccalaureate degree. Although continuing to adhere to its original mission of teacher training, it has expanded its offerings.

Wilberforce University in Ohio and Lincoln University in Pennsylvania are the first two black higher education institutions that offered postsecondary-level instruction and baccalaureate degrees. Both schools remain on their original sites.

Richard Allen, a free black, founded the African Methodist Episcopal (AME) Church in 1799. In 1843 the AME Church founded the Ohio African University. In 1856 the institution was renamed Wilberforce University after William Wilberforce, an abolitionist. With the renaming the institution was chartered to offer a liberal arts education for blacks. In 1857 the school awarded its first baccalaureate degree, making it the first historically black university.

Lincoln University in Pennsylvania has its origins in the Presbyterian Church. Lincoln was established in 1854 as an institution offering postsecondary instruction in the arts and sciences. It awarded its first baccalaureate degree in 1868. In 1873 the university accepted ten students from Liberia. This made Lincoln University the first postsecondary institution in the United States to enroll Africans. Until the late 1960s, it enrolled only males.

The history of the first three black institutions of higher learning in the United States is representative, in many ways, of the history of all historically black colleges and universities. All HBCUs were born out of the exclusionary and discriminatory laws and practices of the dominant white society. Free and or freed blacks, abolitionists, the Freedmen's Bureau, and the Morrill Acts contributed to the establishment of HBCUs. Many began as the equivalent of elementary and high schools and evolved into postsecondary institutions. Their names and curricula changed to reflect their evolutions. Several HBCUs began as institutions for training blacks in trades and agriculture and eventually became institutions that educated and trained black intellectuals, scholars, and professionals. Many do not currently operate on their original sites.

HBCUs are not academic monoliths. Their beginnings, missions, affiliations, and locations are factors that give each their own unique character. Yet, as pointed out by Jackson (2001), they are committed to the education, training, and development of blacks. They provide a nurturing, supportive, affirming environment for aspiring black youth. For many young blacks HBCUs offer the only time in their lives when they can experience an environment free of racial discrimination and tension. HBCUs introduce a large number of black men and women into the nation's mainstream and are the educational institutions that most contributed to the creation and continued expansion of a black middle class in the United States. HBCUs are authentic custodians of the archives of black history and life. They are the political and social centers for black communities.

In this chapter, four aspects of HBCUs are described. First, the history of HBCUs is reviewed in context to social and political events in the United States. Second, the mission and role of HBCUs in higher education in the United States are explained. Third, the status of HBCUs is discussed. This discussion includes leadership, admissions and retention, facilities, and fiscal concerns, to name a few. Finally, the need for HBCUs in the twenty-first century is examined.

WHO ARE THE HBCUS?

For over 160 years, historically black colleges and universities have served as the educational, intellectual, political, cultural, and social centers of African American communities in the United States, especially in the Southeast. There are several definitions of HBCUs. In this book, HBCUs are private and public two-year, four-year, graduate, and professional degree institutions that were established specifically for the postsecondary education of people of African ancestry in the United States.

Of the 103 HBCUs currently operating, approximately 75 percent were established between 1865 and 1899, and over 90 percent are located in the South. HBCUs began as a response to two realities in the United States. Both realities are steeped in the laws, traditions, and practices of the institution of racism in the United States. In the South, primarily, as well as in other parts of the United States, state laws prohibited blacks from attending established historically white colleges and universities. In the North, primarily, as well as in other parts of the United States, blacks were denied access to white institutions due to customs, practices, and traditions (Jackson 2001).

The Carnegie Foundation for the Advancement of Teaching has developed a classification system for all colleges and universities in the United States. This widely accepted system has nine classifications of postsecondary institutions. The institutions are "degree-granting and accredited by an agency recognized by the U.S. Secretary of Education" (2000, 1). The classification placements from the 2000 report are based on institutional data from 1995–1996 through 1997–1998.

The nine categories and their definitions on pages 1 and 2 of the Carnegie Classification 2000 report follow. The number in parentheses after the definition represents the number of HBCUs that are in that classification according to Carnegie.

Doctoral/Research Universities—Extensive: These institutions typically offer a wide range of baccalaureate programs, and they are committed to graduate education through the doctorate. During the period studied, they awarded fifty or more doctoral degrees per year across at least fifteen disciplines. (1)

Doctoral/Research Universities—Intensive: These institutions typically offer a wide range of baccalaureate programs, and they are committed to graduate education through the doctorate. During the period studied, they awarded at least ten doctoral degrees per year across three or more disciplines, or at least twenty doctoral degrees per year overall. (6)

Master's Colleges and Universities I: These institutions typically offer a wide range of baccalaureate programs, and they are committed to graduate education through the master's degree. During the period studied, they awarded forty or more master's degrees per year across three or more disciplines. (25)

Master's Colleges and Universities II: These institutions typically offer a wide range of baccalaureate programs, and they are committed to graduate education through the master's degree. During the period studied, they awarded twenty or more master's degrees per year. (4)

Baccalaureate Colleges—Liberal Arts: These institutions are primarily undergraduate colleges with major emphasis on baccalaureate programs. During the period studied, they awarded at least half of their baccalaureate degrees in liberal arts fields. (14)

Baccalaureate Colleges—General: These institutions are primarily undergraduate colleges with major emphasis on baccalaureate programs. During the period studied, they awarded less than half of their baccalaureate degrees in liberal arts fields. (33)

Baccalaureate/Associate's Colleges: These institutions are undergraduate colleges where the majority of conferrals are below the baccalaureate level (associate's degrees and certificates). During the period studied, bachelor's degrees accounted for at least 10 percent of undergraduate awards. (1)

Associate's Colleges: These institutions offer associate's degrees and certificate programs but, with few exceptions, award no baccalaureate degrees. This group includes institutions where, during the period studied, bachelor's degrees represented less than 10 percent of all undergraduate awards. (10)

Specialization Institutions (There are nine categories for these institutions. Only three of the categories apply to HBCUs.)

Theological seminaries and other specialized faith-related institutions: These institutions primarily offer religious instruction or train members of the clergy. (2)

Medical schools and medical centers: These institutions award most of their professional degrees in medicine. In some instances, they include other health profession programs, such as dentistry, pharmacy, or nursing. (2)

Teachers colleges: These institutions award most of their bachelor's or graduate degrees in education or education-related fields. (1)

Although the majority of HBCUs meet the Carnegie classification requirements, they might not benefit from the classifications. For example, in 2001, as part of the proposed settlement for the *United States v. Fordice* case (discussed in Chapter 3), Jackson State University would be "referred to as a 'comprehensive' university . . . but the proposal specifies that classifying Jackson State as such would not signify any change in the institution's mission, nor would it entitle the university to participate in the programs or receive resources often provided to institutions with that label" (Hebel 2001, on-line).

Approximately 300,000 students are currently enrolled in HBCUs. The racial or ethnic breakdown is 82 percent black, 13 percent white non-Hispanic, 2 percent Hispanic, 0.8 percent Asian or Pacific Islander, 0.2 percent American Indian/Alaskan Native, and 2 percent nonresident alien.

Historically black colleges and universities entered the twenty-first century with an earned legacy of accomplishments and predetermined challenges. For over 100 years HBCUs were the avenue to education access and social and economic advancement for blacks. Following is a history of the four types of HBCUs.

HISTORY OF PRIVATE FOUR-YEAR, GRADUATE, AND PROFESSIONAL INSTITUTIONS

"It was clear that in order for the free slaves to be competitive workers after years of forced ignorance, some formal system of education was imperative. Both the North and South had needs for a low-paid, intellectually noncompetitive labor force" (Anderson 1994, 161). W. E. B. DuBois in 1903 attacked the vocational focus of early black education. He believed that only when the "exceptional men" or talented tenth of the black race received training in leadership through intellectual accruement and liberal arts would the black race be elevated. Manual vocations were not going to meet this end (Good and Teller 1973). It is from the vying issues of Northern and Southern whites' need for blacks in the labor force, and the education that blacks desired to advance black people, that private HBCUs were founded.

The majority of the private HBCUs were founded during the Reconstruction period following the Civil War. The institutions began mostly with church affiliations and Northern white philanthropists. Foremost among the white church groups was the American Missionary Association (Anderson 1994). The Freedmen's Bureau, created by the federal government in 1863, also aided in the development of black colleges.

The following is a brief profile by state of the fifty-three private four-year, graduate, and professional HBCUs.

Alabama

Concordia College was founded in 1922. It is the only institution of the Lutheran Church established for the education of blacks. The idea of the college was conceived by Rosa Young, a Lutheran convert who in 1916 wanted to provide religious education to black children.

Miles College was founded in 1905 by the Colored Methodist Episcopal Church, now known as the Christian Methodist Episcopal (CME) Church. It was named in honor of Bishop William H. Miles.

Oakwood College was established in 1896 as Oakwood Industrial College. It was a small school originally providing industrial and vocational training. It became a two-year junior college in 1917 and a senior college in 1943. After 1958 the school was owned and operated by the General Conference of Seventh-Day Adventists.

Selma University was established in 1878 by the Alabama State Baptist Convention. In 1881 it was incorporated by an act of the state legislature.

Stillman College was founded in 1876 by the Presbyterian Church as Tuscaloosa Institute to educate black men for the ministry. The school's name was changed to Stillman Institute in commemoration of its founder, Reverend Charles Allen Stillman, following his death. In 1899 the admission policy was broadened to allow males who were not interested in pursuing the ministry and female day students to enroll. In 1927 it became a junior college, and in 1951 it became a four-year liberal arts institution.

Talladega College was founded in 1876 by freedmen William Savery and Thomas Tarrant, and assisted by General Eager Swayne of the Freedmen's Bureau and the American Missionary Association. It was the first school in Alabama to admit students without regard to race.

Tuskegee University was founded in 1881 by Booker T. Washington. He received a $2,000 appropriation by the Alabama legislature to educate African American students. The school was originally called the Tuskegee Normal School for the Training of Black Teachers. The school experienced several name changes, and in 1985 it was named Tuskegee University. George Washington Carver conducted his renowned agricultural research from 1897 to 1943 at the Tuskegee Experiment Station, where he served as director.

Arkansas

Arkansas Baptist College was founded in 1884 and is affiliated with the American Baptist Churches. The original name was Minister's Institute. In 1885 it received its current name.

Philander Smith College was founded in 1877 by the Little Rock Annual Conference of the Methodist Episcopal Church. It was originally called Walden Seminary. The name was changed to commemorate a gift given by the widow of Philander Smith, a supporter of the work of the church in the South.

District of Columbia

Howard University was founded in 1867 as a private institution through an act of the U.S. Congress. Named after General Oliver Otis Howard, commissioner of the Freedmen's Bureau, the first name was Howard Normal and Theological Institute for the Education of Teachers and Preachers. Howard University is unique because is it the only HBCU established by the federal government. Alain Locke, the first black Rhodes scholar, taught at Howard from 1912 to 1953.

Florida

Bethune Cookman College was established in 1931 with the merger of Cookman Institute for Men, founded in 1872 by the Reverend D. S. B. Darnell, and Daytona Normal and Industrial Institute for Women, founded in 1904 by Dr. Mary McLeod Bethune.

Edward Waters College was founded in 1866 as Brown Theological Institute. It is the oldest HBCU in the state of Florida. It is affiliated with the African Methodist Episcopal (AME) Church.

Florida Memorial College was established in 1879. In 1941 Florida Baptist Institute and Florida Baptist Academy merged to form the Florida Normal and Industrial Memorial Institute. The institution became a four-year college in 1945. Its present name was adopted in 1963. It was relocated to Miami in 1968. "Lift Ev'ry Voice and Sing," known as the African American national anthem, was written at Florida Memorial by James Weldon Johnson.

Georgia

Atlanta University was founded in 1867 by the American Missionary Association with assistance from the Freedmen's Bureau. In 1929 the institution became what was then the only black graduate and professional institution.

Clark Atlanta University was founded in 1989 with the merger of Atlanta University and Clark College.

Clark College was established in 1869 in Clark Chapel, a Methodist Episcopal Church. It was the first Methodist-affiliated college to serve African Americans.

Interdenominational Theological Center was chartered in 1958 as a collaborative, ecumenical school for seminary studies. Six denominations comprise the school: Baptist, United Methodist, African Methodist, Christian Methodist, Presbyterian USA, and Church of God in Christ.

Morehouse College was founded in 1867 by the Reverend Edmund Turney, organizer of the National Theological Institute of Washington; Reverend William Jefferson White, a Baptist minister and cabinetmaker; and Richard C. Coulter, a former slave as the Augusta Institute. The institution was moved from Augusta to Atlanta and renamed the Atlanta Baptist Seminary. In recognition of the secretary of the American Baptist Home Mission Society, Henry Lyman Morehouse, the school was renamed Morehouse College.

Morehouse School of Medicine was established in 1975 with a federal grant to study the feasibility of developing a two-year medical program in concert with Morehouse College. In 1985 the school became an independent degree-granting institution and fully accredited to award medical degrees.

Morris Brown College was founded in 1881 by the AME Church. It is the only surviving college founded by blacks in Georgia.

Paine College was established in 1882 by the United Methodist Church and the CME Church.

Spelman College was founded in 1881. It is the nation's oldest undergraduate liberal arts college for black women. The campus was originally nine acres of drill ground and barracks used for federal troops after the Civil War.

Kentucky

Simmons University was established in 1873. The baccalaureate institution is owned and operated by the black Baptists of Kentucky.

Louisiana

Dillard University was founded in 1869 as Straight University. It is affiliated with the United Church of Christ and the United Methodist Church.

Xavier University of Louisiana, founded in 1915, is the only HBCU with a Roman Catholic affiliation. It was established as a college preparatory school, and in 1917 a teacher's school was added. In 1925 a college of arts and sciences and a college of pharmacy were established.

Mississippi

Rust College was established in 1866 by the Freedmen's Aid Society of the Methodist Episcopal Church and chartered in 1870 as Shaw University in honor of a financial gift from Reverend S. O. Shaw. In 1892 the name was changed to honor Richland S. Rust, secretary of the Freedmen's Aid Society. In 1920, Dr. M. S. Davage became the first black to serve as president.

Tougaloo College was established in 1869 by the American Missionary Association of New York. The association purchased 500 acres near Jackson, Mississippi, to establish a school for the training of young people regardless of religion and race.

North Carolina

Barber-Scotia College was founded as a women's college in 1867 by Reverend Luke Darland of the Presbyterian Church (USA) as Scotia College. Scotia College merged with Barber College in 1930, and its present name, Barber-Scotia, was adopted in 1932.

Bennett College, established in 1873, is a liberal arts institution affiliated with the United Methodist Church. Progressing from a teacher's school, it became a full-fledged college by 1889 and reorganized as a college for black women in 1926.

Johnson C. Smith University was founded in 1867 as an all-male seminary by Presbyterian ministers. Originally named Biddle Memorial Institute, it was rechartered as the Johnson C. Smith University in 1923 to honor the husband of Mrs. Jane Berry Smith of Pittsburgh, Pennsylvania, who endowed most of the buildings. Female students were admitted in 1932.

Livingston College was founded in 1879 by AME Zion clergy. Originally named Zion Wesley Institute, the name was changed by the North Carolina legislature to honor David Livingston, a British missionary active in Africa.

Saint Augustine's College was founded in 1867 as a coeducational liberal arts institution. It is affiliated with the Episcopal Church.

Shaw University, the oldest HBCU in the South, was founded in 1865 by a New England missionary. Elijah Shaw, a Massachusetts entrepreneur for whom the university is named, joined with others to contribute funds for the establishment of a school for instruction in the Bible of newly freed slaves to start churches and church organizations. In 1881 the school began operating the first four-year medical school in the United States. A law school was established in 1886, and a school of pharmacy followed in 1891. Graduates of Shaw University founded North Carolina Central, Elizabeth City State and Fayetteville State Universities, and North Carolina A&T State University, all public HBCUs. North Carolina A&T University began on Shaw's campus.

Ohio

Wilberforce University, founded in 1856 as the first coeducational college for blacks, was named for the abolitionist William Wilberforce. Due to the Civil War, the school was closed in 1862. However, efforts by the AME Church enabled Bishop Daniel A. Payne to purchase the property, incorporate it, and reopen it in 1863.

South Carolina

Allen University, the oldest HBCU in South Carolina, was founded in 1870 under the auspices of the AME Church.

Benedict College was founded in 1870 to train teachers and preachers. It was originally located in a former slave owner's dilapidated mansion.

Claflin College was founded in 1869 by two Methodist laymen from Massachusetts, William and Lee Claflin. It was initially funded in part by the Morrill Act of 1862.

Morris College was established in 1908 as a coeducational liberal arts institution. The college is owned and operated by the Baptist Educational and Missionary Convention of South Carolina.

Voorhees College was founded in 1897 as the Denmark Industrial School. Its founder, Elizabeth Wright, was a graduate of Tuskegee Institute and a protégé of Booker T. Washington. The school was renamed Voorhees Industrial School in 1902 in honor of Ralph Voorhees. Its present name was adopted in 1967.

Tennessee

Fisk University was incorporated in 1867 under the laws of the state of Tennessee to educate and train black men and women. It was first regionally accredited in 1930, making it the first HBCU to be accredited by the Southern Association for Colleges and Schools.

Knoxville College was founded in 1875 by the United Presbyterian Church of North America. It now has two campuses. In 1989 the Morristown College campus was purchased by Knoxville College.

Lane College was founded in 1882 by a former slave and the Colored Christian Methodist Episcopal Church, which is now the Christian Methodist Episcopal (CME) Church. It began as a high school and became Lane College, a four-year college, in 1895.

LeMoyne-Owen College was founded in 1871 by the American Missionary Association of the Congregational Church. Its original mission was the elementary education of "contraband" blacks and freedmen. Owen College was a junior college founded in 1954 by the Tennessee Baptist Missionary and Educational Convention. In 1968 LeMoyne College and Owen College merged.

Meharry Medical College was founded in 1876 as the Medical Department of Central Tennessee College. The mission was to educate health professionals to serve the black population. In 1915 Meharry became an independent medical college. One-third of the black physicians and dentists practicing in the United States graduated from Meharry.

Texas

Houston-Tillotson College was formed by a merger of two schools in 1952: Tillotson College, founded in 1875, and Samuel Houston College, founded in 1876. The United Methodist Church and the United Church of Christ support the college.

Jarvis Christian College, a coeducational institution, was founded in 1912. It is affiliated with the Christian Church, called Disciples of Christ.

Paul Quinn College was founded in a one-room building in 1872 by a group of African American Episcopal circuit riders. They wanted to provide a trade school to teach the newly freed slaves. In 1988 the college moved to the campus of Bishop College, which had closed earlier that year.

Southwestern Christian College was established in 1949 as a two-year institution. It became a four-year institution in 1984.

Texas College was established in 1894 as a liberal arts college. It is affiliated with the CME Church.

Wiley College was founded in 1873. It is the oldest HBCU chartered by the state of Texas. It is affiliated with the United Methodist Church.

Virginia

Hampton University, formerly known as Hampton Institute and Hampton College, was founded in 1868 by General Samuel Chapman Armstrong. Booker T. Washington graduated from Hampton Institute and modeled Tuskegee after Hampton.

St. Paul's College was founded in 1888 as St. Paul's Normal and Industrial School. In 1947 a four-year degree program began being offered, and in 1957 the name was changed to St. Paul's College.

Virginia Union University was founded in 1865 by the American Baptist Home Mission Society. It began as a branch of the National Theological Institute.

HISTORY OF PUBLIC FOUR-YEAR, GRADUATE, AND PROFESSIONAL INSTITUTIONS

Public education systems evolved slowly and experimentally, the result of constitutional and legislative provisions. There are two types of public postsecondary institutions. The distinction between the two types of public institutions is whether the institutions are land-grant.

In the case of public HBCUs, Roebuck and Murty note, "Public HBCUs were created by the southern state governments for three reasons: to get millions of dollars in federal funds for the development of white land-grant universities, to limit black education to vocational training, and to prevent blacks from attending white land-grant colleges" (1993, 27).

Black Land-Grant Institutions

Land-grant institutions were established on public land that was specifically designated for higher education. Typically, one land-grant institution was established in each state. However, some states have more than one. Land-grant institutions were to concentrate on teaching "such branches of learning as are related to agriculture and the mechanic arts, in such manner as the legislatures of the States may respectively prescribe, in order to promote the liberal and practical educations of the industrial classes in the several pursuits and professions in life" (Brown and Mayhew 1965, 23–24). In addition to the stated concentrations they offered liberal arts educations as well.

Several public HBCUs have their beginning with the Morrill Act of 1890. Passed by the U.S. Congress, the act required states with segregated higher education systems to establish land-grant institutions for blacks. The Morrill Act of 1862 had established land-grant schools for whites. Seventeen of the nineteen land-grant HBCUs were established as a result of the 1890 act, and they still exist. The 1890 Morrill Act required states that were determined to maintain racially segregated higher education systems to establish black land-grant institutions.

Some HBCUs were established prior to the 1890 act and later became land-grant schools. Four states established black land-grant schools through the funds of the Morrill Act of 1862. Walther (1994) gives the following accounting:

Mississippi—Alcorn University was established in 1871 using funds acquired through the 1862 Morrill Act. This was the first black land-grant institution in the United States. In 1874 its name was changed to Alcorn Agricultural and Mechanical College. It is now Alcorn State University.

Virginia—Hampton Normal and Agricultural Institute, later known as Hampton Institute and now Hampton University, was established in 1872 using one-half of Virginia's Morrill Act of 1862 funds. In 1920 the Virginia legislature transferred the funding from Hampton to Virginia Normal and Industrial College. Virginia N&I, founded in 1882, became Virginia's black land-grant college. It is now Virginia State University.

South Carolina—Using all of its funding from the 1862 Morrill Act, South Carolina assisted in establishing Claflin College in 1872. Claflin is a private college. When a white land-grant institution was established in 1879, Claflin received one-half of the funds. In 1896 a black public land-grant institution was established. It was named Colored Normal, Industrial, and Agricultural College of South Carolina, now named South Carolina State University. When the black public land-grant institution was established, funding was withdrawn from Claflin College.

Kentucky—Kentucky did not assign any of its land-grant funds to a black college until 1897, when it utilized funds from the 1862 Morrill Act to establish the Kentucky State Industrial School. It is now Kentucky State University.

Because of its academic philosophy and beginnings, Alabama's Tuskegee Normal and Industrial Institute, later named Tuskegee Institute and now Tuskegee University, is usually considered to be a black land-grant institution. Tuskegee N&I was established in 1881 by the Alabama legislature. In 1893 "the state granted the school its independence and incorporated a semiprivate board of trustees to govern it. Thus, Tuskegee University is not a land-grant college, despite the fact that it was granted 25,000 acres of land by the [U.S.] Congress in 1899" (Cooperative State Research, Education, and Extension 2000, on-line).

Following are the seventeen HBCU land-grant institutions, as identified by the Cooperative State Research, Education, and Extension (2000, on-line). They are listed by their current names.

Alabama A&M University
Alcorn State University, Mississippi
Delaware State University
Florida A&M University
Fort Valley State University, Georgia
Kentucky State University
Langston University, Oklahoma
Lincoln University, Missouri
North Carolina A&T State University
Prairie View A&M University, Texas
South Carolina State University
Southern University and A&M, Baton Rouge, Louisiana
Tennessee State University
University of Arkansas at Pine Bluff
University of Maryland: Eastern Shores
Virginia State University
West Virginia State College

According to the National Association of State Universities and Land-Grant Colleges, Florida A&M University, Tennessee State University, and Southern University and A&M are the leading HBCU land-grant schools whose graduates received doctorates.

Today, the student enrollments at Kentucky State University, Lincoln University in Missouri, and West Virginia State College are 50 percent or more white. Yet these institutions continue to be classified as HBCUs and receive funding from the federal government as HBCUs.

Although the concentration in agricultural and the mechanic arts was clear whether the institutions were a HBCU or historically white, the breadth, depth, and scope of their curricula were very different. HBCU land-grant schools would focus on vocational and technical teacher training. Historically white land-grant institutions would concentrate on research.

Black Non–Land-Grant Institutions

Historically, the U.S. Army and the federal government undertook to teach as well as to protect the freed slaves. In 1862, General Ulysses S. Grant appointed Colonel John Eaton, who became the second U.S. Commissioner of Education, to act as commissioner to freed slaves in Arkansas. Military leaders were often appointed to provide detailed educational directives. Education for blacks basically consisted of "rudimental instruction for the freedmen" under military protection. "This was a form of compulsory education previously unknown in the United States" (Good and Teller 1973, 258).

Many black public universities began as poorly equipped seminaries or as vocational or normal (teacher training) schools. Black public schools were often substandard because the government failed—or refused—to provide equal aid to black institutions. Given the political climate when these schools were established, Southern politicians could ignore the request from blacks for greater educational opportunities.

Following are the twenty-three non–land-grant HBCUs by state or territory, and a brief profile.

Alabama

Alabama State University began as a private education institution for blacks and was founded in 1874 as a public institution. It is the oldest public HBCU in the United States.

District of Columbia

The University of the District of Columbia was established in 1977. It was created through the merger of District of Columbia Teachers College, Federal City College, and Washington Technical College. Its origins can be traced to 1851 when Myrtilla Miner opened a school to prepare black women to teach.

Georgia

Albany State University was established in 1903 as a private school for religious and mechanical training of blacks. In 1932, when the Georgia Board of Regents was established, it became part of the University of Georgia system.

Savannah State College was established in 1890, making it the oldest state-funded institution in Georgia. In 1930 it offered its first baccalaureate degree.

Louisiana

Grambling State University was founded in 1901 to provide agricultural and industrial training for blacks. In 1928 it was a public junior college for blacks, and in 1940 it became a four-year college.

Southern University in New Orleans began in 1959. It is part of the Southern University and A&M System, which is the largest HBCU system in the United States.

Maryland

Bowie State University was founded in 1865 by the Baltimore Association for the Moral and Educational Improvement of Colored People. It began in an African Methodist Church. In 1908 it became a publicly funded institution for blacks, and in 1988 it gained university status.

Coppin State College was founded in 1900 as a teachers college. It was started by the Baltimore City School Board as a one-year training course for preparation of black elementary school teachers. In 1950 the college became part of the University of Maryland System.

Morgan State University was established in 1867 as the Centenary Bible Institution to train clergy for the African Methodist Episcopal Church. In 1939 it was bought by the state of Maryland. In 1975 it received university status.

Mississippi

Jackson State University was founded in 1877 by the American Baptist Home Mission Society. The state of Mississippi took control of the institution in 1940.

Mississippi Valley State University was established in 1946 by the Mississippi State legislature.

Missouri

Harris-Stowe College was founded in 1857 as a teacher training institution. It was the first teacher-training institution west of the Mississippi River. In 1979 it became part of the state public higher education system.

North Carolina

Elizabeth City State University was founded in 1891 as a normal, or teacher training, school. In 1972 it became part of the University of North Carolina System.

Fayetteville State University was established in 1867 by seven black men as a teachers college. It is considered the oldest teachers college for blacks in the South. In 1969 it became part of the University of North Carolina System.

North Carolina Central University was founded in 1910 as a private school for religious training. In 1923 it became a public institution. It was the first state-supported liberal arts college for blacks in the United States. In 1972 it was made part of the University of North Carolina System.

Winston-Salem State University was founded in 1892 as the Slater Industrial Academy. In 1925 the North Carolina Board of Education gave the institution authority to confer baccalaureate degrees.

Ohio

Central State University began in 1887 as a department at Wilberforce University. In 1941 it became an independent degree-granting institution. In 1951 it was authorized to offer baccalaureate degrees, and in 1965 the Ohio General Assembly gave it university status.

Pennsylvania

Cheyney University of Pennsylvania was established in 1837. It is the oldest U.S. institution for the higher learning of blacks.

Lincoln University–Pennsylvania was established in 1854 as the first college for blacks. It began as a male institution. In 1965 it became coeducational.

Texas

Texas Southern University began in 1927 as a private junior college. In 1947 it became a public institution named Texas State University for Negroes and offered baccalaureate degree programs. In 1951 a bill passed by the Texas legislature changed its name to Texas Southern University.

Virgin Islands

The University of the Virgin Islands was established in 1962 through Act No. 862 of the legislature of the United States Virgin Islands. It was originally called College of the Virgin Islands.

Virginia

Norfolk State University was established in 1882 as a junior college that was part of Virginia Union University. In 1956 it became a four-year public degree-granting institution.

West Virginia

Bluefield State College was established in 1895 by the West Virginia legislature. It began as a teacher training college.

HISTORY OF BLACK COMMUNITY COLLEGES AND JUNIOR COLLEGES

Routinely, discussions about HBCUs do not include the eight black public community colleges and the four black private junior colleges that operate today. Yet these schools are an integral part of the network of black postsecondary education.

Community and junior colleges are two-year postsecondary institutions that offer associate's degrees. They serve as a bridge between high school and collegiate aspirations or vocational training.

Black community and junior colleges multiplied during the late 1940s through the mid-1960s. This was not unique to the education of blacks, as during this period, community and junior colleges were being established throughout the United States. The black public community colleges were established, as is the case with the establishment of all HBCUs, because of segregated education laws and practices in the states in which the schools exist.

Generally, community colleges were an extension of the local public school districts. To meet the educational needs of the local community, individuals and church organizations established private junior colleges.

The twelve black community and junior colleges that operate today represent a microcosm of the number that once existed. Unfortunately, most of the history is lost.

Florida is the only known state that provides a published history of its black community colleges. Between 1949 and 1967, Florida had twelve black community colleges. These colleges were located in cities with high black populations that could support the schools. Although the idea of a community college had to be initiated by the local school board, the schools were "planned jointly by the State Department of Education, the local school board, and a local advisory committee" (Smith 1994, xvii). The black community colleges were located in the black community, named after blacks, and had black presidents.

All of Florida's black community colleges were merged with the white community colleges by 1967. The mergers resulted in a loss of the institutions' racial identity. The black colleges moved from the black community. The black schools took the names of the white institutions. All of the presidents of the white institutions became the presidents of the merged schools (Smith 1994).

The National Center for Education Statistics (2001a, on-line, 2001b, on-line) reported that in 1999, over 5.5 million students were enrolled in two-year colleges. Of those enrolled, approximately 40 percent were black. One percent of those blacks were enrolled in black two-year colleges (National Center for Education Statistics 2000, on-line). Nationally, only 15 percent of all blacks who graduate from two-year colleges transfer to a four-year college. For HBCU two-year institutions the percentage of transfers to four-year colleges is approximately 35 percent (Jackson 2001).

One might ask, Why would blacks who aspire to a baccalaureate degree go to a two-year black college? The answer is no different than why a large number of whites who plan to obtain a baccalaureate degree first attend a two-year college: money. Traditionally, tuition for two-year colleges is less than that charged at four-year colleges. Students are able to complete their first two years of college at less expense. Additionally, some individuals are not able to be mobile immediately after high school due to family or other personal circumstances, and local two-year colleges allow them to continue their education without relocating.

Following are the twelve community and junior colleges that are currently operating, by state and a brief profile.

Alabama

Bishop State Community College began in 1937. It offered a two-year degree as part of the University of Alabama. It became an independent community college in 1965.

J. F. Drake State Technical College was founded in 1961 as a vocational and technical training school for blacks.

Lawson State Community College began in 1963. In 1972 the Alabama State Board of Education established it as the only state-supported two-year institution as well as the only public HBCU in central Alabama.

Trenholm State Technical College was established in 1963 by the Alabama State legislature.

Arkansas

Shorter College was founded in 1886. It is affiliated with the African Methodist Episcopal Church.

Louisiana

Southern University at Shreveport was founded in 1967 as part of the Southern University and A&M System.

Michigan

Lewis College of Business, a private school, was established in 1929. It remains consistent with its original purpose, providing business science education.

Mississippi

Coahoma Community College was founded in 1949 for black vocational training.

Hinds Community College–Utica Campus was founded in 1903 for training blacks in vocational education.

Mary Holmes College was established by the Presbyterian Church in 1892.

South Carolina

Clinton Junior College was founded in 1894. The African Methodist Episcopal Zion Church supports it.

Denmark Technical College was established in 1947 as a trade school for blacks. It became part of the South Carolina Technical Education System in 1969.

THE MISSION OF HBCUS

After decades of painstaking efforts, sacrifice, and scrambling and scraping for only the minimal resources allotted to keep [HBCUs] viable and effective, after some 150 years of fighting against the rampant racism that was the cause for HBCUs to be established in the first place—after enduring and surviving all manner of social and racial mistreatment and yet emerging from all this highly respected educational institutions, black colleges are now confronted by the injustice of proposals to phase them out of existence. (Thomas and Green 2001, 245)

HBCUs are virtually ignored and in many instances financially neglected as part of the higher education landscape. By not being acknowledged and recognized they are frequently left to use the sparse resources they are given to develop and to meet the educational aspirations of blacks, until the white-dominated society decides they have exceeded the boundaries set for HBCUs. In spite of their accomplishments, HBCUs remain in back of the big house—that is, historically white institutions.

By opportunity and necessity, HBCUs created their own higher education landscape within the context shaped by whites. The blueprint for black higher education was not solely the choice of blacks. "Various contending forces sought either to repress the development of black education or to shape it in ways that contradicts blacks' interest in intellectual development" (Anderson 1988, 285). The contemporary contending forces are most evidenced in court cases and in federal and state appropriations to HBCUs.

Within the context given them, HBCUs forged an education system that would enable black youth to understand and function in two worlds—black and white. Benjamin E. Mays, president emeritus of Morehouse College (Ga.), a private male HBCU, comments on how HBCUs accomplish the duality. "It is not enough for black colleges to teach their students the economics of capitalism. The graduate of a black college must also understand the problems of the small black capitalist and be able to help him [and her]" (1978, 28). Now more than ever before, black college students must understand the national and international social, political, and economic systems. They must be able to translate that knowledge into meaningful interpretations as black Americans. HBCUs remain the only higher education institutions that specifically provide this type of education for blacks and other dominated groups.

Although it would be easy to blame all of the challenges that HBCUs currently face on whites and the system, the blame has to be shared. Some blacks have contributed to the precarious status and condition of HBCUs. It would be difficult to find a black family in the United

States with college graduates who does not have an HBCU graduate in its lineage. In all likelihood that graduate was the first generation to be college educated.

Beginning in the mid-1970s and continuing now, there are blacks who avow that HBCUs are second-rate or that HBCUs are no longer needed because the vestiges of segregation no longer exist. Some of these blacks are nationally anointed by whites as authorities on the educational needs and aspirations of blacks. The words and actions of these blacks validate whites' justification and systematic substandard support of HBCUs. Carter G. Woodson, a distinguished black historian, considered these blacks "mis-educated Negroes" and the "weak link in the chain" because of their lack of support for valid black institutions (Woodson [1933] 1991, 42).

Paulo Freire states, "Only as they discover themselves to be 'hosts' of the oppressor can they contribute to the midwifery of their liberating pedagogy. As long as they live in the duality in which *to be* is *to be like,* and *to be like* is *to be like the oppressor,* this contribution is not possible" ([1970] 2001, 48). Freire's statement is applicable to HBCUs. In large part HBCUs will fail because all blacks will not give HBCUs the political, economic, and moral support they need and deserve.

Benjamin Mays states, "If America allows black colleges to die, it will be the worst kind of discrimination and denigration known in history. To decree that colleges born to serve [blacks] are not worthy of surviving now that white colleges accept [blacks] would be a damnable act" (1978, 27).

If HBCUs are allowed to cease to exist, what educational systems will meet the mission of these institutions? The missions of HBCUs are (1) education opportunity and access, (2) perpetuation of the black culture, and (3) search for synergy that focuses on interdisciplinary intellectual and training and skill development for future employment and race advancement.

The 1971 report of the Carnegie Commission for Higher Education suggested that the role of HBCUs should be to serve as custodians for the archives of black Americans and as centers of systemic study of both the challenges and achievements of black people.

The issue of access cannot be overemphasized when discussing the mission of HBCUs. Whites in the United States have historically provided access to a better way of life for white people. They have been able to do this through the advantages and privileges of being white in the United States, combined with and at the expense of others through injustice and oppression.

HBCUs attempt to level the education playing field and open opportunities for access and attainment. In the twenty-first century, the education playing field is not level, and access and attainment opportunities are still restricted.

HBCUs correct false race doctrines. Historically white schools are not motivated to, are not interested in, and are not concerned about producing blacks who complete college and obtain Ph.D.s in the sciences, engineering, and other disciplines. It would destroy the stereotype that blacks are stupid and incompetent. HBCUs are the only postsecondary institutions that want to and do cultivate and produce large percentages of blacks who complete college and aspire to further educational attainment.

Douglas V. Davidson confirms that African Americans are more than a racial or ethnic group; they are also members of a culture. The culture is made up of "social institutions, behavioral values, norms, expectations, and rituals which form the core of African American culture" (2001, 194).

HBCUs strengthen and ground young blacks in their culture in the same way historically white institutions strengthen and ground young whites in their culture. The African American culture that HBCUs transmit "is not one grounded in reproducing black misery but one which allows African Americans to express their creativity in a friendly, warm, supportive, empowering environment; something blacks have never experienced in this country" (Davidson 2001, 194).

Arthur E. Thomas states that from their beginning, "the mission that most black leaders [and people] hold for historically black colleges and universities [has been] to maintain access to a better life through education for African Americans and the other poor and oppressed people" (Jackson 2001, 137). Black schools have given past and present generations, as well as future generations, courage, intellectual acumen, and determination.

At HBCUs young black adults achieve the social relevance of higher education by:

1. Hearing the best black minds in the world regularly
2. Knowing the real history of black people
3. Valuing the importance of voting, recognizing that the Voting Rights Act is about to expire and is in jeopardy, and comprehending the political process
4. Identifying with the black community and their relation and obligation to it for the uplifting of all blacks

THE DEBATE OVER CURRICULUM

In 1860, the year before the start of the Civil War, blacks made up 14.1 percent of the population in the United States. Of that percentage, 89.5 percent were slaves (Gonzales 1990). In the majority of the states where slavery was legal, blacks were prohibited by law to learn to read and write. In the years immediately following the Civil War, nine out of ten newly freed slaves were illiterate. The first curriculum for blacks thus focused on learning to read and write.

By 1870, 21 percent of freed blacks were literate. By 1900, 55 percent of the black population was literate, and approximately 2,600 had postsecondary degrees. In the thirty-five years between the end of the Civil War in 1865 and 1900, the educational needs of blacks had changed. HBCUs' curricula were evolving from primarily elementary and high school level education to liberal arts and professional education preparation. Although the professional curricula offerings began primarily in the fields of teacher training and theology, they rapidly expanded to include medicine, law, business, journalism, and the sciences, to name a few.

Freed slaves and free blacks knew that education would provide true liberation. The *type* of education that was appropriate was of greatest concern. On one hand was an education that would provide immediate economic development, such as vocational and industrial skills. On the other hand was a liberal arts education that could develop leaders to guide the elevation of blacks in the United States. This would require a more long-term focus. These two educational perspectives and their relationship to the needs of blacks resulted in a curriculum debate between two esteemed black educators, W. E. B. DuBois and Booker T. Washington.

DuBois and Washington had differing views on the type of education needed to further the advancement of black people. Two conclusions could be made for their differing perspectives. One conclusion is from a political standpoint: that DuBois is a radical and Washington is a conservative. The other conclusion is from a sociological standpoint: that their perspectives emanated from their very different backgrounds.

DuBois was an erudite professor and activist. Born a free black in Massachusetts in 1868, he received his baccalaureate degree from Fisk University; a private HBCU founded by the Congregationalist American Missionary Association in Nashville, Tennessee, and was the first black to receive a Ph.D. degree from Harvard University. His dissertation, titled "The Suppression of the Slave Trade," was published in 1896. Most

of his teaching career was at Atlanta University, the first HBCU established solely for graduate and professional education. In addition, he
studied at the University of Berlin in Germany. In 1905 he formed the
Niagara Movement, which was the foundation for the National Association for the Advancement of Colored People (NAACP). For several years
he served as the director of the NAACP and editor of it magazine, *The
Crisis*. He promoted the concept of the "talented tenth," meaning that a
portion of blacks should have liberal arts for the development of leadership. DuBois was a prolific writer and researcher. In 1963 he left the
United States, forfeiting his U.S. citizenship, and moved to Ghana; he
died shortly thereafter.

Washington was born a slave in Virginia in 1856. Perhaps the
most seminal experience for him was his matriculation at Hampton Institute, a black industrial training institution in Virginia, in the years following the Civil War. He was asked by General Samuel Armstrong, head
of Hampton, on the behalf of whites from Tuskegee, Alabama, to establish a school similar to Hampton. Tuskegee Institute was established in
1881. Washington spent his life advancing Tuskegee and advocating vocational and industrial education for blacks. He was the founder and
first president of the National Negro Business League. He received national recognition from blacks and whites for his work and was influential in post–Civil War Republican Party politics concerning the South.
His most noted publication is his autobiography, *Up from Slavery*. He
died in 1915.

Given their backgrounds, it is not surprising that DuBois advocated liberal arts education for blacks, and Washington promoted vocational and industrial education. DuBois stated,

> If we make money the object of man-training, we shall develop money-
> makers but not necessarily men; if we make technical skill the object of
> education, we may possess artisans but not, in nature, men. Men we
> shall have only as we make manhood the object of the work of the
> schools—intelligence, broad sympathy, knowledge of the world that
> was and is, and the relation of men to it—this is the curriculum of that
> Higher Education which must underlie true life. On this foundation we
> may build bread winning, skill of hand and quickness of brain with
> never a fear lest the child and man mistake the means of living for the
> object of life. (1966b, 518)

Washington stated,

There was a general appreciation of the fact that industrial education of the black people had direct, vital and practical bearing upon the life of each white family in the South; while there was no such appreciation of the results of mere literary training. If a black man became a lawyer, a doctor, a minister, or an ordinary teacher, his professional duties would not ordinarily bring him in touch with the life of the white portion of the community, but rather confine him almost exclusively to his own race. While purely literary or professional education was not opposed by the white population, it was something in which they found little or no interest, beyond a confused hope that it would result in producing a higher and better type of Negro manhood. ([1907] 1966, 409)

Nationalism versus Assimilation

DuBois was a champion of nationalism. He considered assimilation a means to keeping blacks inferior to whites and believed that blacks should not have to be submissive to whites. For DuBois, nationalism meant "three things. First, political power; Second, insistence on civil rights; Third, higher education of Negro youth" ([1903a] 1966a, 514). Washington preferred assimilation and believed that blacks should adapt to fit into white society. "No race can prosper till it learns that there is as much dignity in tilling a field as in writing a poem," he wrote. "It is at the bottom of life we must begin, and not at the top. Nor should we permit our grievances to overshadow our opportunities" ([1895] 1966, 357).

Liberal Arts Education versus Vocational Education

DuBois believed that the forward movement of blacks was based on the development of the mind and work. "Education and work are the levers to uplift a people. Work alone will not do it unless inspired by the right ideals and guided by intelligence" ([1903b] 1966b, 533). Washington was convinced that black elevation was based on the development of industrial or vocational skills and how whites perceived and benefited from it. "The minute it was seen that through industrial education the Negro youth was not only studying chemistry, but also how to apply the knowledge of chemistry to the enrichment of the soil, or to cooking, or to dairying . . . then there began to appear for the first time a common bond between the two races and co-operation between the North and South" ([1907] 1966, 409–410).

Talented Tenth versus the Masses

DuBois's concept of the "talented tenth" was based on the premise of developing leadership first. "From the very first it has been the educated and intelligent of the Negro people that have led and elevated the mass, and the sole obstacles that nullified and retarded their efforts were slavery and race prejudice; for what is slavery but the legalized survival of the unfit and the nullification of the work of natural internal leadership?" ([1903b] 1966b, 519). Washington held that it was more important to provide education for the masses. "It is possible to create in every part of the South a friendly sentiment toward Negro education, provided it can be shown that this education has actually benefited and helped in some practical way the masses of the Negro people with whom the white man in the South comes most in contact" ([1911] 1966, 441).

DuBois did not fully oppose the need for industrially trained black workers, as strongly advocated by Washington. However, he saw no need to reject liberal arts and advanced academic programs, which would embrace a more classical curriculum. This included Latin, Greek, Hebrew, English composition, trigonometry, and Greek history (Banks 1996). Although liberal arts were discussed, for economic reasons blacks still depended on vocational training. Washington viewed liberal arts or a classical education as suitable for some blacks, but he clearly was convinced that basic educational training and manual skills would be adequate and practical for most people. Such an accommodating attitude was nonthreatening to Northern white funders and wealthy businessmen. Yet Washington sent his daughter to Radcliff College in Massachusetts and acknowledged a role for higher learning in the black agenda.

Manning Marable notes that the vocational education training that blacks were receiving did not keep pace with the "changing status of black workers in the labor force. Vocational schools continued to train black students as blacksmiths, wheelwrights, masons, plumbers, and . . .other trades that no longer offered employment to blacks. Some of these skills became obsolete with the development of new technologies, but many others, such a brickmansory, eliminated blacks with the expanding racial segregation of organized labor" (1998, 38). Washington's anti-union stance and the accepted belief by whites that he was the black leader who spoke for all blacks "provided racists inside organized labor with a justification for expelling black members" (37).

In some ways the Morrill Act of 1890 eased the tension in the debate over vocational versus liberal arts education. As noted earlier, the act provided federal funds for the establishment of black land-grant postsecondary institutions. With this act, vocational education was elevated to a position in higher education for the training of professionals. Even so, the debate would not be resolved until the 1920s, as a result of student, faculty, and alumni unrest at HBCUs, discussed later in this chapter.

In describing the "educational emphases" of HBCUs, Kannerstein concludes, "black colleges believe in a liberal arts education, but they also insist on the utility of the liberal arts and do no fear to combine them with career education" (1978, 47).

OUTSIDE FORCES ON THE MISSION AND CURRICULA

Outside forces and influences also have shaped the education of blacks. Anderson points out, blacks "entered emancipation with fairly definite ideas about how to integrate education into their broader struggle for freedom and prosperity, but they were largely unable to shape their future in accordance with their social vision" (1988, 285).

To a large degree, the final decisions on the type of education that would be afforded blacks were out of their hands. Whites from the North and South were also considering the scope of black education. Bullock contends that many whites wanted to maintain a caste system and convince blacks to accept and be satisfied with it. The concern remained among whites that educated blacks would not accept and be satisfied with such a system (1967).

The shift from liberal arts aspirations to industrial adequacy was a direct outgrowth of the need for economic development of newly freed blacks. Racial confinement maintained the agricultural industry as the dominant means for employment. As such, many private HBCUs' early beginnings were as industrial institutes, for example, Tuskegee Institute (Ala.), Hampton Institute (Va.), and Benedict Institute (S.C.). State-supported African American institutions, many of them land-grant institutions, and some private institutions identified in their names the area or areas of focus with letters "A" for Agricultural, "M" for Mechanical, "T" for Technical, "I" for Industrial, and "N" for Normal (normal schools trained teachers). Although some public HBCUs continue to have these designations in their names, today their academic offerings are not limited to those areas (Jackson 2001).

While some HBCUs were moving in the direction of vocational and industrial education, private seminaries also were being established. Usually they began with high school–level education. These seminaries would later become four-year colleges. For example, Walden Seminary became Philander Smith College (Ark.), Atlanta Baptist Seminary became Morehouse College (Ga.), Atlanta Baptist Female Seminary became Spelman College (Ga.), and Bennett Seminar became Bennett College (N.C.).

The biracial society in the South specifically and in the United States generally, fostered the need for HBCUs to move closer to their original focus—liberal arts education. As Bullock attests, "the many daily needs of the segregated Negro community justified giving young Negroes higher professional training" (1967, 164). Leadership, which was needed in all professional fields of endeavor, required a liberal arts education.

ROLE OF HBCUS IN HIGHER EDUCATION

The roles of higher education institutions in the United States includes passing on the heritage and intellectual ideologies of a society and group of people; cultivating an insight into the political, social, and cultural underpinnings of societal institutions; verbal and mathematical accomplishment; development of self and one's relation to others and society; and career preparation. Pascarella and Terenzini state that postsecondary educations assist individuals in "fully appreciat[ing the] goals of socializing the individual for effective functioning in the middle class and acting as an important entrée to positions of status, influence, and wealth in American society" (1991, 2). Society and higher education institutions measure the quality and caliber of postsecondary institutions' academic program by the achievements and accomplishments of their graduates.

In general the difference in the roles of HBCUs and historically white institutions in higher education in the United States is not in the roles themselves, but in the nature of the students who are served, how they are served, and the purpose for serving them. HBCUs are intended to educate blacks. HBCUs serve to advance the self-concept and group identity of black youth and to cultivate the community and political activism of blacks for blacks locally, nationally, and globally. This is done with a full understanding of Eurocentric ideologies. HBCUs are the only postsecondary institutions in the United States that offer truly multicultural curricula rather than monoculture or parallel track curricula. Benjamin Mays notes that HBCUs have two roles:

> The black colleges have a role to play that is unlikely to be carried out if they do not do it. The white colleges are designed primarily to meet the needs of white America; their curricula are so designed. The black colleges have a double role. They must be as much concerned with Shakespeare, Tennyson, and Marlowe as the white colleges. But the [black] institutions must give equal emphasis to the writing of Paul Dunbar, Countee Cullen, and Langston Hughes. As much emphasis as white colleges to white sociologists, but equal attention to black sociologists like E. Franklin Frazier and Charles S. Johnson. The black colleges must include works of great white historians like Schlesinger and Toynbee, but they must also include the works of John Hope Franklin, Carter G. Woodson, and Charles Weslely. (1978, 27–28)

POLITICAL ASPECTS OF HBCUS

Cook (1978) points out, "Unlike white colleges, black colleges can hardly foster a love of, and a passion for, the status quo" (54). Activism and community service are considered part of the education of HBCU students and moral obligations to be honed at HBCUs. These obligations are rooted in the principle that graduates of HBCUs will assume the mantel for the political, social, and economic development of blacks, and in turn of the United States and the world. For HBCUs, activism and community service are mutually reciprocal: black activism and service to black communities, specifically, and to the entire community in which the HBCUs are located are part of the mission, role, and curriculum. Community service projects involve faculty and students.

Community Service

HBCU outreach varies. Some are funded by federal government agencies, and others are funded by grants from private foundations. HBCUs reach out to the surrounding community by providing preschool programs, radio stations, renovation of housing, welfare-to-work programs, grant writing assistance for community-based organizations, teleconferences and distance education classes, noncredit continuing education, community development initiatives, health programs, programs for the elderly, and environmental programs. They have formed partnerships with public school systems for mentoring, tutoring, and cultural activities. They have cultural events of music, dance, art, and theater.

Early Activism

There have been periods of time when activism at HBCUs have received national attention. More often than not, students were at the vanguard.

Unrest in the 1920s

Unrest on HBCU campuses had been festering for some time. Wolters reports that in 1914 "students at Alabama's Talladega College went on strike 'in protest against the paternalism of some of their white teachers and the indifference of others'" (1975, 276). Three years later a four-day strike at Morehouse College in Georgia occurred. This strike was for the same reasons as Talladega.

By the beginning of the 1920s there were approximately seventy-seven HBCUs with a total enrollment of 14,000. Most HBCUs, public and private, were still controlled by whites. The members of the boards of trustees were white. The presidents and administrators were white. The majority of the faculty where white. One blatant example was at Lincoln University in Pennsylvania, where blacks were *prohibited* to serve on the faculty (Wolters 1975). Many of the institutions had accepted in whole or in great portions Booker T. Washington's doctrine of vocational education curricula. Between 1923 and 1929, HBCUs were the center of protests that involved black students, some administrators and faculty, and black communities, which included alumni. The black students protested, realizing that they could be expelled and with full knowledge of the sacrifices that their families had made for them to be in college. Administrators and faculty who supported the protest did so with full knowledge that they could be fired. Black communities that supported the protest did so with full knowledge that violence could flow from the campus to the town. Yet, for these protesters the cause was bigger than themselves. The cause was the advancement of the race. Blacks were not satisfied with their caste position in the United States. They wanted the full privileges and rights of American citizens.

A number of events and movements that occurred nationally foreshadowed the protests on HBCU campuses. In 1919 there occurred what James Weldon Johnson called the "Red Summer." More than twenty race riots occurred that year between June and December. Marcus Garvey's Back to Africa movement, the growing influence of the NAACP and Urban League, the Harlem Renaissance, and the expansion of black journalism also added to the growing dissatisfaction with the status quo at HBCUs (Wolters 1975).

At the core of the HBCU unrest was the recognition by black college students, alumni, and some faculty that for blacks to direct their futures they had to control their education. Blacks knew that as the population migrated from the farm to the cities, an education that consisted of more than vocational training, no matter how it was veiled, was needed. As Wolters notes, "Throughout the black college rebellions of the 1920s there was a rejection of the condescending belief that whites unerringly knew the best methods of [black] education and an insistence that black youth must be trained according to principles endorsed by the black community" (1975, 18).

Unrest in the 1960s and 1970s

The Civil Rights movement of the 1960s is discussed in the next section. However, it was in part the catalyst for the late 1960s and early 1970s wave of student unrest at HBCUs. Black students were demanding full enfranchisement in the United States and a voice in their education. This was the era of the Vietnam War, and student unrest was seen on campuses across the United States. Vietnam was the fourth foreign war in the twentieth century in which blacks had fought for the freedom of others, and yet they could not obtain the same rights and privileges at home. A disproportionate number of soldiers in Vietnam were black. They fought, died, or returned home altered psychologically, spiritually, and physically or some combination of the three. HBCU students knew them personally. As Wolters explains,

> A growing number of [black students] turned away from protest against discrimination in the larger society and instead demanded that their colleges be reorganized. . . . Most black college protests of the late 1960s and early 1970s had a decidedly separatist thrust and have been based on the belief that blacks could not make real progress until they renounced their cultural and psychological allegiance to middle-class Euro-American values and developed a unique national consciousness. (1975, 343–344)

The weeklong "lockup" of the Morehouse College Board of Trustees during the spring of 1969 is just one example of how HBCU students fought for reorganization. Morehouse, a male college in Georgia, is one of six HBCUs that make up the Atlanta University Center. The other schools are Spelman College, a female college; Morris Brown College, an AME college; Interdenominational Theological Center, a seminary of six denominations; Clark College; and Atlanta University, the first HBCU solely for graduate and professional education. All of the schools are private and had separate boards, presidents, faculty, and student populations. Although the lockup was initiated by Morehouse students and only involved the Morehouse Board of Trustees, the weeklong demonstration involved students from all of the undergraduate colleges in the Atlanta University Center, as well as faculty and community members. Gibbs outlines the "demands" that were made by the students:

1. In these times it is improper for black schools to be named after obscure white persons;
2. The separate colleges in the A.U. Center probably could not celebrate a second centennial as small independent colleges;
3. The colleges should undergo fundamental changes, in terms of their function and how they relate to the surrounding black community;
4. At least a majority of the Boards of Trustee members controlling black institutions should be black;
5. Students should participate in the decision-making processes which govern their lives; and
6. *More and better black curriculum is needed. (1999, 227)*

Following the lockup it was agreed that the majority of the Morehouse Board of Trustees would be black, a board member could not serve for more than six consecutive years, students would gain "real and equitable power to determine the destiny of their institutions," and the board would support consolidation of the schools in the Atlanta University Center if agreed upon by all of the institutions (Gibbs 1999, 231).

As a footnote, in 1989 Clark College and Atlanta University merged due to fiscal constraints and as a means of keeping both institutions open. The institution is now Clark Atlanta University.

Civil Right Movement of the 1960s

To care for the interests of recently freed blacks, the federal government in 1863 created the Bureau for Refugees, Freedmen, and Abandoned Lands, known as the Freedmen's Bureau. The bureau provided social service and medical and educational assistance to freedmen in the South. As Lomax notes, many of the schools established by the bureau "produced today's rebels" who participated in the freedom rides and sit-ins of the 1960s (1962, 21). The schools included Howard University (D.C.), Hampton University (Va.), Fisk University (Tenn.), and Johnson C. Smith University (N.C.).

HBCU students galvanized the Civil Rights movement of the 1960s. Their passion for and dedication to civil rights was the actualization of the principle they had been taught at home—bettering of self and the circumstances of others. Yet when they acted on this principle, it was often received with consternation by parents and other elders. John Lewis's account of his mother's reaction to the first time he was jailed, in spring 1960, exemplifies this concern:

> When my parents got word that I had been arrested—I wrote them a letter from the Nashville jail explaining what had happened and that I was acting in accordance with my Christian faith—they were shocked. Shocked and ashamed. My mother made no distinction between being jailed for drunkenness and being jailed for demonstrating for civil rights. "You went to school to get an education," she wrote me back. "You should get out of this movement, just get out of that mess." (1998, 115)

The young people had a different interpretation of bettering themselves and the conditions of others. They were going to do it beyond their home communities. They were going to do it across the nation and the world. They were going to begin with where they found themselves at that time. They would, perhaps, find new vocations. Lewis, originally from Alabama, was a student at Fisk University in Tennessee. Studying to be a "preacher," he has held the seat of representative for the 5th U.S. Congressional District of Georgia since 1987.

HBCU student involvement in the Civil Rights movement is marked as beginning in early 1960. Carson, Garrow, Gill, Harding, and Hine (1991) chronicle the beginning of student involvement as February 1, 1960, in Greensboro, North Carolina. Franklin McCain, David

Richmond, Joseph McNeil, and Ezell Blair Jr. were students at North Carolina A&T University. In their dormitory, after extensive discussions, they planned and carried out a sit-in at the Woolworth store's lunch counter and asked to be served. In March 1960, students from the Atlanta University Center schools formed the Atlanta Committee on Appeal for Human Rights. The committee's declaration was published as a paid advertisement in the *Atlanta Constitution.* This open declaration initiated student sit-ins in Atlanta. In April 1960, student sit-in leaders from HBCUs across the South as well as students from Northern schools met at Shaw University (N.C.) to organize their efforts. The result of this meeting was the establishment of the Student Nonviolent Coordinating Committee (SNCC), which came to organize many of the decade's defining protests and marches in support of civil rights.

Eleanor Nunn, a student at Shaw University, was one of the students at the meeting. She recounts the following:

> As a Southerner I witnessed the many contradictions of the segregated South of the 1950s and 1960s. I could shop on Raleigh's main street, Fayetteville Street, at Hudson-Belks, a local department store, and at F. W. Woolworth. I could even work in these stores. Yet if I were hungry I dare not sit down to be served. If I were thirsty, there were clearly marked water fountains: "White Only" and "Colored." However, as a high school student, who served as student body president and also president of the youth division of the NAACP in my community, I was comfortably armed with appropriate adult leadership and support to strategically address segregation. More importantly, the value that I placed on myself negated all doctrines of white superiority and black inferiority. I had grown up attending community meetings with my parents and sisters, listening attentively yet growing more impatient with the presentations, charts and graphs from white people on plans for the black community.
>
> Participating in educational and community discussions, sit-ins and marches in a quest to improve the plight of blacks provided me with an excellent foundation to become an active participant in the establishment of the Student Nonviolent Coordinating Committee, or SNCC, my freshman year at Shaw University. I remember how wonderful it was to see Ella Baker, a Shaw graduate and a female, stand in Greenleaf Auditorium before over 150 students to discuss the planning strategies for the attack on segregation. Most of the movement leaders were males. Thus SNCC was established. Today a historic marker is placed at the Shaw campus to commemorate this

event. Strategic planning, knowledge, skills, self worth, communication, collaboration, assertiveness, nonviolence, and patience, all terms used to describe components of my life; many of which were enhanced via my civil rights experiences. Serving as a Peace Corps Volunteer, public service appointments, political appointments and professional positions have been extensions of my desire to be helpful and value humankind.

Contemporary Activism

Are civil rights movements for blacks passé? Are community actions and activism not needed? If community actions and activism were needed, would today's HBCU students be ready to participate? Could they be at the vanguard of the movement? Do they have the burning desire, creativity, and courage to plan and implement a better life for themselves and others? What do HBCU students talk about in their dormitories and in the student unions? Are HBCU students networking across HBCUs to establish an activist agenda and a critical mass of support?

The answers to all of these questions are not known. However, a few can be answered. First, a civil rights movement is still necessary. Second, there are at least two concrete areas needing student activists.

HBCU students can begin to address the systematic frontal assault on the elimination of public HBCUs and the covert attack to starve many private HBCUs out of existence. The activism of black students is credited to the loss of the plaintiffs in the *Wooden* case, discussed in Chapter 3. The intervention of black students in this case had two effects. First, they thwarted anti–affirmative action admissions standards in Georgia's public HBCUs. Second, they "defeated the plaintiffs' efforts to maintain a class action" suit (Shaw 2000, on-line). Are HBCU students in other states taking notice of this intervention? Is there a national HBCU student movement to protect HBCUs? A particularly reassuring answer to the last question is, "Perhaps." In 2002 twenty-one HBCU student leaders and 400 students and nationally recognized blacks met at Tennessee State University for three days for the first HBCU "think tank" on the future of HBCUs (Hefner 2002, 10). Interestingly, a small portion of HBCU students espoused the view that "HBCUs were either no longer necessary in an integrated world or were at risk of being obsolete because they primarily were serving a social function rather than an academic one" (2002, 11). The answers to the questions cannot be known at this time. Whether the "HBCU think tank" is effective is yet to be seen.

Blacks remain the only group in the United States that have to have their right to vote renewed. President Lyndon B. Johnson signed the Voters Right Act of 1965. Yet the signing of the act did not make it a law. Through an amendment of the act by President Ronald Reagan in 1982, blacks' right to vote was extended for twenty-five years. In 2007 this act will come before the U.S. Congress again. Are blacks so secure in the United States that it can be assumed that an extension will occur or that the act is not needed? Where are the children, and yes, the grandchildren of the Civil Rights movement of the 1960s, who are picking up this mantel and moving it forward?

FULFILLMENT OF THE MISSION AND ROLE

Ivy League colleges and major research universities are known for the national and international recognition their faculty receive and for the accomplishments and prominence of their graduates. The achievements, attainment, and earning of the graduates, coupled with the recognition of the faculty lead many to hypothesize that the curriculum, academic programs, and instruction are excellent. As Cynthia L. Jackson notes, however, most of these nationally and internationally recognized faculty have virtually no contact with undergraduate students and very little contact with graduate students except for the few doctoral students with whom they choose to work. For these institutions and the faculty, research, not teaching, is the primary concern. The majority of the undergraduate and the predoctoral graduate-level teaching is done by doctoral students who have associate positions, entry-level faculty, and adjuncts. Other historically white institutions that focus more on teaching than research can also boast of the accomplishments, achievements, and earnings of their graduates, and it is hypothesized that the curriculum, academic programs, and instruction are of quality. However, these hypotheses of excellence and quality have not been tested. Therefore, based on the achievements, accomplishments, and earnings of HBCU graduates as well as the nationally and internationally known faculty at some HBCUs, it can be asserted that the curriculum, academic programs, and instruction are equally excellent (Jackson 2001).

HBCU supporters are vexed by the very presumption of a question of the continued need for HBCUs and the press to justify their role in higher education in the United States. Questions are raised about the quality of the education, the preparedness of HBCU graduates to function in the mainstream of the United States, and the necessity of HBCUs given the supposed opening of admissions to historically white institutions. As evidenced by data, the definitive answer is that the dual role of HBCUs in the twenty-first-century United Stated higher education system is to continue to increase the number of African American youth who are awarded baccalaureate degrees and to imbue black youth with their culture.

Because higher levels of educational attainment are associated with higher levels of income, the black middle class is expanding along with black leadership. Cook points out, "It is hardly an accident that Martin Luther King Jr. was an alumnus of Morehouse College rather than of Harvard College and that the overwhelming majority of the leaders of the civil rights movement—nationally and locally—are graduates of black colleges" (1978, 52).

The available data leads one to conclude that (1) the quality of the education at HBCUs is sound; (2) that graduates of HBCUs are neither isolated nor limited in their ability to be active, vital, productive, and contributing citizens in United States and world societies; and (3) that historically white institutions are not definite accessible educational opportunities for most blacks.

William Trent concludes that HBCUs are fulfilling their role in U.S. postsecondary education. "Black colleges continue to be a primary source of degrees for blacks, and in some major fields, they produce more than would be expected" (1991, 59). HBCUs fulfill the dual role noted by Mays as well as the roles of all higher education institutions in the United States.

HBCUs constitute 3 percent of all postsecondary institutions in the United States. They enroll 16 percent of all blacks in higher education. Of this 16 percent, 26 percent are in four-year HBCUs. Twenty-eight percent of baccalaureate degrees awarded to all blacks in the United States and one out of six graduate and professional degrees earned by blacks are awarded from HBCUs. Although the graduation rates are down from the 34 percent in 1976, Catherine LeBlanc, former executive director of the White House Initiative on Historically Black Colleges and Universities, states, "The graduation rate is significant. In some Southern states, HBCUs graduate even greater percentages of African Americans. According to the [Department of Education], HBCUs graduate more than 50 percent of the black students who receive bachelor's degrees in Alabama (50.1), Louisiana (67.3), Mississippi (57.0), North Carolina (58.7), and Virginia (50.1)" (2001, 48). Enrollment trends in the 1990s forecasted that over 300,000 blacks will graduate from historically black colleges and universities between 1993 and 2018

(Roebuck and Murty 1993, 4). There is no reason to conclude that the trend will change.

HBCUs provide an environment that enfranchises all of its students in the institutions and prepares them for full participation in the society of the United States. They afford many graduates with the foundation and aspiration for professional and post-baccalaureate educational attainment, which would otherwise not have been realized. By 1991, HBCUs had educated 70 percent of all African Americans holding baccalaureate degrees. By 1995, 60 percent of blacks with doctorates received their baccalaureate degree from an HBCU.

The U.S. Department of Education, Office of Civil Rights reported in 1999 that HBCUs produced more than 80 percent of all African Americans who were conferred degrees in medicine and dentistry. The two institutions were Howard University (D.C.) and Meharry Medical College (Tenn.). Currently, 19.7 percent of the medical and dentistry degrees awarded to African Americans are from these two institutions. Morehouse School of Medicine (Ga.), established in 1975, is adding to the medical and health professional legacy. Office of Civil Rights reports from those same years also show that HBCUs provided undergraduate training for three-fourths of all blacks holding a doctorate degree, three-fourths of all black officers in the armed forces, and four-fifths of all black federal judges. The reports show that HBCUs lead in institutions awarding baccalaureate degrees to black students in the life sciences, physical sciences, mathematics, and engineering and that they continue to rank high in terms of the proportion of graduates who pursue and complete graduate and professional training. Finally, the reports of the Office of Civil Rights show that HBCUs account for 50 percent of black faculty in traditionally white research universities (1991, on-line).

In major U.S. corporations, 45 percent of blacks having positions of vice president or higher are graduates of HBCUs (Clarke 1998). Forty-five percent of the 107th United States Congress graduated from HBCUs. Just in the past thirty years, HBCU graduates include United Nations ambassadors, surgeon generals, an astronaut, Nobel laureates, a U.S. Supreme Court justice, U.S. Court of Appeals justices, state supreme court justices, secretaries of U.S. cabinet departments, U.S. ambassadors, a governor, numerous mayors, and the first black woman member of the American College of Physicians, just to name a few.

Of the top fifteen baccalaureate institutions of black Ph.D. degree recipients, twelve are HBCUs (*Black Issues in Higher Education* 1999). Three out of four African American females who earned a doctorate degree in the sciences between 1975 and 1992 received their baccalaureate degrees from an HBCU (Leggon and Pearson 1997).

Jill Constantine conducted a study on the long-term wage level of African Americans who received their baccalaureate degrees during the 1970s. The researcher found "that students who attended HBCUs in the 1970s later enjoyed substantially higher value added to wages than black students who attended historically white or racially mixed four-year institutions" (1995, 541). The finding was attributed to the higher post-baccalaureate degree attainment of blacks who graduate from HBCUs as compared to those who graduate from historically white institutions.

Because HBCUs have never excluded nonblacks, they also have served as postsecondary opportunity and access for other youth of color, and some whites. In fall 1998, student enrollment in the 103 HBCUs was 273,472. Blacks represented 82 percent of enrollees. Eighteen percent were other racial and ethnic groups (National Center for Education Statistics 2000, on-line).

HBCUs accept the responsibility and provide remedial assistance for students who need it, including academic and social assistance. These students are prepared for collegiate pursuits and equipped with the necessary social skills for entrance into the mainstream of the United States and its workforce.

Approximately 80 percent of HBCU students are from economically disadvantages backgrounds and are the first generation to attend college. The remaining 20 percent are second, third, and fourth generations to attend college, and their parents are professionals. Some HBCUs are positioning themselves to attract the best and brightest black students. Candidates for admission to the School of Business and Industry at Florida A&M University, for example, must have a minimum SAT score of 1100; in 1993, the school graduated the sixth largest number of African Americans (219) receiving a business degree. About 30 percent of all blacks earning degrees in business graduate from HBCUs. Colleges and universities like Florida A&M University, Howard University, Morehouse College, and Spelman College can recruit the best and brightest of black students because many of their programs are accredited and highly competitive, as are their recruitment standards.

Although most HBCU students are from the South, many come from across the country as well as around the world. Following recent attacks on affirmative action, black students have been more apt to search for friendlier collegiate environments. A report published in 2000 by the United Negro College Fund (UNCF) states that "California sends the largest number of students to UNCF schools after the states in which the institutions are located (mostly southern)" (LeBlanc 2001, 46).

The data presented in this section make clear that graduates of HBCUs influence people's lives every day—not just black people, but all Americans and people throughout the world. The data should also put to rest any rancor and inquisitions about the quality of HBCU educations and the ability of its graduates to operate in the mainstream of American society.

STATUS OF HBCUS

Graduates of black colleges must be competitive with the graduates of white colleges for professional positions in the mainstream of American society. Black institutions cannot compete in the broad sweep of American life without being competent agents for the transmission of topflight skills, genuine learning, and intellectual excitement. Black colleges must be more than black; in order to survive and prosper, they must be centers of excellence (Cook 1978, 55).

The status of HBCUs is in many ways an uneven terrain. Historically and now, they are underfunded, whether public or private. In spite of the underfunding they have made great strides in advancing the higher education and lifestyles of blacks. Racial identification, accreditation and program quality, leadership, faculty, admissions and retention, technology, facilities, fiscal concerns, and national student honors are discussed in this section, which concludes with an examination of the continued need for HBCUs in the twenty-first century.

Racial Identity

Race is a designation and an issue that is being watered down to mean ethnicity. Race and racial identity, the designation of people of common ancestry, tells who a person is. It connects and distinguishes people by a certain history and heritage and can, depending on one's racial identity, result in fortunate or unfortunate treatment in the United States. William S. Jackson, former dean of Atlanta University School of Social Work, writes, "Blacks achieve a sense of their own identity from their own experiences. Being black is a state of mind reflecting the unique experiences shared by blacks, varied as they are, that set them apart from any other group and results in a certain kind of psychological adjustment that other groups do not have to make" (1970, 2).

Theodore Shaw, associate director-counsel of the NAACP Legal Defense and Educational Fund, Inc., writes:

> In the year 2000, race in America still has a powerful impact on life experiences. Race affects mortality rates of black babies, the quality of education of black children, where blacks live, how they interact with the police, the kind of employment opportunities or health care available to them—in short, life experiences from cradle to grave. . . . In the legal struggle to determine whether the impact of race upon the lives of minority students will be seen, at the very least their voices must be heard. (2000, on-line)

Except for the black churches, HBCUs are the only social institutions in the United States that support, reinforce, and amplify the racial identity of blacks.

At three public land-grant historically black colleges and universities, whites comprise 50 percent or more of the student population. These schools are West Virginia State College, Kentucky State University, and Lincoln University in Missouri. Bluefield State College is an HBCU in West Virginia that also has whites as the majority of its student population. All of these institutions continue to maintain the HBCU designation. By doing so, these institutions continue to receive federal funding allocated for HBCUs. Thus, federal funding designated to strengthen HBCUs and redress the historical disparity of funding is being used to educate white students.

Bluefield State College is representative of the politics of a public HBCU achieving the goals of the *Fordice* decision—racial neutrality. (The *Fordice* decision is discussed in Chapter 3.) Though Bluefield State is identified as an HBCU, little remains that supports that identification. It is the only HBCU with a white president. In 2003, 8 percent of its student population is black. Of the eighty-two faculty members, two are black.

When the *Brown v. Board of Education* Supreme Court decision was handed down in 1954, Bluefield State began desegregating. In 1968, the passing of a state referendum closed its dormitories. The referendum was a result of a student protest for input in university policies and the academic curriculum. Keep in mind that this was the time of the Vietnam War and that campus protest frequently occurred. This same year a white president was hired. With the dormitories closed, and remaining closed today, Bluefield State is a commuter school. The black population in West Virginia is less than 5 percent. Like West Virginia State College, Bluefield State relied on attracting out-of-state black students to enroll. With the dormitories closed, out-of-state recruitment efforts became useless (Jackson 2001).

Accreditation and Program Quality

Six regional accrediting agencies are recognized by the U.S. Department of Education as the entities to appraise the quality of education and instructional support systems of postsecondary institutions in the United States. Accreditation by these agencies makes a postsecondary institution eligible to participate in federal grant and assistance programs. In addition, institutions in one region recognize the accreditation of institutions in another region.

According to Evelyn Carroll (1982), prior to 1935 no HBCU was regionally or professionally accredited. They are now appraised by three of the six regional accrediting agencies. They are (1) Middle States Association of Colleges and Schools: Commission on Higher Education, (2) North Central Association of Colleges and Schools: The Higher Learning Commission, and (3) Southern Association of Colleges and Schools: Commission on Colleges. As of December 2001, the data from the websites of the three regional accrediting agencies indicated that ninety-five of the 103 HBCUs, or 92 percent, were accredited by their respective regional accrediting agencies.

In addition, academic professional associations accredit certain academic programs by recognizing the academic quality of postsecondary institutions' training for particular professions. An example is undergraduate business programs. Prior to 1991, the American Assembly of Collegiate Schools of Business (AACSB) accredited only seven HBCUs. The institutions were North Carolina A&T State University, Clark Atlanta University (Ga.), Howard University (D.C.), Jackson State University (Miss.), Morgan State University (Md.), Norfolk State University (Va.), and Tennessee State University. Few HBCUs were accredited because the process favored larger institutions. However, in 1991, the AACSB revised its accreditation process. Eleven more HBCUs became candidates for accreditation within five years. Thus, most of the HBCUs with AACSB accreditation received it after the accreditation process was modified.

Queister Craig is a professor at North Carolina A&T State University and the first black to serve as president of the AACSB. He reports that the new accreditation process improved inclusion for a broad spectrum of institutions as well as the perception of what makes a quality institution. The new standards are based on institutional missions. Although aspects of the missions of HBCUs differ from that of traditionally white institutions, if performed according to professional standards, the outcomes will be of quality, and accreditation can be earned.

HBCUs realize the necessity for academic profession accreditations. These specialized accreditations play a role in the institutions attracting the best and brightest black as well as nonblack students.

Following are a sample of HBCUs and the area of their specialized accreditations provided by the National Association for Equal Opportunity in Higher Education (1999):

Alcorn State University (Miss.)—music, teacher education, nursing, industrial technology

Clark Atlanta University (Ga.)—business, social work education, library science, pubic affairs and administration, medical records, physical therapy, dietetics, health education, clinical laboratories

Delaware State University—aviation

Dillard University (La.)—nursing

Fayetteville State University (N.C.)—teacher education

Fisk University (Tenn.)—music, teacher education, chemistry

Grambling State University (La.)—teacher education

Jackson State University (Miss.)—teacher education, social work education, chemistry, music, computing sciences, industrial technology, public affairs and administration, journalism and mass communication

J. F. Drake State Technical College (Ala.)—occupational education

Johnson C. Smith University (N.C.)—teacher education

Kentucky State University—social work education, teacher education, nursing, music

Lincoln University (Mo.)—teacher education, nursing, music

Norfolk State University (Va.) —corrective therapy, clinical laboratory sciences, nursing, social work education, music, medical records, dietetics, psychology, allied heath education, business, computing sciences, industrial technology, chemistry

Philander Smith College (Ark.) —teacher education

Tennessee State University—business

Tuskegee University (Ala.) —architecture, chemistry, dietetics, teacher education, engineering, extension service,

nursing, occupational therapy, social work education,
veterinary medicine
Virginia Union University—theology

As far as program quality is concerned, HBCUs have witnessed great inequities in professions such as health care. This is an area of particular significance to blacks. As Ronald Roach states,

> Minorities are less likely to be given appropriate heart medications or to undergo bypass surgery. Minorities are less likely to receive kidney dialysis or transplants. Several students revealed significant racial differences in who received appropriate cancer diagnostic tests and treatments. Minorities also are less likely to receive the most sophisticated treatments for HIV infection, which could forestall the onset of AIDS. In contrast to getting sophisticated treatments, minorities are more likely to receive certain less-desirable procedures, such as lower limb amputations for diabetes. (2002, 26)

Directly addressing the medical conditions and diseases that specifically or significantly affect blacks, for example HIV/AIDS, sickle-cell anemia, and diabetes, has as much to do with the conditions and diseases as it does with the social and cultural factors of blacks in the United States. Having medical professionals who can empathize with the social and cultural factors of patients can be a contributing factor in who receives medical services and how the medical services are provided. Between 1867 and 1904, nine medical schools were established to train African Americans. Duke University's Medical Center Library website (1999) lists seven of them: Flint Medical College of New Orleans (La.), Howard University Medical School (D.C.), Knoxville Medical College (Tenn.), Leonard Medical School of Shaw University (N.C.), Meharry Medical College (Tenn.), Chattanooga National Medical College, and University of West Tennessee College of Physicians and Surgeons. Two additional schools were reported to the authors. These are Kansas Medical College and Louisville Medical College (Ky). By 1923 only two of the nine schools remained—Howard University Medical School and Meharry Medical College. The closing of the other medical schools is attributed to the standards set for training medical professionals in the 1910 *Flexner Report on Medical Education*. The seven medical colleges were unable to meet the standards. As of 2003, Howard and Meharry, in addition to Georgia's Morehouse School of Medicine (founded as part of

Morehouse College and an independent institution in 1985), are the only three historically black medical schools in the United States.

Research concerning black health and medical issues is more likely to be conducted by black medical and health care researchers. Robin Smiles reports that between 1950 and 1997, only 250 blacks who graduated from medical school reported their primary responsibility as being research. Smiles cites Lauren Wood, the principal investigator for the National Cancer Institute and National Institutes of Health, as saying, "Historically the focus has been on service, because the need has been so great, referring to the long need for more minority practicing physicians to serve minority communities. But those who train health care professionals also need to emphasize that 'real service to the community' is going to come from doing research on what impacts that community" (2002, 24–25). Historically black medical schools as well as historically black colleges and universities, generally, can play a major role in producing the medical and health care researchers.

In the area of substance abuse, some HBCUs have the potential of addressing the service and research needs of blacks. HIV and AIDS have reached epidemic levels in the black community. This is particularly true for young blacks between the ages of eighteen and thirty. Whereas blacks make up 12 percent of the population in the United States, the National Center for HIV/AIDS and Prevention reported that in 1998, blacks accounted for 45 percent of HIV/AIDS cases. The U.S. Centers for Disease Control and Prevention in 1999 reported that 57 percent of "all new AIDS cases involve blacks" (Roach 1999, 22). Eight out of ten African American babies are born with HIV.

Research has found a significant relationship between HIV/AIDS and the abuse of some illegal drugs. People of color represent 68 percent of clients in substance abuse clinics. Sadly, the number of black professionals providing services in substance abuse programs is minimal (Coggins 2001, 10).

Between the 1970s and 1980s three HBCUs—Atlanta University School of Social Work, Jackson State University, and Coppin State College (Md.)—were awarded funds to develop master's degree programs in substance abuse. In spring 2002 the University of Arkansas at Pine Bluff began its master's degree program in substance abuse (Coggins 2001).

In 2001, Patrick Coggins was the chair of the site visits and technical assistance services committee for the National HBCU Consortium on Substance Abuse. The consortium has an HBCU membership of sixty-nine institutions. The purpose of the study conducted for the consortium was to determine the progress of the member institutions in developing and implementing substance abuse course and degree programs for the past five years, and the progress made in course and degree programs being licensed by the state and accredited by the professional substance abuse association. Coggins shared the conclusions of the 2001 study with the authors:

First, advance degrees are a necessity for growth in any field. The experience gained from a higher level of education would in effect make the individual more prepared, as well as more knowledgeable and competitive in a field predominated by white practitioners. Because over 68 percent of the clients/patients are minorities, African Americans and other minority practitioners will be able to work and assist substance abusers of the same race and ethnic group or nationality, and to feel culturally connected and comfortable on their road to recovery.

Second, bachelor's and master's degrees are needed for professional positions in substance abuse fields. The data show that only 5–7 percent of the sixty-nine HBCUs surveyed in this study offer a bachelor's degree in substance abuse and that 3–4 percent of those HBCUs offer a master's degree in substance abuse. This lack of a significant number of HBCUs offering master's degree programs indicates the need for HBCUs to be an integral part of the effort to increase the number of African American and other minority professionals. These graduates will possess the requisite skills and competencies to address the epidemic of drugs and HIV/AIDS, which are devastating African Americans and other minorities.

Third, HBCU institutions need to promote substance abuse as a viable field of study. The minority population comprises a disproportionate number of people who are afflicted by substance abuse and HIV/AIDS, yet the number of trained professionals lags far behind. Thus, HBCUs have an excellent opportunity to be an integral part of increasing the pool of qualified substance abuse counselors, researchers, and other providers.

Fourth, minorities enrolled in the substance abuse program at HBCUs are faced with the problem of licensing /certification in the field of substance abuse. Less than 4 percent of the HBCUs offering courses and degrees have approved substance abuse courses that are accredited by state licensing bodies. The result is that after completion of coursework at an HBCU, the graduate then has to negotiate with the state licensing body. Therefore, HBCUs should develop curricula that will incorporate the process for certification and licensure by the state as a substance abuse counselor or other professional.

Fifth, because only three HBCU institutions (Coppin State College, Jackson State University, and University of Arkansas at Pine Bluff) offer the master's degree with a specialization in substance abuse, it is paramount that other HBCU institutions develop master's degree programs in order to provide minorities with the competitive edge in the field. The national data show that while many institutions offer graduate-level courses, only 3 percent of the 103 HBCUs offer the master's degree in substance abuse. Another trend that should be examined is that the master's degree training appears to be becoming the minimum qualification for supervisory and key management positions in the substance abuse field.

Sixth, the doctorate degree is not offered at any of the HBCUs who responded to this survey, and the consortium is not aware of any of the 103 HBCUs offering a doctoral degree with specialization in substance abuse. Certainly, the National HBCU Consortium on Substance Abuse should explore regional doctorate programs to the ever-increasing need for both teaching faculty and researchers in the area of drug abuse and HIV/AIDS. The idea is that this advanced degree offering would address the national need for individuals of African American descent and other ethnic backgrounds to fill the labor shortage of doctoral-level practitioners in the substance abuse fields of treatment, research, policy developing, and analysis.

Seventh, the Center for Substance Abuse and Treatment (CSAT) and other federal agencies must focus resources and efforts on providing concerted site visits and technical assistance to the HBCUs. The University of Arkansas at Pine Bluff, Clark Atlanta University, Dillard University, Southern University at New Orleans, Mississippi Valley State College, and other HBCUs provided an indication that such site visits and technical assistance result in institutions moving rapidly to develop and complete the approval of a degreed substance abuse program.

Eight, HBCUs must consider a comprehensive approach, which includes:

1. Offering continuing education in substance abuse and HIV/AIDS for staff, faculty, students, and community practitioners
2. Conducting scientific research on diverse issues in substance abuse treatment and prevention

3. *Linking research to the courses and degree offerings in substance abuse (i.e., include a series of research projects as part of the course offerings)*

Leadership

Leadership is a key variable in setting the tone and climate of the organization. The tone and climate are established in part by what leaders say, do, tolerate, and ignore.

Carlton E. Brown, president of Savannah State University in Georgia, has identified several attributes of effective HBCU presidents in the twenty-first century: "The new leader needs to be broadly knowledgeable, have a strong grasp of finance, technology and teamwork, and needs to be a perpetual change agent" (*New Black College Presidents* 1999, 84). Teamwork will be the saving grace of HBCUs, which can no longer afford to be paternalistic organizations in which the president acts as the benevolent parent who knows what is best for the institution, its faculty, and students. Openness to new and different ideas and possibilities from all sectors in HBCUs is needed.

The authors have had frequent opportunities to talk with HBCU faculty and administrators and to observe HBCU presidents. Conversations with them, along with our own observations, indicate a tendency for many HBCU presidents to exhibit an authoritarian and autocratic leadership style.

Although not writing about HBCU leaderships specifically, Manning Marable in *Black Leadership* (1998) makes observations of black leadership that parallel the conversations about and observations of HBCU presidents. "[Blacks need to] move away from the charismatic, authoritarian leadership style and paternalistic organizations toward the goal of 'group-centered leaders' and grassroots empowerment. In short, instead of leadership from above, democracy from below. The time for all voices to be heard is long overdue" (xvii).

The challenge of leading higher education through the twenty-first century is a monumental task for many educational institutions and is a huge challenge for most HBCUs. Notwithstanding the extreme fiscal challenge, HBCUs are confronted with critical issues that include curriculum limitations, infrastructure needs, and accreditation uncertainties. To meet these challenges, HBCU leaders need leadership styles that will serve a competitive environment in this information and technology age.

The observed leadership style of many HBCU presidents is grounded in the historical context in which HBCUs were established. By 1900, blacks who served as HBCU leaders were aware of their inability to alter their institutions. They had little power and no control over resources (Banks 1996). Black leaders of educational institutions were often faced with huge year-end debts, thus forcing them to adapt to the demands of white philanthropists, who provided a source of funds and often were not pleased to see liberal arts curricula interfere with industrial educational programs. Clearly, the concept of industrial education was extremely appealing to white employers and wealthy men: black labor was needed. Vocational education ruled, and most black education leaders chanted the rhetoric of vocational education for blacks. Even so, a few black leaders risked their jobs and, we would argue, their funds by attempting to add liberal arts programs. One example is John W. Davison, president of Fort Valley Normal College in Georgia, who in 1900 "was removed when Washington loyalists accused him of deviating from the industrial education model" (Banks 1996, 46).

Except for HBCUs affiliated with black church organizations, the majority of the early presidents of HBCUs were white. For example, Rust College in Mississippi obtained its first black president in 1920. This was *fifty-four years* after the college was founded. By the 1930s, the number of black presidents had increased. However, in the late 1950s there remained whites who were presidents of HBCUs.

Many early black educational leaders were greatly compromised by lack of funds and control of their institution. The all-black campuses were like sterile fortresses, closely monitored by state officials, white corporate philanthropists, or black religious denominations. Naturally, educational leaders were very clear on the source of their legitimacy and power; thus black college administrators were often very authoritarian. Academic freedom was virtually nonexistent; faculty was hired by the president, who in turn served at the pleasure of the board of trustees or governing board.

Currently, HBCUs, especially public HBCUs, are experiencing a rapid turnover of presidents. Within the public institutions, this is primarily attributed to a hostile political environment. For all HBCUs it is suggested that the high turnover rate is due to expectation incompatibility between the presidents and the boards of trustees (Maggett 1996).

Contemporary leaders of HBCUs must fulfill the schools' missions while dealing with inadequate budgets, stereotypical attitudes of black inadequacy, insensitive politicians, and, in many cases, faculty and staff members who are insensitive to the needs and mission of the institutions. It is imperative that leaders of HBCUs have a keen insight into the problems the institutions face in relation to comparable white institutions. Leaders of HBCUs walk a thin line daily between compassion for and understanding of the students and the realities of administrative and fiscal accountability. The HBCU leader is further hampered by the question, Are these schools necessary?

Despite this daunting task, many HBCU presidents have performed magnificently in both the public and private HBCUs. They have stood the test with accreditation agencies, federal and state agencies, foundations, boards of regents and boards of trustees, the corporate and private sectors, and the public.

In the twenty-first century, HBCUs continue to offer tangible opportunities for blacks to have a leadership role in higher education. The American Council on Education reported in its 2000 edition of *The American College President* that in 1998 blacks represented 6 percent of *all* higher education presidents. The majority of the black presidents are in public baccalaureate and master's degree institutions. In 1999, 19 percent of HBCU presidents were female (National Association for Equal Opportunity in Higher Education 1999). This is the same percentage of female presidents nationally (Lively 2000). The significance of these percentages is that except for HBCUs, male and female black college students have (1) few opportunities to see and know black mentors in leadership roles; (2) few tangible examples of blacks being in charge; and (3) little exposure to black role models in college presidencies, whereby it becomes a future career option. This last point is important to the future of HBCUs.

Faculty

HBCUs are tangible examples of staff and faculty diversity in higher education. In 1993, the most recent data available, 24 percent of the total staff at HBCUs was nonblack, and 34 percent of the total faculty at HBCUs was nonblack (Jackson 2001). No historically white colleges and universities can report similar percentages for staff or faculty diversity.

Yet, faculty diversity does not always work to the advantage of HBCUs. One of the plaintiffs in the *Wooden* case, discussed in Chapter 3, serves as an example: She decided it was not prestigious to teach in an institutions that is predominately black and wanted to work in an "interracial" environment. As another example, Cynthia L. Jackson recalls an encounter with a white chair of a department of an HBCU at a national network conference for HBCU faculty. The department chair asked her why she was at the conference. She explained that she was the Graduate College dean at The Union Institute and was promoting a program designed to increase the number of black faculty with doctorates at HBCUs. The chair responded, "Why do they need doctorates, all they are doing is teaching." When Jackson asked him, "Isn't that what you do?" he did not reply. These two examples are a sample of the number of nonblacks who have negative attitudes about working at an HBCU and their black colleagues. How can people with this attitude promote the mission of HBCUs? Many nonblacks at HBCUs are there because they could not obtain a position at traditionally white institutions. Yet HBCUs hire them because the nonblacks have the credentials needed for accreditation.

It would be unfair to assume that all qualified blacks would be capable and effective HBCU faculty and that all qualified nonblacks teach at HBCUs while they wait for something better or because they cannot do better. Consider Victoria L. Valentine, editor of *The Crisis*, the magazine of the NAACP, who notes how nationally recognized black faculty considered leaving Harvard University after the Harvard president raised questions about them maintaining the scholarship and research requirements of faculty at the institution. She wonders if these blacks would be willing and/or able to adapt to the more restricted environment and expectations of lower salaries, regular teaching schedules, constant mentoring of students, extremely limited support staff, and limited resources at other universities, specifically HBCUs (2002). There are also nonblack faculty who are capable and willing to meet the challenges and academically thrive at HBCUs. This is noted in Frank W. Wu's book *Yellow: Race in America Beyond Black and White*. Wu is an Asian American law professor at Howard University.

Faculty at public HBCUs are paid less than faculty at public historically white institutions. In the 1990s, increases in faculty salaries at HBCUs "generally kept pace with those at other colleges, though salaries at HBCUs remained somewhat lower" (National Center for Education Statistics 1996, on-line). In 1993–1994, female faculty at HBCUs "earned 86 percent of the average for all female faculty members compared to male HBCU faculty, who earned 79 percent of the average for all male faculty. Within HBCUs, men's salaries averaged 12 percent higher than women's salaries, compared to a 24 percent difference for all institutions."

Given the tendency for many HBCU presidents to be authoritarian and autocratic, faculty at some HBCUs contemplate unionizing. One such case is at LeMoyne-Owen College in Tennessee. In September 2002, the faculty of LeMoyne-Owen College formally declared their intent to form a union to ensure that they have a voice in the future of the college:

> Professors at LeMoyne-Owen College have won the right to form a union, but the administration . . . is refusing to bargain and continues to wage a legal battle against the effort. . . . A regional director of the National Labor Relations Board found that professors neither possess absolute control over any facet of the school's operation, nor effectively recommend policies affecting its administration. And in some cases the president has circumvented the standing committees by appointing people to special committees. . . . Even the Faculty Assembly does not function independently of the administration . . . since the dean of faculty calls the meetings and set the agendas. (Smallwood 2002, on-line)

The college's immediate past president contended that faculty "have considerable influence during the college's accreditation process and also supervise other programs," thus implying that faculty have managerial status and therefore are not covered by federal labor laws to unionize. However, the regional director of the National Labor Relations Board found that "decision-making authority of the LeMoyne-Owen faculty is routine, lacking the breadth and the discretion necessary to give the professors managerial status" (Smallwood 2002, on-line). The college administration requested a review by the full National Labor Relations Board in Washington, D.C., in October 2002.

Admissions and Retention

HBCUs have a higher retention rate of African American college students than do historically white institutions (Constantine 1995). The high retention rate is attributed generally to two factors: (1) a supportive environment, and (2) the readiness of HBCUs to provide remediation for students who need it. A key factor that attributes to the high retention and graduation rate is the small classes, which provide individual attention (Jackson 2001). The average student-to-teacher ratio in HBCU undergraduate classes is 14:1. In relation to the small class size, the U.S. Department of Education, Office of Civil Rights (1991, on-line) notes, "Traditionally, the faculties at many HBCUs place as much, or more, emphasis on teaching and students service activities as on research. This permits more time for personal and high quality student-teacher interactions."

LeBlanc (2001) estimated that in fall 2002, approximately 300,000 students would matriculate at the 103 HBCUs. The enrollment numbers at HBCUs are gradually increasing. LeBlanc attributes this to three circumstances. First, an anti–affirmative action climate has "sent black students hunting for friendlier environments." Second, black students who transfer from traditionally white institutions to HBCUs "report that the social and cultural support they find [at HBCUs]—so important to intellectual and emotional development—are often missing on [white campuses]." Finally, "white students and other nonblacks [are] looking for [a] good education at affordable prices" (47–48).

HBCUs and Technology

To be on par, HBCUs have to be ahead of any curve. This follows the age-old requirement that blacks have to be twice as good just to be considered average. Although circumstances have continued to place HBCUs several steps behind historically white institutions, the introduction of technology into higher education compounds the circumstances.

Internet access, specifically, and technology, generally, are critical to HBCUs remaining competitive. Although several HBCUs have the capacity, there remain many that have not been able to focus their full attention to this educational resource and administrative tool. This is particularly true of many small, private HBCUs (Jackson 2001).

The National Association for Equal Opportunity in Higher Education (NAFEO) conducted an assessment of the computing resources, networking, and connectivity of HBCUs. The study was funded by the U.S. Department of Education (2000). According to the NAFEO report, approximately two-thirds of all HBCUs responded to the survey. The findings from the assessment are considered a point of reference to determine the "degree to which [HBCUs] are keeping pace with change." A summary finding from the report is that HBCUs' "overall status on the information superhighway [was] more positive than originally assumed. However, there are serious areas of *digital divide* in the area of student access, high speed connectivity and insufficient infrastructure, particularly at smaller, rural institutions" (1).

Less than 25 percent of HBCU students owned personal or laptop computers at the beginning of the twenty-first century (NAFEO 1999). In 2000, the president of Morris Brown College required all faculty and students to have laptop computers. This was a first for an HBCU (Dilonardo 2002). How and whether this requirement was implemented has not been reported. However, the requirement raises a couple of concerns. First, requiring all students to have laptop computers is an admirable expectation. Perhaps it is an attempt to close the digital divide. Yet, given the financial constraints of the majority of HBCU students just to stay in college, it is in all probability not a realistic response if students are expected to defray the cost of the required laptops. Second, faculty having laptops without training on how to use them is useless. "Work is needed [with faculty] in the area of integrating technology in the classroom" (NAFEO 2000, v).

Although technological changes have influenced all higher educational institutions, the gross limitations of fiscal, physical, and human resources have created a gap in the science capacity at minority institutions (Nunn 2001). Johnson and Packer (1987) in a national report, *Workforce 2000: Work and Workers for the Twenty-First Century,* stated that the ability of the United States to remain competitive in a global economy is directly related to the educational opportunities and training provided to those groups who have historically been underrepresented and underserved.

Not all students—and especially not all blacks—have access to quality facilities and instructions in science. The result has been a population that is inadequately prepared to fulfill the needs of a technologically competent workforce (Clark 1996). America's historically black colleges and universities continue to play a significant role in the production of bachelor's degrees earned by blacks, generally, and in the sciences, specifically, despite the percentage of black students at historically white institutions. Thus strengthening the undergraduate programs and infrastructure at HBCUs would provide a significant resource of skilled, diverse talent for the rapidly changing technological workforce (Nunn 2001).

The ability of HBCUs to offer online courses and degrees is dependent on their technological infrastructure, coupled with the mission of the institution. Public HBCUs and large private HBCUs are more likely to offer online access to education. Public HBCUs are encouraged and receive funding from the respective state to offer online education. The large private ones can use their monetary resources to offer online education. Those offering online education are more likely to offer courses rather than degrees. For several years the primary form of distance education for HBCUs was "teleconferences." A 1999 NAFEO study states that "58 percent of black institutions participated in some form of distance education, but that 85 percent of them were not offering degrees online" (vi).

> Small private HBCUs are less likely to offer online education. One reason is the lack of funding. Of equal importance is a lack of compatibil-

ity between distance education and the institutional mission. These schools will integrate technology in the classroom, libraries, and dormitories but believe that online or distance education does not provide the nurturing, socially cultivating and individualized atmosphere that is the hallmark of HBCUs. (Arnone 2002, on-line)

NAFEO's study was based on a combination of public and private HBCUs. A study conducted by the Thurgood Marshall Scholarship Fund provides a more positive picture for its forty-four HBCUs public member institutions. Roach (2001) summarizes the findings:

> Eight institutions have more than 50 percent of their classes actively using the Web to enhance student learning; 61 percent have a formal group advocating technology education for faculty; only two institutions have more than 50 percent of their classes with material on the Web; eight out of ten institutions have classes that conduct research and make limited usage of emerging technologies; more than half of the 44 member institutions have hired a chief information officers; 42 institutions have a campus network; most have sophisticated IT infrastructures. (35)

Arnone (2002, on-line) gives the following sample of on-line opportunities provided by HBCUs. In keeping with the NAFEO and Marshall Fund studies, it is not surprising that only two private HBCUs are in the sample.

> Clark Atlanta University (Ga.) offers twenty courses
> Elizabeth City State University (N.C.) offerings range from fifteen to twenty-three courses, depending on the semester
> Hampton University (Va.) offers one bachelor's degree program and seventeen courses
> Lawson State Community College (Ala.) offers twelve courses
> North Carolina A&T State University offers one bachelor's degree program, one master's degree program, and fifty to sixty courses during various semesters
> North Carolina Central University offers one doctoral degree program and twenty-three courses
> Norfolk State University (Va.) offers fourteen courses
> South Carolina State University offers fifty-eight courses

West Virginia State College offers one to two courses depending on the semester

The army's Historically Black Colleges and Universities/Minority Institutions program is one avenue for HBCUs to increase and enhance their technology capacity. The objective is to provide "scientific and technical information products and services at no charge to faculty, staff, and students by assisting with development and improvement of HBCU scientific and technical curriculum and research programs and to strengthen their ability to compete for federal grants and contracts" (Historically Black Colleges and Universities /Minority Institutions, on-line).

In addition, the army program provides distance education to enlisted soldiers through U.S. universities and pays their tuition. Arnone reports that North Carolina State A&T, the first HBCU to participate, cited "infrastructure issues" as well as participation being "awfully demanding on . . . resources," which caused them to consider leaving the program. In 2002 Alabama A&M University, Bethune–Cookman College (Fla.), Florida A&M University, Grambling State University (La.), Morgan State University (Md.), and North Carolina Central University formed the "Virtual HBCU consortium" by deciding to participate in the program (Historically Black Colleges and Universities/Minority Institutions, on-line).

Facilities

With the freeing of slaves one of the first acts was to build formal schoolhouses. Their crude construction was a monument to the hopes and aspirations of a people to acquire knowledge, overcome poverty, and be accepted as human beings.

Today some HBCUs still stand as majestic, yet substandard, monuments to the hope for a better life through education. However, in the twenty-first century poorly equipped, inadequately funded institutions—the case with many HBCUs—will not serve students well in the highly technological society. Though change in education, particularly higher education, is always slow, no educational institution is immune from major forces impacting society. Technological advances are among the major forces influencing education. HBCU facilities must be constructed or renovated to prepare students for a life in a technological society and knowledge-based economy that is increasingly complex and filled with change (Nunn 2001).

Fiscal Concerns

There are now 103 identified historically black colleges and universities in the United States. There were once more. The number of public black two-year colleges declined primarily due to mergers, as discussed earlier in this chapter. In addition, the number of private four-year black colleges has decreased, with nine black colleges closing since 1976 (Joiner 1998). Bishop College (Tex.), which was established in 1881 and affiliated with the Baptist Church, closed in 1988. In 1990 Paul Quinn College (Tex.) acquired and moved its main campus to the former site of Bishop College. Mississippi Industrial College, a private institution founded in 1905, closed in 1986. Daniel Payne College (Ala.), a private four-year college founded in 1889 in Birmingham, closed in 1977. Lomax-Hannon Junior College (Ala.), founded in 1893 as a two-year college affiliated with the African Methodist Episcopal Zion Church, closed in 1984. Natchez Junior College (Miss.), a private two-year college founded in 1884, closed in 1989. Prentiss Institute (Miss.), a private two-year college founded in 1907, closed in 1990.

The closing of many HBCUs, and the precarious existence of many others, is related to the symbiotic relationship between fiscal deficits and regional accreditation. Achieving regional accreditation is to a great degree contingent upon institutions meeting certain "quality" standards in academic programs and institutional support systems. These systems include leadership, faculty credentials, library and other educational contents, facilities, and fiscal soundness. An institution that is operating with a fiscal deficit is unlikely to be able to meet the accreditation standards. Thus, it loses accreditation and the potential of federal funding. Without the available federal student loans on which many HBCUs students are dependent, students are less likely to attend a school.

Financial resources are a two-prong issue. One issue is student expenditure; the other is faculty salary. The National Center for Education Statistics (1996, on-line) reports that "during the 1993–1994 academic year per student expenditures at public HBCUs [were] lower than those at other public institutions." In addition, due to the slow rate of growth, private HBCUs spent about 14 percent less per student than all private postsecondary institutions.

The U.S. Congress reports in the "Findings" section (Item 9 F) of the Individuals with Disabilities Education Act (IDEA) Amendments of 1997 that "as recently as 1991, historically black colleges and universities enrolled 44 percent of the African-American teacher trainees in the Nation. However, in 1993, historically black colleges and universities received only 4 percent of the discretionary funds for special education and related services personnel training under this Act." This finding is significant when one considers the percentage of African American children who are identified and placed in special education programs.

Most private HBCUs are tuition driven. This means that all or the majority of the operating budget is based on tuition received.

Lottie Joiner reports that in 1996 "at least 25 historically black colleges were operating in the red. Even Howard University (D.C.) had a $6.9 million budget deficit in 1994" (1998, 50). Howard University is the only HBCU classified by Carnegie as a doctoral/research university—extensive.

National Achievement Scholars and Rhodes Scholars

For some of the reasons noted by Catherine LeBlanc in the "Admissions and Retention" section of this chapter, an increasing number of black students with high SAT scores and who are National Achievement Scholars are selecting HBCUs rather than historically white institutions. Florida A&M University currently claims the most black National Merit Scholars. It attracts as many National Merit Scholars as Harvard University (*Black Issues in Higher Education* 2001).

Christopher Elders is a 2001 Rhodes scholar from Morehouse College in Georgia. He chose to attend Morehouse instead of Dartmouth College or Northwestern University, where he was also accepted. At a hearing on HBCUs before the U.S. Congress in 2002 he was questioned about his choice for college. His response illuminates why black students of all academic readiness levels opt for HBCUs: "Of course, there is not one type of college for everyone. With surface distinctions removed, the subtle distinctions among African-American students became apparent. . . .The all-black environment creates a sense of freedom for many students to assume roles and responsibilities they might otherwise not pursue at another institution (Mollison 2002).

Since the first selection of Rhodes scholars in 1903, 2,950 Americans have won scholarships from 304 colleges and universities. There have been four Rhodes scholars from HBCUs: In 1986, Howard University was the first HBCU to have a Rhodes scholar, a communications major named Mark Alleyne. In 1993, Morehouse College student Nima

Warfield, an English major, was awarded the scholarship. Carla Joy Peterman, a student at Howard University majoring in history, was awarded the scholarship in 1999. In 2001, Christopher Elders, the political science major from Morehouse College who appeared before Congress, was selected. Morehouse has established a special program to prepare students for competitive scholarships and fellowships.

THE CONTINUED NEED FOR HBCUS IN THE TWENTY-FIRST CENTURY

Safety, a sense of belonging, and a belief in the potential of students are essential to academic success. Yet too many black students at historically white institutions have not been privy to these academic success essentials.

A Harvard University professor attributes the concept of grade inflation at historically white institutions to a conspiratorial scheme to bolster black students' self-esteem. He states, "When grade inflation got started, in the late 60s and early 70s, white professors, imbibing the spirit of affirmative action, stopped giving low or average grades to black students and, to justify or conceal it, stopped giving those grades to white students as well" (Maysfield 2001, B24). A professor at Colgate University (N.Y.) has charged "that professors on his campus give minority students 'undeservedly high grades' and let them discuss their 'feelings' in class rather than encourage them to offer 'reasoned opinions'" (Wilson 2001, A10).

At Auburn University (Ala.) two white fraternities dressed in Ku Klux Klan robes or blackface for Halloween. Pictures from the parties were made public. "In some of the pictures, [the white] students in blackface can be seen wearing copies of Omega Psi Phi's [a black fraternity] T-shirts—as well as fake Afros—while mimicking gang signs. Several [of the white] students carrying rifles or wearing Ku Klux Klan robes hold a noose around the neck of a [white student] in blackface. . . . Some of the photos are posed in front of a Confederate battle flag" (Kellogg 2001, on-line).

In 2002, the police supervisor at Auburn University was found to be a member of the Ku Klux Klan who recruited other officers to join the Klan. The supervisor gave an officer "a compact disk of music with lyrics advocating white supremacy and violence against blacks" (Flores 2002, on-line).

For a year, an unknown person at Indiana University–Purdue sent over 100 e-mails with racist messages to students, faculty, and staff. The individual has not been apprehended (Carnevale 2002, on-line).

In 2003, students at the University of Louisville (Ky.) received T-shirts printed with "10 Reasons Why a Beer Is Better than a Black Man" on the front. The shirts were distributed by Bank One as part of its on-campus promotion campaign for students to receive credit cards from the bank (Pitsch 2003, on-line).

These incidents are only a microcosm of situations black students encounter at historically white institutions today. In *The Agony of Education: Black Students at White Colleges and Universities* (1996), Feagin, Vera, and Imani provide a sociological examination of the discouraging, painful, and frequently degrading experiences of black students at public historically white institutions.

Educational anthropologists have found consistently in international comparative studies conducted in the 1980s and 1990s that the dominant group in a society has higher IQ test scores and grades than the dominated groups. This was found with research groups of Koreans in Japan, Aborigines in Australia, Maoris in New Zealand, and Irish in England (Jackson 2001). Analysis of those studies identifies three factors that contribute to the dominant group surpassing the dominated group in IQ test scores and grades. First, the dominated group is targeted for discrimination in all aspects of the dominant society, and the discrimination begins with the education afforded the dominated group. Second, curricula that are developed by and for the dominant group disenfranchises the dominated group. Third, the historical link between the dominant group and the dominated group determines the severity of the first two factors. Dominated groups whose original connection with the dominant group was in apartheid conditions such as slavery and colonization are more likely to collectively score lower on IQ tests and have lower grades, as compared to the dominant group. Carter Woodson agrees, noting that

> the most important thing in the uplift of [blacks] is almost entirely in the hands of those who have enslaved them and now segregated them. . . .The present system under the control of the whites trains the [African American] to be white and at the same time convinces him [and her] of the impropriety or the impossibility of becoming white. ([1933] 1991, 22–23)

Woodson's statement remains accurate in the twenty-first century. It also serves as the basis for the continued need of HBCUs.

There are approximately 280 black independent precollege schools, which serve an estimated 8 percent of black school-age children. Approximately 2 percent of school-age black children are in parochial or private white schools. The other 90 percent are in public schools (Jackson 2001).

Even when the public school systems' student population are predominately African American, whites control them. The curricula of public school systems as well as parochial and private white schools promote an extremely Eurocentric curriculum that is grounded in the history, traditions, contributions, and ideologies of people of European ancestry. Such curricula at the most exclude and at the least marginalize the history, traditions, contributions, and ideologies of people of African ancestry and other people of color. Some public school districts recently have attempted to offer multicultural curricula, where the subject matter is to be grounded in the history, experiences, traditions, contributions, and ideologies of multiple racial and ethnic groups. However, the implementation of the multicultural curricula principles is either supplemental or incidental. In 1996, just 18.9 percent of kindergarten through twelfth-grade teachers and 15.8 percent of principals and assistant principals were black. Unfortunately, as the number of black students in public schools increases, fewer blacks in college are choosing education as a profession (Jackson 2001). The percentages remain consistent with current statistics.

Cynthia L. Jackson notes, "Research and observations conclude that the public schooling of African American children systematically requires them to forfeit their cultural ties, demeans their self-esteem, and has them relinquish their diverse forms of expression. This is attributed, in large part, to the reality and experience gulf between white teachers and black students" (2001, 60). Black school-age children continue to be overrepresented in special education classes and disproportionately suspended and expelled. These actions result in the separation and exclusion of a large percentage of black students from the general student population and/or the school on a regular basis. Thus, 92 percent of black school-age children have few educational experiences that affirm them.

Clearly, vestiges of separate education programs for blacks are evident today within educational systems. This is illustrated by the resegregation of students by aptitude and attitude, disproportionate denial and repositioning of black teachers and administrators, and discipline of black students for minimal infractions when they disrupt the "comfort zone" of white teachers and students, to name a few.

In postsecondary institutions, there is an evolutionary strategy evolving that is designed to shift certain students, most probably black, Hispanics, and poor whites, to selected educational institutions. No doubt, many of these "selected" institutions will be HBCUs and other non–flagship universities. Yet such a strategy, real or contrived, suggests an even greater reason for HBCUs to be preserved and enhanced and for them to strive for academic and administrative excellence.

Education, family, and community are the framework for the support system that is vital to sociopsychological development, and educational achievement and attainment, for all youth, but especially dominated groups, such as blacks. HBCUs rebuild what public school desegregation dismantled for most black students. HBCUs reconnect the education of blacks with the black family and the black community.

In the thirty-eight years between 1960 and 1998, the percentage of African Americans receiving high school diplomas increased approximately 60 percent. In spite of the increase in high school graduations, only 14.7 percent of African Americans completed four or more years of college (Jackson 2001).

Schooling is the interplay between and among the institutional environment, climate, and culture in which learning is to occur. *Institutional environment* is the curriculum, instructional practices, strategies and methods, assessment decisions, administrative and instructional staff, and students. *Institutional climate* is the intangible sense that people have about whether they feel they belong or are alienated, feel trust or distrust of people in the institutions, and are involved or uninvolved in the life of the institution. *Institutional culture* is the beliefs, values, and assumptions that people within the institution make about each other (Jackson 2001). The institutional factors of environment, climate, and culture also contribute to the individuals' self-concept, self-esteem, group identity, participation, and, most important, academic success and future educational attainment.

The mission of an educational institution and the exercise of authority determine how the interplay occurs, and to whose advantage. Given blacks' historical link to whites in the United States, the institutional environment, climate, and culture are critical factors to blacks' academic achievement and educational attainment. Black students at HBCUs report a more positive relationship with organizational environment, climate, and culture than do blacks at historically white institutions (Allen, Epps, and Haniff 1991; Feagin, Vera, and Imani 1996; Jenkins 2000).

HBCUs have consistently liberated the black mind and intellect. William Gray, the president and CEO of the United Negro College Fund, provides a concise explanation of the continued need for HBCUs: "Just as the religious and ethnic colleges of early immigrants—Georgetown, Yeshiva, Brigham Young—provided doorways for their rejected communities, HBCUs continue to serve all [blacks]. They have a vital role to play. From their halls have come—and will continue to come—the business persons, physicians, scientists, engineers, architects, teachers, public servants, and artists [blacks] need to be strong in the twenty-first century" (1997, on-line).

REFERENCES

Allen, Walter R., Edgar G. Epps, and Nesha A. Haniff, eds. 1991. *College in Black and White: African American Students in Predominantly White and in Historically Black Public Universities.* Albany, NY: State University of New York Press.

Anderson, Claud. 1994. *Black Labor, White Wealth.* Edgewood, MD: Duncan & Duncan, Inc.

Anderson, James D. 1988. *The Education of Blacks in the South, 1860–1935.* Chapel Hill, NC: University of North Carolina Press.

Arnone, Michael. 2002. "Historically Black Colleges Grapple with Online Education." *The Chronicle of Higher Education,* http://chronicle.com/weekly/v48/i30/30a0270.1htm (cited April 20, 2002).

Banks, William M. 1996. *Black Intellectuals.* New York: W. W. Norton.

Black Issues in Higher Education. 1999. "Top 15 Baccalaureate Institutions of Minority Ph.D.s." *Black Issues in Higher Education* 16, 19: 41.

———. 2001. "FAMU Ties Harvard in Recruitment of National Achievement Scholars." http://www.blackissues.com//020101/binews8.cfm (cited February 16, 2002).

Brown, Hugh S., and Lewis B. Mayhew. 1965. *American Higher Education.* New York: Center for Applied Research in Education, Inc.

Bullock, Henry Allen. 1967. *A History of Negro Education in the South: From 1619 to the Present.* Cambridge, MA: Harvard University Press.

Carnegie Commission for Higher Education. 1971. *From Isolation to Mainstream: Problems of the Colleges Founded for Negroes.* Upper Saddle River, NJ: Carnegie Commission for Higher Education.

Carnegie Foundation for the Advancement of Teaching. 2000. *The Carnegie Classification of Institutions of Higher Education: A Technical Report.* New York: Carnegie Foundation for the Advancement of Teaching.

Carnevale, Dan. 2002. "Anonymous Racist E-Mail Floods a College Campus." *The Chronicle of Higher Education,* http://chronicle.come/free/2002/04/2002040501t.htm (cited April 20, 2002).

Carroll, Evelyn C. J. 1982. "Priorities in Philanthropic Support for Private Negro Colleges and Universities, 1930–1973." Ph.D. diss., University of Michigan (UMI No. 8214970).

Carson, Clayborne, David J. Garrow, Gerald Gill, Vincent Harding, and Darlene Clark Hine, eds. 1991. *Eyes on the Prize Civil Rights Reader: Documents, Speeches, and Firsthand Accounts from the Black Freedom Struggle.* New York: Penguin Books.

Clark, Julia V. 1996. *Redirecting Science Education.* Thousand Oaks, CA: Corwin Press.

Clarke, Robyn D. 1998. "Partnering for Success." *Black Enterprise* 29, 2: 112–116.

Coggins, Patrick. 2001. *Analysis of Substance Abuse Degree Programs Offered by HBCUs.* Unpublished report, Stetson University, Deland, FL.

Constantine, Jill M. 1995. "The Effect of Attending Historically Black Colleges and Universities on Future Wages of Black Students." *Industrial and Labor Relations Review* 48, 3: 531–546.

Cook, Samuel DuBois. 1978. "The Social-Ethical Role and Responsibility of the Black College." Pp. 51–67 in *Black Colleges in America: Challenge, Development, Survival.* Edited by Charles V. Willie and Ronald R. Edmonds. New York: Teachers College Press.

Cooperative State Research, Education, and Extension. 2000. *1890 Land Grant Colleges and Universities: History of the 1890 Programs.* http://www.reeusda.gov/1890/history.htm (cited January 21, 2002).

Davidson, Douglas V. 2001. *Ethcaste: PanAfrican Communalism and the Black Middleclass.* Lanham, MD: University Press of America.

DuBois, William E. B. [1903a] 1966a. "Of Mr. Booker T. Washington and Others." Pp. 509–518 in *Negro Social and Political Thought, 1850–1920: Representative Texts.* Edited by Howard Brotz. New York: Basic Books.

———. [1903b] 1966b. "The Talented Tenth." Pp. 518–533 in *Negro Social and Political Thought, 1850–1920: Representative Texts.* Edited by Howard Brotz. New York: Basic Books.

Duke University Medical Center Library. 1999. http://mclibrary.duke.edu/hot/blkhist.html (cited March 14, 2003).

Feagin, Joe E., Herman Vera, and Nikitah Imani. 1996. *The Agony of Education: Black Students at White Colleges and Universities.* New York: Routledge.

Fields, Cheryl D. 1996. "Taking Care of Business." *Black Issues in Higher Education* 13, 21: 12–22.

Flores, Christopher. 2002. "Auburn U. at Montgomery Fires Police Supervisor After Allegations of Racist Behavior." *The Chronicle of Higher Education,* http://chronicle.com/daily/2002/02/2002022504n.htm (cited March 23, 2002).

Freire, Paulo. [1970] 2001. *Pedagogy of the Oppressed.* New York: Continuum International Publishing Group Inc.

Gibbs, Spencer C. 1999. *Above Our Heads: The Making of a Morehouse Man.* New York: Hamilton House Publishers, Ltd.

Gonzales, Juan L., Jr. 1990. "The Black Experience in America: From Slavery to Freedom." Pp. 79–107 in *Racial and Ethnic Groups in America.* Dubuque, IA: Kendall/Hunt Publishing Company.

Good, Henry, and James D. Teller. 1973. *A History of American Education.* New York: Macmillan Press.

Gray, William H., III. 1997. *The Case for All-Black Colleges.* http://www.eric.ed.gov/resources/ericreview/vol5no3/black.html (cited March 25, 2002).

Hebel, Sara. 2001. "A Settlement and More Division in Mississippi." *The Chronicle of Higher Education,* http://chronicle.com/weekly/v47/i34/34a0231.htm (cited February 5, 2002).

Hefner, David. 2002. "One Struggle, One Battle, One Survival." *Black Issues in Higher Education* 19, 2: 10–11.

Historically Black Colleges and Universities/Minority Institutions. http://www.dtic/mil/dtic/hbcumi/index.html (cited April 24, 2002).

Howard University Charter Day. 1999. http://founders.howard.edu/charterday99/swygert (cited February 16, 2002).

Jackson, Cynthia L. 2001. *African American Education: A Reference Handbook.* Santa Barbara, CA: ABC-CLIO.

Jackson, William S. 1970. *Thoughts on the Black Experience.* Unpublished manuscript.

Jenkins, Erica Denise. 2000. "Who Is More Satisfied? A Comparison of African American Graduates of Historically Black Colleges and Universities and Predominantly White Institutions." Ph.D. diss., University of Iowa. Abstract in *Dissertation Abstracts International* 61: 12 A.

Johnson, W. B., and A. Packer. 1987. *Workforce 2000: Work and Workers for the Twenty-First Century.* Indianapolis, IN: Hudson Institute.

Joiner, Lottie L. 1998. "Historically Broke Colleges and Universities. *Emerge* (September), 48–53.

Kannerstein, Gregory. 1978. "Black Colleges: Self Concept." Pp. 29–50 in *Black Colleges in America: Challenge, Development, Survival.* Edited by Charles V. Willie and Ronald R. Edmonds. New York: Teachers College Press.

Kellogg, Alex P. 2001. "Auburn U. Considers Expelling 2 Fraternities after Party with Mock Lynching, Blackface." *The Chronicle of Higher Education,* http://chronicle.com/daily/2001/11/2001110705n.htm (cited March 23, 2002).

LeBlanc, Catherine W. 2001. "State of the HBCUs." *The New Crisis* 108, 5: 46–49.

Leggon, Cheryl B., and Willie Pearson Jr. 1997. "The Baccalaureate Origins of African American Female Ph.D. Scientists." *Journal of Women and Minorities in Science and Engineering* 3, 4: 213–224.

Lewis, John. 1998. *Walking with the Wind: A Memoir of the Movement.* San Diego, CA: Harcourt Brace and Company.

Lively, Kit. 2000. *Diversity Increases among Presidents.* http://plsc.iark.edu/FW/diversity_increases_among_presid.htm (cited February 28, 2002).

Lomax, Louis E. 1962. *The Negro Revolt.* New York: Harper and Row.

Maggett, Linda L. 1996. "The HBCU Presidential Pressure Cooker." *Black Issues in Higher Education* 13: 26–28.

Marable, Manning. 1998. *Black Leadership.* New York: Columbia University Press.

Mayfield, Harvey C. 2001. "Grade Inflation: It's Time to Face the Facts." *The Chronicle of Higher Education* 47, 30: B24.

Mays, Benjamin E. 1978. "The Black College in Higher Education." Pp. 19–28 in *Black Colleges in America: Challenge, Development, Survival.* Edited by Charles V. Willie and Ronald R. Edmonds. New York: Teachers College Press.

Mollison, Andrew. 2002. *Black Colleges Heard on Hill.* http://www/accessatlanta.com/ajc/epaper/editions/thrusday/news_c3b616de231f60d000c3.html (cited February 16, 2002).

Morehouse College News. 2001. http://newsrelease/2001/december/newrhodescholar (cited February 16, 2001).

National Association for Equal Opportunity in Higher Education. 1999. *Institutional and Presidential Profiles on the Nations' Historically and Predominantly Black Colleges and Universities: Bridging the New Millennium, 1999–2000.* Silver Springs, MD: National Association for Equal Opportunity in Higher Education.

National Center for Education Statistics. 1996. *Historically Black Colleges and Universities: 1976–1994.* Washington, DC: National Center for Education Statistics. Available at http://nces.ed.gov/pubs/96902.htm (cited February 26, 2002).

————. 2000. *Fall Enrollment in Institutions of Higher Education: Integrated Postsecondary Education Data System.* Washington, DC: U.S. Department of Education. Available at http://nces.edu.gov/pubs2001/digest/dt223.html. (cited February 26, 2002).

————. 2001a. *Fall Enrollment in Colleges and Universities Survey: Integrated Postsecondary Education Data System.* Washington, DC: U.S. Department of Education. Available at http://nces.ed.gov/pubs2001/proj01/tables/table16.asp (cited February 26, 2002).

————. 2001b. *Fall Enrollment in Colleges and Universities Survey: Integrated Postsecondary Education Data System.* Washington, DC: U.S. Department of Education. Available at http://nces.ed.gov/pubs2001/proj01/tables/table18.asp. (cited February 26, 2002).

New Black College Presidents. 1999. *Ebony* 54 (October), 84–98.

Nunn, Eleanor F. 2001. *Biotechnology Education and Training in North Carolina Public Historically Minority Universities: A Five-Year Evaluation.* Ph.D. diss., Union Institute.

Pascarella, Ernest T., and Patrick T. Terenzini. 1991. *How College Affects Students: Findings and Insights from Twenty Years of Research.* San Francisco: Jossey-Bass, Inc.

Pitsch, Mark. 2003. *Offensive T-Shirt Stirs Anger at U of L: Credit Card Solicitors Banned after Incident.* http://www.courier-journal.com/localnews/2003/01/29/ke012903s357881.htm (cited March 14, 2003).

Roach, Ronald. 1999. "The Race to Save Lives." *Black Issues in Higher Education* 16, 21: 22–16.

————. 2001. "Marshall Fund Releases IT Study on Public HBCUs." *Black Issues in Higher Education* 18, 7: 35.

————. 2002. "Unequal Treatment: Confronting Racial and Ethnic Disparities in Health Care." *Black Issues in Higher Education* 19, 7: 26.

Roebuck, Julian B., and Komanduri S. Murty. 1993. *Historically Black Colleges and Universities: Their Place in American Higher Education.* Westport, CT: Praeger.

Shaw, Theodore M. 2000. *The Debate over Race Needs Minority Students' Voices.* University of Maryland. http://www.inform.umd.edu/EdRes/Topic/Diversity/Specific/Race/General/Reading/deba999999.html (cited February 26, 2002).

Smallwood, Scott. 2002. "NLRB Office Approves Faculty Union at Private College in Tennessee." *The Chronicle of Higher Education,* http://chronicle.com/daily/2002/09/2002092402n.htm (cited February 26, 2002).

Smiles, Robin V. 2002. "Race Matters in Health Care." *Black Issues in Higher Education* 19, 7: 22–29.

Smith, Walter L. 1994. *The Magnificent Twelve: Florida's Black Junior Colleges.* Tallahassee, FL: FOUR-G Publishers.

Thomas, Arthur E., and Robert L. Green. 2001. "Historically Black Colleges and Universities: An Irreplaceable National Treasure." Pp. 245–265 in *African American Education: A Reference Handbook.* By Cynthia L Jackson. Santa Barbara, CA: ABC-CLIO.

Trent, William T. 1991. "Focus on Equity: Race and Gender Differences in Degree Attainment: 1975; 1980–81." Pp. 41–59 in *College in Black and White: African American Students in Predominately White and in Historically Black Public Universities.* Edited by Walter R. Allen, Edgar G. Epps, and Nesha Z. Haniff. Albany, NY: State University of New York Press.

U.S. Department of Education. 1996. *Table A1: Fall Enrollment in Historically Black Colleges and University, by Institution, Race/Ethnicity, and Percent of Black Students.* http://www.ed.gov/offices/OERI/PLLI/HBCU/table a1.html (cited February 5, 2002).

U.S. Department of Education. Office of Civil Rights. 1991. *Historically Black Colleges and Universities and Higher Education Desegregation.* Washington, DC: U.S. Department of Education. Available at http://www/ed/gov/offices/OCR/hq9511.htm. Updated December 28, 2000 (cited January 21, 2002).

Valentine, Victoria L. 2002. "What About the HBCUs?" *The New Crisis* 109, 3: 1.

Vlach, John Michael. 1993. *Back of the Big House: The Architecture of Plantation Slavery.* Chapel Hill, NC: University of North Carolina Press.

Walther, Erskine S. 1994. *Some Readings on Historically Black Colleges and Universities.* Greensboro, NC: Management Information and Research.

Washington, Booker T. [1895] 1966. "Atlanta Exposition Address." Pp. 356–359 in *Negro Social and Political Thought, 1850–1920: Representative Texts.* Edited by Howard Brotz. New York: Basic Books.

———. [1907] 1966. "The Fruits of Industrial Training." Pp. 406–417 in *Negro Social and Political Thought, 1850–1920: Representative Texts.* Edited by Howard Brotz. New York: Basic Books.

———. [1911] 1966. "The Mistakes and the Future of Negro Education." Pp. 434–445 in *Negro Social and Political Thought, 1850–1920: Representative Texts.* Edited by Howard Brotz. New York: Basic Books.

White House Initiative on HBCUs. 1996. *A Century of Success: Historically Black Colleges and Universities, America's National Treasure.* Washington, DC: White House Initiative on HBCUs.

Wilson, Robin. 2001. "Colgate Professor Sparks Furor with Comments on Minority Students' Achievement. *The Chronicle of Higher Education* 48, 15: A10.

Wolters, Raymond. 1975. *The New Negro on Campus: Black College Rebellions of the 1920s*. Princeton, NJ: Princeton University Press.

Woodson, Carter G. [1933] 1991. *The Mis-Education of the Negro*. Philadelphia: Hamik's Publications.

Wu, Frank W. 2002. "Why I Teach at Howard." *The New Crisis* 109, 3: 28–32.

Chapter Two

✎ **Chronology**

The chronology of historically black colleges and universities (HBCUs) is inextricably tied to political and social events and educational concerns in the United States. Catalyzed by blacks' quest for educational, political, economic, and social independence, the history and current existence of HBCUs is not only about the birth and maturity of educational institutions but equally about the advancement of a people.

The following chronology is adapted from Cynthia L. Jackson's chronology in *African American Education: A Reference Handbook* (2001). It was modified to address HBCUs specifically. The chronology highlights critical political and social events and educational concerns that influence HBCUs.

1787   The Northwest Ordinance is passed, authorizing sale of public land for support of education, which established the land-grant principle.

1800s   Eighty public and private HBCUs are operating.

1837   Cheyney University of Pennsylvania is founded. It is the first institution of higher learning for African Americans in the United States.

1854   Lincoln University in Pennsylvania is founded. It is the first historically black institution founded specifically for college-level instruction.

1856   Wilberforce University in Ohio is founded. It is closed during the Civil War and reopened by the African Methodist Episcopal (AME) Church. (Richard Allen, a free black, founded the AME Church in 1799.)

1861–1870   The American Missionary Association establishes seven colleges and thirteen normal (teaching) schools for blacks.

1862   The Morrill Act of 1862, passed by the United States Congress, provides federal funds for land-grant institutions of higher education for whites. Some states use parts of these funds to establish education institutions for blacks.

1865   The Thirteenth Amendment to the United States Constitution abolishes slavery.

The United States Bureau of Refugees, Freedmen, and Abandoned Lands, known as the Freedmen's Bureau, is established by Congress to assist newly freed slaves with food, medicine, jobs, contracts, legal matters, and education. It leads to the creation of some HBCUs, including Howard University and Hampton University.

Shaw University in Raleigh, North Carolina, is founded. It is the oldest black postsecondary institution in the South and the first black institution to have a medical school.

One out of ten newly freed slaves can read and write.

1865–1875   Twenty-four private black colleges open.

1867   Howard University is founded through a charter by the United States government to educate African Americans.

1868   The Fourteenth Amendment gives blacks citizenship and "equal protection under the laws."

1870   Twenty-one percent of newly freed blacks are literate.

The Fifteenth Amendment gives blacks the right to vote.

The Freedmen's Bureau is abolished.

1871   Alcorn College is founded in Mississippi. It is the first African American land-grant college.

1876	Meharry Medical College in Tennessee is founded to educate health professionals for blacks. Currently, one-third of all black practicing physicians and dentists graduated from Meharry.
1880	Forty-five percent of blacks in the South are literate.
1887	The Hatch Act is passed, mandating the creation of agricultural experiment stations for scientific research.
1890	The United States Congress passes the Morrill Act of 1890. States with segregated higher education systems are required to provide land-grant institutions for both systems. This Second Morrill Act, as it is called, leads to the creation of seventeen historically black land-grant institutions.
1895	Booker T. Washington's "Atlanta Compromise" speech stresses vocational education for blacks.
1896	The United States Supreme Court in the *Plessy v. Ferguson* decision upholds that states have constitutional authority to provide separate but equal accommodations for blacks.
1900s	Over 100 HBCUs are operating.
1900	Fifty-five percent of the U.S. black population is literate. Approximately 2,600 blacks have postsecondary credentials.
1901	W. E. B. DuBois, author of *The Souls of Black Folks,* presents the concept of the "talented tenth."
1905	The Smith-Lever Act is passed, providing land-grant institutions with federal support for agricultural extension programs in state and local communities.
1914	Talladega College (Ala.) students strike in protest of the attitudes and behaviors of white faculty administrators and faculty toward the black students. Three years later a four-day strike at Morehouse College (Ga.) occurs for the same reasons.

1915   Carter G. Woodson initiates the Association for the Study
            of Negro Life and History. Its name is changed to the Study
            of Afro-American Life and History. Publication of *The Jour-
            nal of Negro History* begins in 1916.

1919   Over twenty race riots occur across the country. (James
            Weldon Johnson named this period "Red Summer.")

1923–1929   HBCU administrators, students, faculty, and alumni as
            well as black communities protest for more black control
            of HBCUs.

1927   Seventy-seven black colleges and universities are operat-
            ing, with a total enrollment of 14,000.

1929   Atlanta University is established as the first African Amer-
            ican institution solely for graduate and professional edu-
            cation.

1932   *The Journal of Negro Education* is founded at Howard Uni-
            versity (D.C.). It publishes research that identifies and de-
            fines the problems and issues in African American educa-
            tion.

1933   Carter G. Woodson's *The Mis-Education of the Negro* is
            published.

1940–1960   The number of black two-year public and private colleges
            grows in keeping with a national increase of two-year col-
            leges.

1944   The United Negro College Fund (UNCF) is incorporated.
            Conceived by Frederick D. Patterson, president of
            Tuskegee Institute (Ala.), now Tuskegee University, it is a
            consortium of thirty-nine private, regionally accredited
            four-year historically black colleges and universities.
            UNCF's purpose is to enhance the quality of education of
            HBCU students, provide scholarships, raise operating
            funds for member institutions, and provide technical as-
            sistance.

1950s   Seventy-five million dollars of public funds each year go to Southern educational institutions that do not admit African Americans.

1950   Congress creates the National Science Foundation.

1958   The National Defense Education Act (NDEA) provides student loans, fellowships, and aid for the improvement in the teaching of science, mathematics, and modern languages.

1960s–1970s HBCU students are at the vanguard of the Civil Rights movement. In addition, there are protests at several HBCUs for more black control and a more black-oriented curriculum.

1960   Sixty-five percent of all black students in higher education are enrolled at HBCUs.

             Four North Carolina A&T State University students sit-in at a Woolworth store lunch counter in Greensboro. This action is considered the beginning of student involvement in the Civil Rights movement.

             The planning meeting for the Student Nonviolent Coordinating Committee (SNCC) is held at Shaw University in Raleigh, N.C.

1961   Report of the United States Commission on Civil Rights titled "Equal Protection of the Laws in Public Higher Education: 1960" recommends that federal funds be disbursed "only to such publicly controlled institutions of higher education as do not discriminate on grounds of race, color, religion, or national origin."

1963   The Higher Education Act (HEA) recognizes the need to provide aid to colleges and universities for the construction of academic facilities.

1964   Affirmative action policies are instituted based on the Civil Rights Act of 1964.

1964 *(con't)*   National Defense Education Act amendments authorize major changes to expand graduate fellowships programs and eliminate discriminatory lending practices to institutions.

1965   President Lyndon B. Johnson signs the Higher Education Act of 1965. The federal government defines historically black colleges and universities. Institutions accredited by accrediting agencies recognized by the secretary of education are eligible for programs and activities to enhance teacher quality, institutional aid, and student financial assistance.

Voting Rights Act of 1965 is signed by President Johnson and reinstated in 1982 by President Ronald Reagan. In 2007 it will come before the U.S. Congress for renewal.

1969   The National Association for Equal Opportunity in Higher Education (NAFEO) is founded. It serves to address the interests of 118 historically and predominately black colleges and universities, primarily as a public policy advocate.

1970s   Thirty-four percent of all black students in higher education are enrolled at HBCUs.

The majority of the black public two-year colleges are merged with historically white two-year colleges or are closed.

1973   The seventeen states that are still operating dual higher education systems are collectively addressed through the *Adams v. Richardson* case. The U.S. Department of Education, Office of Civil Rights (OCR) is accused of not meeting its responsibility to enforce Title VI of the Civil Rights Act of 1964 for higher education desegregation.

1974   A class action suit, *Ayers v. Waller,* subsequently known as *Ayers v. Fordice,* is filed by the Black Mississippians' Council on Higher Education against Mississippi for the state to enforce Title VI of the Civil Rights Act of 1964. When the

U.S. Department of Health, Education, and Welfare (HEW) files suit the case is named *United States v. Fordice*. In the 1992 decision, the U.S. Supreme Court orders the state of Mississippi to dismantle its dual system in higher education. The case is settled in 2002.

1976   Thirty-four percent of all blacks awarded postsecondary degrees earn them from HBCUs.

1977   In the *Adams v. Califano* case the OCR is found lacking in fulfilling its compliance responsibilities for disabilities acts. This finding motivates the OCR to address the desegregation of higher education.

1979   President Jimmy Carter establishes the U.S. Department of Education. This gives education a cabinet seat. Previously, education was part of the Department of Health, Education, and Welfare (HEW).

1980s   Twenty-five percent of all black students in higher education are enrolled at HBCUs.

1980   President Carter, through Executive Order 12232, establishes the White House Initiative on HBCUs. It is to provide a systematic process to help HBCUs access federally funded programs. All subsequent U.S. presidents issue similar executive orders.

1981   President Ronald Reagan calls for a 25 percent cut in federal funds to education. The cutbacks decrease funding to poor students and are detrimental to the future of many black colleges.

1986   Mark Alleyne, a Howard University (D.C.) student, is the first HBCU student to be awarded a Rhodes scholarship.

1987   The Thurgood Marshall Scholarship Fund (TMSF) is created with the Office for the Advancement of Public Black Colleges and Miller Brewing Company. Serving a role similar to the one the UNCF plays for private HBCUs, the TMSF has forty-five public black member institutions. It provides merit-based scholarships to students attending member schools and assists member schools in increasing their endowment through fundraising and marketing campaigns.

1989   President George H. W. Bush establishes the Presient's Advisory Board on Historically Black Colleges and Universities.

1990s   Thirteen HBCUs are in jeopardy of losing their eligibility to participate in the federal student financial aid program due to a student loan default rate of 25 percent or more for three consecutive years. They have until July 1, 2002, to petition to the U.S. Department of Education.

1990   The Credit Reform Act of 1990 enables the U.S. Congress to intervene to address student loan default rates.

1992   President George Bush signs the Higher Education Act amendments, reauthorizing the 1965 Higher Education Act and establishing the Federal Direct Loan Program. The program provides seven forms of student financial assistance through loans and grants and is designed to allow institutions to use federal funds to provide loans directly to students, thereby avoiding private lenders and simplifying the process.

1993   Federal appeals court rules that tax-supported colleges can continue.

        Nima Warfield, a Morehouse College (Ga.) student, is the second HBCU student to be awarded a Rhodes scholarship.

1994   A three-judge panel of the U.S. Court of Appeals unanimously strikes down a University of Maryland scholarship program open to black students. This reverses a 1993 federal court ruling. A Hispanic student denied the right to apply to the program brought the suit in 1990.

1995   Fifteen percent of all black students in higher education are enrolled at HBCUs. This is the plateau in the declining enrollment. Twenty-six percent of all blacks matriculating in four-year institutions are at HBCUs. Twenty-eight percent of bachelor degrees awarded to all blacks are awarded from HBCUs. One out of six blacks earning graduate or professional degrees earn them at HBCUs.

1996   Spelman College's (Ga.) capital campaign reaches $114 million. This is the largest in the history of HBCUs.

Howard University (D.C.) and Hampton University (Va.) lead all HBCUs in the country in recruiting National Achievement Scholars.

Sixteen percent of all black students in higher education are enrolled at HBCUs.

1997   President William Jefferson Clinton formally apologizes for the Tuskegee experiment, a secret governmental study of untreated syphilis in black males. The study began in 1932 and ended in 1972 when uncovered by news reporters.

The Ohio legislature considers closing Central State University due to financial deficits. The university is placed under state financial supervision.

1999   Carla Joy Peterman, a Howard University student, is the third HBCU student to be awarded a Rhodes scholarship.

Dillard University (La.) graduates the largest number of black students of a college in the United States who enter medical school.

2000   Hampton University (Va.) raises $216 million in seven years. This capital campaign fund's goal is to raise $250 million by 2003.

Of the nineteen higher education desegregation cases in the *Adams v. Richardson* case, two states have not reached an agreement on a desegregation plan with the U.S. Department of Education, five states have reached an agree-

2000 *(con't)*   ment with the Department of Education and are being monitored by that department, four stated have reached an agreement with the Department of Education and are being monitored by the Department of Justice, and eight states have reached an agreement with the Department of Education and are declared desegregated (Hebel 2000, online).

A task force of HBCU presidents and U.S. House of Representatives Republican leaders meets to discuss HBCUs and a plan for partnerships with corporations.

2001   Florida A&M University ties Harvard University in recruiting National Achievement Scholars.

President George W. Bush appoints Roderick Paige as the secretary of education for the U.S. Department of Education. Paige is the first black appointed to this position and is an HBCU graduate.

Christopher Elders, a Morehouse College (Ga.) student, is the fourth HBCU student to be awarded a Rhodes scholarship.

A new Congressional subcommittee on Twenty-First Century Competitiveness will oversee all Higher Education Act (HEA) programs except for aid to historically black colleges and universities, Hispanic-serving ones, and other smaller programs.

President Bush's 2003 budget provides limited funding increases for HBCUs.

Virginia, one of the two states that previously had not reached an agreement on a desegregation plan with the Department of Education, signs an agreement with the department, which will monitor it.

2002   President Bush appoints Leonard Spearman, HBCU graduate and former president of two HBCUs, as the executive director of the White House Initiative on HBCUs.

U.S. Secretary of Education Roderick Paige appoints Patrick Swygert, president of Howard University, as the chair of the Historically Black Colleges and Universities Capital Financing Board.

In the 107th United States Congress, 45 percent of blacks in office are graduates of HBCUs.

Oracle Corporation gives over $10 million to the UNCF for the member institutions' technology infrastructure and instruction.

The White House Initiative on HBCUs is relocated from the Department of Education's Office of Post-Secondary Education to the Office of the Secretary of the Department of Education.

The first HBCU student "think tank" on the future of HBCUs is held at Tennessee State University.

President Bush appoints Gerald A. Reynolds as the head of the Office of Civil Rights in the U.S. Department of Education while Congress is in recess. Reynolds, a black, is considered an opponent of affirmative action and civil rights groups. He is responsible for overseeing the enforcement of civil rights and affirmative action issues at all levels of education. If the Senate does not confirm Reynolds to the appointment, then his tenure in the position will conclude.

Central State University in Ohio is released from state financial supervision.

2003   Hoping to increase the number of African American dentists, Tuskegee University and New York University College of Dentistry enter into a collaboration to offer the B.A. and D.D.S degree program. The collaboration is the first of its kind for the two institutions.

Chris Matthews's MSNBC "Hardball College Tour" is broadcast from the campus of North Carolina Central Uni-

2003 *(con't)*   versity. The university is the first HBCU to participate in a "Hardball" broadcast and the first higher education institution to do so that year.

John H. Johnson, publisher and chair of Johnson Publishing Company, gives $4 million to Howard University's School of Communications. Johnson Publishing is the top-ranked black-owned company internationally and publishes *Ebony* magazine and *Jet* magazine.

Delta Sigma Theta Sorority, Inc., establishes a $1 million scholarship endowment to Howard University to honor the sorority's founders. The sorority was established in 1913 at Howard.

Chapter Three

❧ Legal Influences on HBCUs

All branches of the federal government have intervened in the states' governance of public higher education. In this chapter federal interventions that directly or subsequently influenced HBCUs are discussed. More specifically, presented are presidential executive orders, U.S. Constitution amendments, U.S. legislative acts, and federal court cases. The chapter concludes with a discussion of the implications of federal intervention as it relates to HBCUs in the twenty-first century.

GOVERNANCE OF HIGHER EDUCATION

All education systems and institutions in the United States are, to a greater or lesser degree, under the jurisdiction of the state in which they are located. Governance agencies common to all higher education institutions, private and public two-year and higher, are state boards of regents. Regents grant state licenses for institutions to operate within a state. Institutions that want recognition by the U.S. Department of Education seek regional accreditation (discussed in Chapter 1). An institution must have a state license before seeking regional accreditation. The nature of additional governance depends on whether the institution is public or private.

Public postsecondary institutions are governed by the state, in this case, the governor and state legislature, state departments of higher education, and state citizens. In a 1997 report prepared for the California Higher Education Policy Center the authors state that the manner and influence of each constituent is dependent on "the constitutional strength of the Governor, the presence of a strong private higher education sector, constitutional status of public institutions, the existence of a well developed, two-year college sector, collective bargaining, and voter initiatives" (Bowen, Bracco, Callan, Finney, Richardson, and Trombley, on-line). Internally, the governance includes boards of trustees, chancellors and/or presidents, administrative officers, and in varying degrees, faculty and students.

Private higher education institutions receive state licenses, and may obtain regional accreditation, after which their governance is internal. Private institutions are governed by the social, political, legal, and cultural attitudes of their affiliate organizations (including religious bodies) as well as by boards of trustees, presidents, administrative officers, and in some instances faculty and students, in varying degrees.

FEDERAL GOVERNMENT INTERVENTION IN HIGHER EDUCATION

Although governance of public higher education is the responsibility of the states, there are times when the federal government intervenes in the manner in which the state governance system carries out it responsibilities. The three branches of the federal government are executive, legislative, and judicial. As part of their broad range of authority, U.S. presidents can issue executive orders, which are rules, regulations, and instructions with which federal agencies are required to comply. The bicameral legislation is comprised of the House of Representatives and the Senate. As the lawmaking bodies they enact bills and acts, and have the constitutional authority to ratify amendments to the U.S. Constitution. The judicial branch is the multilayered federal court system. The U.S. Supreme Court is the highest court, or the court of last appeal. Its decisions supercede all other court decisions. State courts interpret state constitutions and laws. Federal courts, which include the U.S. Supreme Court, interpret the U.S. Constitution and laws. Their interpretations or decisions establish public policy. Federal judges are appointed by the president of the United States and make their court decisions with influence by the social order of the times and potentially by their political convictions (Jackson 2001).

All states' constitutions, laws, and policies, including those that govern higher education, must operate within the structure of the U.S. Constitution. When state laws and practices violate the provisions of the Constitution, the federal government can intervene.

States with public HBCUs have, in tradition and practice, resisted equitable treatment of public HBCUs compared to the treatment of public historically white institutions. Jackson notes, "The white schools, especially the larger white schools, always had the lion's share of resources and academic opportunities, while the [HBCUs] were short-changed. . . . Historically, [HBCUs] have not been competitive because resources have been distributed unequally, unfairly, and of lesser quality" (Jackson 2001, 158–159). When inequitable treatment is not addressed by the state, HBCUs and their constituents have looked to the federal government for redress.

PRESIDENTIAL EXECUTIVE ORDERS

Affirmative Action

President Franklin D. Roosevelt developed the concept of affirmative action in Executive Order 8802, which was written in 1941. This executive order made it illegal for defense contractors receiving federal funds not to hire blacks because of race (Jackson 2001).

President Lyndon B. Johnson first included the phrase *affirmative action* in Executive Order 11246, written in 1965 and titled "Equal Employment Opportunity." The purpose of the executive order and in turn affirmative action was to redress discriminatory employment practices of organizations that received federal funding. It did this by linking federal funding with employment practices of organizations. Organizations that receive federal funding are required to have employment practices and procedures that provide equal access for consideration of employment as well as the full benefits and rights of other employees. Postsecondary institutions that accept federal money for student financial aid and/or research grants, for example, are to comply with affirmative action policies and guidelines (Jackson 2001).

White House Initiative on HBCUs

President Jimmy Carter signed Executive Order 12232 in 1980. This executive order established the White House Initiative on HBCUs, a federal program that increases and monitors federal funding of HBCUs.

Thirty U.S. departments participate through grants, contracts, and other agreements. Annually, each department is required to present a federal plan and report on how it assists HBCUs. In addition to the U.S. Department of Education, the other federal agencies are the Department of Agriculture; the Agency for International Development; the Appalachian Regional Commission; the Department of Commerce; the

Central Intelligence Agency; the Corporation for National Service; the Departments of Defense and Energy; the Environmental Protection Agency; the Equal Employment Opportunity Commission; the Departments of Health and Human Services, Housing and Urban Development, the Interior, Justice, and Labor; the National Aeronautics and Space Administration; the National Credit Union Administration; the National Endowments for the Arts and the Humanities; the National Science Foundation; the Nuclear Regulatory Commission; and the Departments of State, Transportation, and the Treasury.

President George H. W. Bush established the President's Advisory Board on Historically Black Colleges and Universities with Executive Order 12677 in 1989. As stated in the order, the board advises the president and the secretary of education on HBCUs; provides an annual report to the president "on HBCU participation in federal programs; advises the Secretary of Education on increasing the federal role in strengthening HBCUs; and reports to the President on how to increase the private sector role in strengthening these institutions."

President William J. Clinton in 1993 signed Executive Order 12876. The executive order characterized the mission of the White House Initiative on HBCUs as a means "to advance the development of human potential, to strengthen the capacity of historically black colleges and universities to provide quality education, and to increase opportunities to participate in and benefit from Federal programs."

President George W. Bush signed Executive Order 13225 in 2001. In this executive order he continued the President's Advisory Board on Historically Black Colleges and Universities until September 30, 2003.

U.S. CONSTITUTIONAL AMENDMENTS

In 1865 the U.S. Congress passed the Thirteenth Amendment making slavery illegal in the United States and its territories. Actual slavery was ended because blacks could no longer be considered the tangible property of whites. The vestiges of slavery were not ended through this amendment, however. Blacks were not granted citizenship and the accompanying civil rights. John Hope Franklin and Alfred Moss point out, "Most Southern whites, although willing to concede the end of slavery even to the point of voting for adoption of the Thirteenth Amendment, were convinced that laws should be speedily enacted to curb blacks and to ensure their role as a laboring force in the South" ([1947] 1994, 225).

The laws that curbed blacks were known as Black Codes. Southern whites had the approval of President Andrew Johnson to control blacks as they deemed necessary and appropriate.

The Fourteenth Amendment was ratified in 1866, in a milieu of conflict between President Johnson and Congress. Citizen rights and "the equal protection of the laws" were given to blacks and any individual born or naturalized and living within the jurisdiction of the United States. The response in the South to the Fourteenth Amendment was to establish a de jure segregated society that was maintained through Jim Crow laws. Northern states, for the most part, maintained a de facto segregated society (Franklin and Moss [1947] 1994; Jackson 2001).

Since Southern states and a few Northern states did not consider the Fourteenth Amendment to include the right to vote, it would take the Fifteenth Amendment to specifically address this right of U.S. citizenship. The Fifteenth Amendment, ratified in 1870, granted suffrage to black males without prejudice because of "race, color, or previous condition of servitude." (Women, black or white, were not granted suffrage until the passage of the Nineteenth Amendment in 1920.) Voting rights give blacks, as it does all U.S. citizens, the opportunity to actively participate in the political system, which influences all aspects of their lives including their education (Jackson 2001).

Although the Fifteenth Amendment gave black males the right to vote, whites developed ways to restrict this right. Southern states passed laws that required blacks to pass literacy tests, to pay poll taxes, and to be removed from voting rolls if they were convicted of criminal actions. Criminal convictions of blacks became commonplace. Some Western states used literacy tests. Some Northern states were subtler in barring blacks from voting. The Voting Rights Acts of 1965 strengthened the Fifteenth Amendment by prohibiting "qualification or prerequisite to voting" for any citizen of the United States (Asante and Mattson [1947] 1992; Franklin and Moss 1994; Jackson 2001).

U.S. LEGISLATIVE ACTS

As noted at the beginning of this chapter, education is the jurisdiction of the states. However, education is considered to be included in providing "for the general welfare" clause in the U.S. Constitution. Based on this, the federal government has used its authority to interface with states and their public education institutions (Jackson 2001). Following are the three legislative acts that specifically affect HBCUs.

Morrill Act of 1890

Discussed in detail in Chapter 1, the Morrill Act of 1890 established seventeen public HBCUs. These are known as land-grant institutions. They were "established in each of the [S]outhern and border states. . . . These institutions offered courses in agriculture, mechanical, and industrial subjects, but few offered college-level courses and degrees [initially]." Some began as private schools and eventually came under public control (U.S. Department of Education, Office of Civil Rights 1991, on-line).

Civil Rights Act of 1964

Title VI of the Civil Rights Act of 1964 addressed public education desegregation—precollege and postsecondary. This title attached monetary sanctions to institutions that did not comply with the U.S. Supreme Court *Brown* decision, discussed later in this chapter. Federal agencies and departments that award federal money to programs and other activities must do so in a manner that does not discriminate against race, color, or national origin. Departments and agencies must issue rules, regulations, or orders that are consistent and comply with the objective of the act. Education institutions that are not in compliance can be refused funding (Jackson 2001).

Authorization to request desegregation plans from states that continued to maintain dual educational systems and ignore the *Brown* decisions was established through Title VI. The Office of Civil Rights (OCR) was established in what was then the Department of Health, Education, and Welfare, now the Department of Education. The OCR has the responsibility to oversee compliance with Title VI.

In the 1960s and early 1970s, the OCR "placed its primary compliance emphasis . . . on eliminating unconstitutional elementary and secondary school segregation in the southern and border states" (U.S. Department of Education, Office of Civil Rights 1991, on-line). The OCR's compliance oversight responsibilities expanded to include oversight of desegregation plans in higher education (discussed later in this chapter) as well as oversight of plans that protect the rights of the disabled in educational settings, and the oversight compliance of Title IX, which focuses on sex discrimination in education.

Higher Education Act of 1965

The Higher Education Act of 1965, and subsequent amendments to the act, broadens the intervention of the federal government in postsecondary education to insure quality in and access to higher education. Funds are appropriated for institutions that are accredited by agencies recognized by the secretary of education. These agencies include, but are not limited to, the regional accrediting agencies discussed in Chapter 1.

Through this act, Congress has acknowledged the significant contribution that HBCUs have made in the postsecondary education of African Americans. The discriminatory manner in which the states and the federal government historically dispersed funds to HBCUs was also recognized, amounting to an admission of the role the state and federal governments played in creating the current precarious state of a large number of HBCUs.

Title III of the act contains three programs to remedy the discriminatory practices:

1. Strengthening Historically Black Colleges and Universities Program: provides funds to assist in establishing and strengthening "the physical plants, financial management, academic resources, and endowments of historically black colleges and universities." This funding includes graduate and professional institutions (U.S. Department of Education, on-line).
2. Historically Black Colleges and Universities Capital Financing Program: gives the Department of Education authority to select a private for-profit Designated Bonding Authority (DBA) to issue bonds and make loans to " creditworthy historically black colleges and universities for capital projects related to instruction, research, or housing of students, faculty or staff"; provides financial insurance to guarantee loans to qualifying HBCUs; and establishes the HBCU Capital Financing Advisory Board to advise the secretary of education and DBA on "the most efficient way to implement construction, renovation, or maintenance financing" (U.S. Department of Education, on-line).
3. Minority Science and Engineering Improvement Program: provides grant funding "to effect long-range im-

provement in science education at predominately minority institutions and to increase the flow of underrepresented ethnic minorities, particularly minority women, into science and engineering careers" (U.S. Department of Education, on-line).

COURT CASES

Court cases concerning HBCUs can be divided into two distinct eras: pre-*Brown* and post-*Brown*. In the pre-*Brown* era, courts interpreted laws and based their decisions on the *Plessy v. Ferguson* decision of 1896, which affirmed the doctrine of "separate but equal." Court cases during this era concerned the accessibility of graduate education. In all of the cases the graduate level sought by the black plaintiff was only offered at public historically white institutions.

In the post-*Brown* era, court decisions were based on the 1954 and 1955 *Brown v. Board of Education* cases, which overturned the "separate but equal" doctrine. The *Brown* decision focused on how to remedy de jure segregation in public education. In this era, the focus was on desegregation at all levels of education.

All of the cases concern educational access for blacks and how that should occur. Access includes being able to enroll in a school coupled with receiving, as Carter Woodson defines education, "a real education to inspire people to live more abundantly, to learn to begin with life as they find it and make it better ([1933] 1991, 29). Central to the cases, pre- and post-*Brown,* was the Fourteenth Amendment's "equal protection of the law" clause.

In this section lower court and U.S. Supreme Court cases that are representative of legal decisions that affect HBCUs are presented according to the two eras. The sources for the following synopses are Cynthia L. Jackson's chapter titled "Legal Influences on African American Education" (2001); the Legal Information Institute of Cornell University Law School (http://www/cornell.edu); and FindLaw for Legal Professionals (http://caselaw.lp.findlaw.com). The Legal Information Institute and FindLaw contain the court opinions in their entirety.

Pre-Brown *Era*

Plessy v. Ferguson (1896). The separate but equal doctrine, affirmed in *Plessy v. Ferguson,* required establishing equal facilities for whites and blacks when public funds were involved. Whites were held accountable to insure that the separate but equal doctrine was carried out. The Supreme Court's interpretation of "equal protection of the laws" upheld states' rights to establish segregated societies. It will be seen in subsequent cases that "separate" never equated to "equal," and there was no good faith intention on the part of states or education institution officials for this to occur (Jackson 2001).

Pearson v. Murray (1936). This case appears to have been the first litigation to raise questions about the separate but equal doctrine in higher education. The University of Maryland would not admit Murray, a black, to its law school. Murray had graduated from Amherst College and met all admissions requirements. He "was denied admission on the sole ground of his color," the justices wrote.

The justices of the court of appeals in Maryland, where this case was argued, stressed repeatedly that separate but equal required "equal treatment." They concluded that when a state offers a certain type of education for one race it is required to offer the same type of education for the other race.

In the 1930s, when this case was tried, the University of Maryland had the state's only law school. One option for remedy would be to establish a law school for blacks in Maryland, if the appellants had the authority to do so. However, the appellants for this case were officers of the University of Maryland and did not have that authority. Therefore, given the parameters of this case the justices ordered that Murray be admitted to the University of Maryland Law School.

Missouri Ex Rel. Gaines v. Canada (1938). This case also concerns a black who had met the admissions requirements and was denied admission because of race. Gaines graduated from Lincoln University, Missouri's HBCU. In lieu of admitting him to the law school of the State University of Missouri, a "legislative declaration" was produced agreeing to either pay his tuition and expenses to a law school in a state where blacks could be admitted or establish a law school at Lincoln University. Gaines did not accept either option.

The U.S. Supreme Court decided that requiring Gaines to go out of state for a law education showed an "unmistakable disregard for his rights." In addition, because Gaines was then the first and only black to apply for law school in Missouri, establishing a school just for him was not reasonable. Given these factors, Gaines was admitted to the School of Law of the State University of Missouri.

Sipuel v. Board of Regents of University of Oklahoma (1948). Sipuel, a black, applied to the University of Oklahoma Law School, the only state-supported law school in Oklahoma. She was denied admission because of her race. In this five-paragraph decision, the U.S. Supreme Court overturned the lower court's decision and ordered her to be admitted. In the opinion of the justices, the state was required to provide equal protection afforded by the Fourteenth Amendment for Sipuel to receive a law education, *and* the state would be required to "provide it as soon as it does for applicants of any other group."

McLaurin v. Oklahoma State Regents (1950). McLaurin, a black, applied to the University of Oklahoma education doctoral program, then the only public education doctoral program in the state. McLaurin was denied admission for two reasons: first, his race, and second (and of equal importance in this case), because it was a misdemeanor in Oklahoma for blacks and whites to attend desegregated higher education settings. These settings included classrooms, the library, and the cafeteria.

McLaurin sued, questioning the constitutionality of the law based on the Fourteenth Amendment. The Oklahoma district court held that the law was unconstitutional. The court entrusted compliance with the decision to the state.

The Oklahoma legislature amended the law. Blacks were allowed to attend historically white institutions when the same program to which a black applied was not offered at Langston, the only HBCU in the state.

McLaurin was admitted to the university. However, university officials devised ways to segregate him from white students: They assigned him to a desk in a room next to the classroom where the class occurred, assigned and restricted him to a specific desk on the library mezzanine, and restricted him from using the cafeteria when white students were present. Later he was allowed to sit in the classroom with a roped-off area labeled "Reserved for Colored." The district court found that the despairing treatment did not violate his equal protection rights. McLaurin then appealed to the Supreme Court. By the time the case was heard by the Court, the rope and sign had been removed and he was assigned to a row in the classroom that was specified for black students. He could also use an assigned table on the main floor of the library and eat in the cafeteria at a separate assigned table. Even so, the Court found that the treatment denied him an education as well as equal protection under the law.

Sweatt v. Painter (1950). Tangible equity in education facilities and resources was the focus of this case. Sweatt, a black, applied to the University of Texas Law School for the February 1946 term. He was denied admission because he was black. This was the only state-funded law school in Texas.

Sweatt sued, but instead of admitting Sweatt, the Texas court suspended the case for six months to give the state time "to supply substantially equal facilities" for African Americans. In December 1946, the state trial court denied Sweatt's case because during those six months university officials had arranged to open a law school for blacks beginning in February 1947. When the black law school was opened, Sweatt did not enroll, citing that the educational facilities were not equal to those at the University of Texas Law School.

Sweatt appealed to the Texas Court of Civil Appeals, and the case was returned to the lower court "for further proceedings without prejudice to the rights of any party to this suit." The lower court and subsequently the court of civil appeals found that the black law school had substantially equal facilities to those at the University of Texas. The Texas Supreme Court refused to hear the case.

The Texas courts' concept of "substantially equal facilities" included the following: The black law school did not have its own faculty; rather, four faculty members from the University of Texas Law School taught at both institutions but maintained their offices at the University of Texas. Of the 10,000 books ordered for the black law library, less than a third had been delivered; in addition, the black law library did not have a full-time librarian. The University of Texas Law School library housed 65,000 books and several full-time librarians. The black school was not accredited whereas the University of Texas Law School was.

A few adjustments had been made to the facilities at the black law school and some circumstances had changed when this case was heard by the U.S. Supreme Court. Specifically, five full-time faculty were employed to the law school, which by that time enrolled twenty-three students. The library had 16,500 books and a full-time librarian. The black law school had a practice court and legal aid association, and one graduate who became a member of the Texas Bar. The black law school had applied for accreditation.

The Supreme Court's decision that Sweatt was denied equal protection of the laws rested on three points: (1) Law schools are to provide the knowledge and practices of the legal profession. Individuals cannot be expected to be skilled in the profession if they are isolated from the people and institutions involved with the law. (2) The exchange of views and ideas about the law is fundamental to learning the profession; anything less is "an academic vacuum." (3) Compelling Sweatt to enroll in the black law school excluded him from 85 percent of the state's population. As a member of the Texas Bar he would have to come in contact with that portion of the population in the form of other lawyers, witnesses, jurors, and judges, to name a few. In conclusion, Sweatt was admitted to the UT Law School, and the black school continued to operate.

Post-Brown *Era*

Desegregation of public education was the focus of the post-*Brown* era cases. In the pre-*Brown* era, public HBCUs opened an increasing number of schools and departments so historically white institutions could avoid desegregation. Desegregation was initially intended to "provide blacks access to educational opportunities" that were already in place at white schools (Jackson 2001, 198). However, in the post-*Brown* era and into the twenty-first century, desegregation has become a means to curb the academic offerings of public HBCUs, threatening the very existence of the institutions.

Brown v. Board of Education (1954). The *Brown* case is a consolidation of cases from Kansas, South Carolina, Virginia, and Delaware. The U.S. Supreme Court justices recognized that the facts and localities of the four cases differed. However, they saw similarities in the legal issues. The plaintiffs in these cases wanted black students to be able to attend precollege public schools in the districts in which they lived on a nonracial basis.

The case reversed the 1896 *Plessy* decision of separate but equal, or segregated, education. The justices ruled that though blacks were provided separate education facilities, the support systems for blacks' education was not equal in quality or quantity to that of whites. In addition, the justices found through the testimony of Dr. Kenneth Clark, a black psychologist, that segregated education was psychologically detrimental for blacks, which resulted in blacks' feelings of inferiority. Based on the two findings, they decided that "any language in *Plessy v. Ferguson* contrary to this finding is rejected" and that "in the field of education, the doctrine of 'separate but equal' has no place"; in summary, that segregated education does not afford blacks equal protection of the law.

Having made their decision, the justices contemplated the manner in which their decision would be implemented. They posed two concerns for consideration. One was on the immediacy of allowing students to attend the schools of their choice. The other was on the role of the Supreme Court in guaranteeing compliance with their decision.

They presented three possible opinions: (1) the development of compliance mandates; (2) the appointment of a "special master" to recommend mandates; or (3) empowering the lower courts to development of the mandates. If the Court decided on the third option, additional consideration would be needed on the type of directives and guidelines the Supreme Court would give the lower courts. The case was placed on the docket of the Supreme Court for the next year to hear arguments on the three options.

Brown v. Board of Education (1955). In this case, also known as *Brown II*, arguments on the Court's questions on immediacy of providing choice in school attendance and desegregation compliance were heard.

The Court acknowledged that community circumstances were a factor to be considered in desegregating public school education. It decided that school officials would have the primary responsibility of directing school desegregation and that the lower courts, which heard the individual cases, would have supervisory jurisdiction. The lower courts were to determine if school officials were making "good faith implementation of the governing constitutional principles."

The Supreme Court gave the lower courts the following directives and guidelines: The lower courts were to require school district officials to begin the process of complying with the *Brown I* decision immediately. Desegregation plans were to be developed by the school district officials and submitted to the courts. The plans were to take into consideration impasses concerning administration, facilities, transportation, personnel, attendance areas, and state laws and regulations that impeded the desegregation plans. In reviewing the plans the courts were to determine if the time frame of the plans would produce prompt and reasonable compliance as well as the plausibility and adequacy of responses to impasses.

Adams v. Richardson (1973). For the most part *Brown I* and *II* were seen as applying to precollege education only. When Title VI of the 1964 Civil Rights Act was enacted, nineteen states still had dual higher education systems. These states were Tennessee, Louisiana, Alabama, Mississippi, Ohio, Arkansas, North Carolina, Delaware, Georgia, South Carolina, Missouri, Oklahoma, West Virginia, Florida, Pennsylvania, Texas, Virginia, Maryland, and Kentucky.

Collectively, cases concerning higher education desegregation are known as the *Adams* cases. These cases stem from legal suits that began to be filed in 1970 by individuals and the National Association for the Advancement of Colored People (NAACP). In these cases, the U.S.

Department of Education, Office of Civil Rights (OCR) is accused of not meeting its responsibility to enforce Title VI of the Civil Rights Act of 1964 for state desegregation plans in higher education.

The 1977 district court decision in *Adams v. Califano* affected the nineteen states that operated dual higher education systems. In this case the OCR was found not to be fulfilling its compliance responsibilities concerning the Rehabilitation Act of 1973 and the Americans with Disabilities Act of 1990. In light of this decision the OCR stepped up its enforcement of Title VI (U.S. Department of Education, Office of Civil Rights 1991, on-line).

The OCR published guidelines and regulations on which acceptable desegregation plans were to be developed. The "criteria" highlighted the following:

1. Enhance HBCUs through improvements in physical plants and equipment, number and quality of faculties, and libraries and other financial support.
2. Expand the nonminority enrollment at HBCUs by offering on their campuses academic programs that are in high demand or unavailable at the state system's other campuses.
3. Provide HBCUs with resources that would ultimately ensure they were at least comparable to those at traditionally white institutions having similar missions (U.S. Department of Education, Office of Civil Rights 1991, on-line).

By 2000, the status of the desegregation cases by state were as follows (Hebel 2000, on-line):

1. States without an agreement on a desegregation plan with the U.S. Department of Education: Maryland, Virginia
2. States that are being monitored by the U.S. Department of Education: Florida, Kentucky, Ohio, Pennsylvania, Texas
3. States that are being monitored by the U.S. Department of Justice: Alabama, Louisiana, Mississippi, Tennessee
4. States that the federal government found desegregated: Arkansas, Delaware, Georgia, Missouri, North Carolina, Oklahoma, South Carolina, West Virginia

In 2001, Virginia had reached an agreement with the U.S. Department of Education on a desegregation plan to be monitored by the department (Hebel 2001, on-line). This leaves Maryland as the only state without an agreement.

Regents of the University of California v. Bakke (1978). This case brings into question the legality of admissions programs designed specifically to redress admission practices and policies for people of color, and introduces the concept of reverse discrimination. Reverse discrimination is when whites believe that they are not receiving equal protection of the law because of race.

The Medical School of the University of California at Davis had a special admissions program to increase the number of minority and disadvantaged students. The program was coordinated with the regular admissions program but had a separate admissions committee. The committee for the special program was allocated a specific proportion of slots each year, based on the potential overall class size.

Bakke, a white male, applied to the medical school in 1973 and 1974. Both years he was reviewed through the regular admissions program, interviewed, and denied admission. He sued the university system after being denied admission in 1974. He wanted "mandatory, injunctive, and declaratory relief" to be admitted to the medical school because, as he claimed, he was being discriminated against because he is white, and this violated his equal protection under the laws. The court found that the special program was based on a racial quota because it held a specific number of slots specifically for minorities, and the university could not take race into consideration for admissions. Yet the court did not require that Bakke be admitted because he did not prove that he would have been admitted if a special program did not exist.

When the California Supreme Court ruled that the special admissions program denied nonminority applicants equal protection of the laws and that Bakke should be admitted, the university appealed the decision to the U.S. Supreme Court. The university contended that the decision of the California Supreme Court was inappropriate because white males, such as Bakke, are not a "discrete and insular minority requiring extraordinary protection from the majoritarian political process."

The U.S. Supreme Court justices affirmed Bakke's admission to the school because the university could not prove that Bakke would have been denied admission even if the special program had not existed. However, it reversed the California Supreme Court's decision stating that the special admissions program of the medical school was allowed to continue.

United States v. Fordice (1992). In 1975 Jake Ayers Sr. of Mississippi, parent of a student at Jackson State University, an HBCU, filed suit in district court. He claimed, in what would become a class action suit, that Mississippi did not provide adequate resources to maintain and improve the infrastructure and academic quality of its three public HBCUs. The case was based on violation of the Ninth, Thirteenth, and Fourteenth Amendments as well as Title VI of the 1964 Civil Rights Act.

Originally the case was titled *Ayers v. Waller* (Waller was then Mississippi's governor). When Kirk Fordice became governor of Mississippi, it was renamed *Ayers v. Fordice*. Subsequently, the United States, through the Department of Education, filed its suit stating that Mississippi had not met the requirements of equal protection under the Fourteenth Amendment or the requirements of Title VI.

The 1992 U.S. Supreme Court decision allowed the consideration of race for admissions if in so doing it furthered the elimination of the vestiges of a dual system. The justices concluded that "the fact that the majority of a student population is mostly black or white does not mean, in and of itself, that a dual system exists." What had to be carefully considered is "whether retention of all eight institutions itself affects student choice and perpetuates the segregated higher education system, whether maintenance of each of the universities is educationally justifiable, and whether one or more of them can be practically closed or merged with other existing institutions." To make this decision the policies and practices of the university system have to be considered in their entirety. The consideration was if the policies and practices are "race-neutral." Oversight of the desegregation plan was the responsibility of the lower court.

In January 2002, the U.S. district judge agreed to a plan that was supported by the Mississippi legislators. Some of the plaintiffs are considering an appeal. The highlights of the plan, which make no stipulations on the historically white institutions in Mississippi, follow:

1. Each HBCU must have an enrollment of at least ten percent nonblack.
2. Funds are to be apportioned over seventeen years by the State for each of the HBCUs. These funds are to be used a) to improve current academic programs and offer new ones, b) capital improvements, and c) endowments.

3. Each HBCU's ability to control its portion of the principal of the endowment is contingent on each maintaining the minimal nonblack student enrollment percentage for three consecutive years. (Hebel 2002a, on-line)

Hopwood v. Texas (1992). Based on the 1978 *Bakke* decision where race could be considered in admissions to redress prior discrimination admissions practices and policies, and in accordance with a federal desegregation order in 1983, Texas had established an admissions program to increase the enrollment of people of color in postbaccalaureate education. In 1992, Hopwood and other whites filed against the University of Texas. They stated that they had been denied admissions to the law school because of preferential treatment afforded people of color. In 1992, the district court found that race could be considered for admissions when it furthers diversity of the student population. In 1996, the Fifth U.S. Circuit Court overturned this finding and ruled that considering race as a factor for admissions violated others' equal protection of the law rights in the Fourteenth Amendment. This decision made race as a factor for admissions unconstitutional. The U.S. Supreme Court would not hear the appeal.

Wooden et al. v. Board of Regents of the University System of Georgia (1999). In this case four plaintiffs, for varying reasons, claimed that the existence of the three public HBCUs in Georgia is evidence of a segregated university system and, as a result, that they have "suffered an injury."

The plaintiffs were:

1. Wooden, a black teacher in Camden County School District. He did not receive his bachelor's degree or master's degree from one of the three public HBCUs. His two children did not attend one of the HBCUs. He admitted that "he has never been discriminated against by any University System institution." He claimed that he "wants to help Georgia children receive an equitable education."
2. Harris, a white teacher in the Glynn County School System. Her baccalaureate degree is from the University of Georgia, and her mater's degree is from Georgia Southern University. She admitted that she never "personally suffered [any] injury as a result of the defendant's allegedly discriminatory policies." Her reason for participating in the suit was "to represent, as an educator,

students who have attended or are attending University System institutions."

3. Bratcher, a white instructor of developmental studies at Fort Valley State University (FVSU), an HBCU. She stated that because of her support of Newt Gingrich and Rush Limbaugh (two politically conservative public persons), she was "treated unfairly by the FVSU administration." However, she admitted that she had not been discriminated against personally at FVSU. Her participation in the suit was "as an HBI [historically black institution] employee interested in eliminating any vestiges of the *jure* segregation within the University System." She stated that because the majority of the faculty and students at FVSU are black, the prestige of being a faculty member at FVSU is lower. She claimed that she was being denied the opportunity to work in an interracial environment. Finally, she stated that she was representing "her students, whom she claims are afraid to challenge the current status quo on their own."

4. Jarvis, a white resource coordinator in the Crawford County School System. He holds a bachelor's degree and master's degree from the University of Georgia and was a student at FVSU in pursuit of a certificate in school counseling. He was representing "himself and other FVSU students, as well as the Middle Georgia community in general." Although he admitted that he had not been treated in a discriminatory manner, he joined the suit because he received "poor quality of instruction" at FVSU. Therefore, he claimed, "The 'stigmatic effect' of attending an institution still hindered by the vestiges of the *jure* segregation . . . lowers the value of any FVSU credential [he] might attain."*Wooden et al. v. Board of Regents of the University System of Georgia* (1999)

Prior to handing down his decision, the U.S. district court judge gave the following explanations of the law:

General Standing Principle—"A plaintiff must show, as a constitutional minimum, that he [or she] has 'suffered an injury in fact'—an invasion of a legally protected interest which is (a) concrete and particularized and (b) actual or imminent, not conjectural or hypothetical."

Injury Requirement—"The 'direct injury' requirement ensures that a plaintiff has a personal stake in the matter. . . . Individualized stigmatic injury resulting from unlawful discrimination is a sufficient injury to establish standing . . . [b]ut courts recognize as 'stigmatically injured' only those who have actually been subject to unequal treatment due to discriminatory conduct. . . . Hence mere 'deprivation of the benefits of interracial association' is not an injury sufficient to establish standing to sue."

Third Party Standing—"While a plaintiff generally may only assert his [or her] own interests, in limited situations he [or she] can advance third party rights. But to do so he [or she] must show that he [or she] (1) also has suffered an injury in fact and (2) had a close relationship with the third party. Finally, the third party must be unable to vindicate his [or her] own rights."

Based on these aspects of the law, the judge denied all claims and rendered the following orders: Wooden and Harris did not have affiliations with the HBCUs. Therefore they have not been injured. In addition, they cannot represent third parties. Bratcher did not suffer any injury by teaching in a predominately black setting. "Students may have standing to complain about discriminatory hiring of teachers," the decision noted, but Bratcher could not be a third-party representative because it was only her word that students had this concern, and she did not indicate that students asked her to represent them. The judge noted, "Interestingly, Bratcher insists she does not even care what her students think about the lawsuit."

Jarvis's enrollment in FVSU made his claim more creditable than that of Wooden and Harris. However, his claim was a "general grievance," which does not show "an injury in fact." He has not been injured through stigmatic injury because he did not claim that the injury was due to racial discrimination, "but rather on mere attendance at FVSU." In addition, Jarvis gave no evidence that public HBCUs and historically white public institutions use different standards to hire faculty. The judge stated, "Indeed, he relies only upon his personal belief in concluding that his teaching at FVSU was 'inadequate' and that FVSU has inferior teaching standards." Jarvis's word alone was not sufficient.

Gratz et al. v. Bollinger et al. (2003) and *Grutter v. Bollinger et al.* (2003). These two cases, popularly known as the University of Michigan cases, became the first U.S. Supreme Court decisions in the twenty-first century on affirmation action in higher education. The cases focused on the constitutionality of racial preference programs for admission. In both cases the university's central argument was that its admissions policies were in keeping with its mission of attempting to maintain an ethnically and racially diverse student population.

Although its supporters heralded the 2003 decision in the *Grutter* case as a victory for affirmative action, the victory should be celebrated with some caution. The 2003 decision is based on the view that Justice Lewis Powell wrote in the Court's 1978 *Bakke* decision, which has been the determining factor in what courts can hear regarding affirmative action in higher education. In the opinion, Justice Powell makes it clear that the only cases that can be heard are those in which obtaining or maintaining a diverse student population is at issue. It is important to emphasize that Justice Powell placed this view in the Court's *Bakke* opinion and it was not formally agreed upon by the other eight justices. It is conceivable; therefore, that this could be seen as a loophole in the future. Justice Sandra O'Connor states in the opinion she wrote for the *Grutter* case, "Since *Bakke*, Justice Powell's opinion has been the touchstone for constitutional analysis of race-conscious admissions policies...Courts, however, have struggled to discern whether Justice Powell's diversity rationale is binding precedent."

CONCLUSION

"Desegregation," states Jackson, "became something that was done *to* blacks and not *for* blacks (2001, 198). She was referring specifically to the desegregation of precollege school systems, but the statement also applies to postsecondary education desegregation.

As though forecasting the plausible future, Benjamin E. Mays wrote in 1978, "Integration must never mean the liquidation of black colleges" (27). Yet, in many ways integration or desegregation is meaning just that.

Desegregation and affirmative action were not originally focused on diversity. Both were intended to redress the inequities that the "separate but equal" doctrine created. The inequities were not grounded in the racial diversity of a classroom or school but in the inadequate funding, resources, and facilities of schools that blacks attended. They also were grounded in the systematic practices, policies, and traditions that perpetuated the inadequacies (Jackson 2001).

The *Coleman Report* changed the meaning of desegregation in precollege education to mean the busing of blacks to white schools (Jackson 2001). The practices and policies in precollege desegregation would become similar in postsecondary desegregation. Black colleges would be closed or merged.

In the Bakke case five of the nine Supreme Court justices agreed with the spirit of affirmative action. Thus it was decided that special admissions for medical students of color were not unconstitutional. However, notes Dahlia Lithwick, Justice Lewis Powell's "swing vote" opinion shifted the focus of affirmative action from redressing past inequities and discrimination to diversifying student populations. "Powell—and thus the entire *Bakke* majority—made student-body diversity the singular goal of affirmative action programs," she writes. "Judges may not hear arguments about the importance of a 'level playing field.' . . . The only permissible question before them anymore is whether the school in question is promoting 'diversity'" (2002, on-line).

What is interesting about desegregation for both precollege and higher education is that it becomes the burden of blacks. However, in both situations the real concern was equal access and distribution of state funding—tax money—for education. This is something blacks never seem to obtain, although they are taxpayers.

There has been no consistency in the decisions concerning desegregation and no clarity of principles for determining the courts' decisions. This is most evident in the post-*Brown* era decisions, as well as in the desegregation plans approved by the OCR. Allowing for "community circumstances" in relation to desegregation allows for a great deal of ambiguity on what is desegregation and how it should occur.

Based on the results of precollege desegregation, there is no reason to believe that higher education desegregation will be any different. In precollege desegregation, black schools were closed. In higher education desegregation, black schools have merged; merging is another form of closure. Throughout the precollege desegregation process blacks were not "involved in defining the concept of desegregation" (Jackson 2001, 198). The black Mississippians' Council on Higher Education, the plaintiffs in *Fordice*, have argued "that they were not adequately represented in the settlement talks" (Hebel 2002a, on-line).

Forty-five years after the *Brown* decision, precollege education is almost as segregated as it was before the decision. Yet the school districts that were under court order to desegregate have been released because repeatedly judges found that all vestiges of segregation were removed from the districts (Orfield and Eaton 1997). Based on the results of precollege desegregation as well as the decisions in higher education desegregation, it is reasonable to conclude that desegregation is a euphemism for dismantling all vestiges of any educational structures that support and promote the advancement of blacks through education. Tangible evidence of this can be found in the claims and allegations in the *Wooden* case.

Frederick S. Humphries, president of the National Association for Equal Opportunity in Higher Education, a national HBCU policy advocacy organization, expresses concern about funding to HBCUs once federal monitoring for desegregation plans in higher education end. "State legislatures still are largely dominated by alumni from predominantly white institutions, and without outside intervention . . . that could eventually lead them to repeat the past cycles of unequal funding (Hebel 2002b, on-line.)

Historically black colleges and universities fulfilled the educational aspirations of blacks when no other educational systems were available. Prior to the Civil War, blacks were denied access to education. After the Civil War, support for blacks to engage in some form of an education system became evident first in the establishment of HBCUs and later with the adoption and expansion of policies and statutes prohibiting racial discrimination in education. Yet all of these statutes, policies, and laws are merely symbols of legal racial legitimacy. When desegregation court orders are compiled and analyzed, it will be found that they simply created separate educational programs for black students within schools that were desegregated in name only (Bell 1992). It is obvious that the numerous U.S. desegregation cases, laws, policies, and practices of the previous decades have failed to protect the inalienable right of blacks to have equal access to education (Gates and West 1996).

Clearly, the quest for educational freedom continues because desegregation has not and is not likely to provide educational freedom for blacks. Blacks must find tactics other than desegregation for educational freedom.

Paulo Freire states,

> The oppressed, having internalized the image of the oppressor and adopted his guidelines, are fearful of freedom. Freedom would require them to eject this image and replace it with autonomy and responsibility. Freedom is acquired by conquest, not by gift. It must be pursued constantly and responsibly. Freedom is . . . the indispensable condition for the quest for human completion. ([1970] 2001, 47)

Reflecting on some of the past actions of the courts and legislatures, there appears to be a very skilled and purposeful effort to sidetrack or limit real equality of educational opportunities for blacks. In the pre-*Brown* era, this was done by agreeing to allocate more funds to black colleges and universities, establishing new graduate programs and professional schools, although limited in academic scope, and other seemingly programmatic benefits. The subliminal message is obvious. In effect, the absence of overt discrimination does not mean that exclusionary practices have ended; rather, the character of discrimination has changed (Massey and Denton 1994).

Visionaries should not view the change in how discrimination is characterized as an absolute negative. Responsible visionary black leaders should seize this opportunity to dismantle this historical cycle of overt or covert denial of equal access for HBCUs to be academically competitive. Who has truly benefited from the laws, policies, executive orders, or statutes designed to provide equal educational opportunities to all? The answer remains, "Whites."

Undoubtedly, blacks are still attempting to extrapolate their educational gains. Yet national, state, and local elected and appointed gurus continued to discuss, design, and debate virtual educational opportunities for blacks and HBCUs while real opportunities are being implemented for non-HBCUs. Thus, any discussion on laws influencing HBCUs should serve as a benchmark or catalyst to determine what exactly these laws have provided. It is critical that HBCUs use the first decade of the twenty-first century to vigorously pursue academic and administrative excellence constantly and responsibly.

Derrick Bell does not consider educational freedom to be an idea that is not located outside of the individual; nor is it an idea that becomes myth. It is the indispensable condition for the continued quest for human completion (1992). Or, in the words of the U.S. Constitution, "The inalienable rights of life, liberty and the pursuit of happiness."

HBCUs' responses to the current desegregation court decisions will determine the future of public HBCUs. A fact that is never mentioned in court decisions—or anywhere else—is that HBCUs have always been affirmative action organizations. Their doors have always been opened to all. Thus, it is difficult to understand how the issue of "race-neutral" policies and practices leave HBCUs having to carry the burden of higher education desegregation.

M. Christopher Brown examines higher education desegregation from the principles of a democracy. He writes,

> The democratic question remains whether public historically black colleges should survive and be allowed to continue to promote their unique mission in a unitary system of higher education. . . . Democratic collegiate desegregation is not the mixing of racial groups for the sole purpose of mathematical ratios or racial balance, especially when the process increases or creates more and/or different sets of inequities

(e.g., public black college closure or merger). Democracy embodies the concepts of parity and equity. (1999, 103–104)

Demographers project that by 2020, one-third of the U.S. population will be black or Hispanic. By 2050, more than one-half of the U.S. population will be people of color. Perhaps these demographics will force the concept and processes of desegregation to resemble parity and equity. As Douglas V. Davidson notes, "Given the history of non-white people and their educational experiences in this country eventually a system of liberal apartheid or meritocratic apartheid is going to be created" (Jackson 2001, 42). In the next eighteen years, how many public HBCUs will be lost due to desegregation plans that have nothing to do with democracy?

Given the previous history with school desegregation, it is possible that by 2047, fifty-five years after the *Fordice* decision, a number of public HBCUs will be closed or merged. This would leave only private HBCUs to meet the missions of these institutions—and leave a substantial void in the U.S. higher education landscape.

Asante and Mattson note, "Initially, Lincoln [College in Pennsylvania] and Hampton [in Virginia] were founded to serve both Native Americans and African Americans" (1992, 134). A committee report for the Historically Black Institutions and the Status of Minorities in the Profession states that as of 1995, 13.1 percent of students enrolled at HBCUs were white, 1.5 percent were Hispanic, and "fractional percentages were Asians or Pacific Islanders, American Indians, or Alaskan Natives" (Committee L on the Historically Black Institutions and the Status of Minorities in the Profession 2002, on-line). Given these baseline statistics as well as the historical connections with nonblacks, public HBCUs, to address the nonblack racial quota, should give serious consideration to actively targeting recruitment and retention of people of color whose history in the United States is similar to blacks.

REFERENCES

Adams v. Richardson, 480 F.Supp. 92 (D.C. Cir. 1973).

Asante, Molefi K., and Mark T. Mattson. 1992. *Historical and Cultural Atlas of African Americans.* New York: Macmillan Publishing Company.

Bell, Derrick. 1992. *Faces at the Bottom of the Well.* New York: Basic Books.

Bowen, Frank M., Kathy Reeves Bracco, Patrick M. Callan, Joni E. Finney, Richard C. Richardson, and William Trombley. "State Structures for the

Governance of Higher Education: A Comparative Study." http://www.policycenter.org/comparative/comparative.html (cited January 21, 2002).

Brown, M. Christopher, II. 1999. *The Quest to Define Collegiate Desegregation: Black Colleges, Title VI Compliance, and Post-Adams Litigation.* Westport, CT: Bergin & Garvey.

Brown v. Board of Education, 347 U.S. 483 (1954).

Brown v. Board of Education, 349 U.S. 294 (1955).

Committee L on the Historically Black Institutions and the Status of Minorities in the Profession. 2002. http://eric-web.tc.columbia.edu/hbcu/report.html (cited January 26, 2002).

Franklin, John Hope, and Alfred A. Moss Jr. [1947] 1994. *From Slavery to Freedom: A History of African Americans.* 7th ed. New York: McGraw-Hill.

Freire, Paulo. [1970] 2001. *Pedagogy of the Oppressed.* New York: Continuum International Publishing Group.

Gates, Henry L., and Cornel West. 1996. *The Future of the Race.* New York: Vintage Books.

Gratz et al. v. Bollinger et al. (02–516) (2003).

Grutter v. Bollinger et al. (02–241) (2003).

Hebel, Sara. 2000. "A Pivotal Moment for Desegregation." *The Chronicle of Higher Education,* http://chronicle.com/weekly/v47/i09/09a02601.htm (cited March 29, 2002).

———. 2001. "Virginia Reaches Agreement on College-Desegregation Plan." *The Chronicle of Higher Education,* http://chronicle.com/weekly/v48/i14/14a02301.htm (cited March 29, 2002).

———. 2002a. "Mississippi Legislators Back Proposed Settlement of Desegregation Case." *The Chronicle of Higher Education,* http://chronicle.com/daily/2002/01/2002012104n.htm (cited February 10, 2002).

———. 2002b. "Desegregation Lawsuits Wind Down, But to What Effect?" *The Chronicle of Higher Education,* http://chronicle.com/weekly/v48/i31/31a02801.htm (cited May 14, 2002).

Hopwood v. Texas, 78 F.3d 932 (5th Cir. 1996).

Jackson, Cynthia L. 2001. *African American Education: A Reference Handbook.* Santa Barbara, CA: ABC-CLIO.

Lithwick, Dahlia. 2002. *The Legal Fiction of "Diversity."* Available at http://slate.msn.com/?id=2065878.

Massey, Douglas S., and Nancy A. Denton. 1994. *American Apartheid: Segregation and the Making of the Underclass.* Cambridge, MA: Harvard University Press.

Mays, Benjamin E. 1978. "The Black College in Higher Education." Pp. 19–28 in *Black Colleges in America: Challenge, Development, Survival.* Edited by

Charles V. Willie and Ronald R. Edmonds. New York: Teachers College Press.

McLaurin v. Oklahoma State Regents, 339 U.S. 637 (1950).

Missouri Ex Rel. Gaines v. Canada, 305 U.S. 337 (1938).

Orfield, Gary, and Susan E. Eaton. 1997. *Dismantling Desegregation: The Quiet Reversal of* Brown v. Board of Education. New York: New Press.

Pearson v. Murray, 169 Md. 478 (1936).

Plessy v. Ferguson, 163 U.S. 537 (1896).

Regents of the University of California v. Bakke, 438 U.S. 265 (1978).

Sipuel v. Board of Regents of University of Oklahoma, 332 U.S. 631 (1948).

Sweatt v. Painter, 339 U.S. 629 (1950).

United States v. Fordice, 505 U.S. 717 (1992).

U.S. Department of Education. *Historically Black Colleges and Universities Capital Financing Program.* Available at http://www.ed.gov/OPE/HEP/idues/hbcu_kap.html. Last updated September 24, 2001 (cited January 27, 2002).

———. *Minority Science and Engineering Improvement Program.* Available at http://www.ed.gov/offices/OPE/OHEP/idues/msi.html. Last updated January 16, 2002 (cited January 27, 2002).

———. *Strengthening Historically Black Colleges and Universities Program.* Available at http://www.ed.gov/offices/OPE/HEP/idues/title3b.html. Last updated October 11, 2001 (cited January 27, 2002).

U.S. Department of Education, Office of Civil Rights. 1991. *Historically Black Colleges and Universities and Higher Education Desegregation.* Washington, DC: U.S. Department of Education. Also available at http://www/ed/gov/offices/OCR/hq9511.html. Last updated December 28, 2000 (cited January 27, 2002).

Wooden et al. v. Board of Regents of the University System of Georgia, 457 GA 43 (1999).

Woodson, Carter G. [1933] 1991. *The Mis-Education of the Negro.* Philadelphia: Hamik's Publications.

Chapter Four

✎ Philanthropy and Government Relations

This chapter will cover the historical and contemporary relationship and influence of philanthropy and government funding for HBCUs. These two entities are integral to understanding fiduciary aspects of HBCUs. Understanding the historical relationship between HBCUs and philanthropy provides insights into the contemporary relations between the two. Unfortunately, research on this relationship is almost nonexistent.

PHILANTHROPY DEFINED

Philanthropy is the gifting of money, labor, and other assistance for the good of others. It is a fundamental aspect of funding in higher education. Endowments are established, buildings are built, and scholarships and fellowships are provided through philanthropic funds. In some cases, philanthropy is a necessity in maintaining the solvency of an institution's operating budget.

Usually when one thinks about philanthropy the first idea that comes to mind is a foundation. Foundations are the financial organizations that are established to disperse funds to organizations, institutions, or individuals that further the interest or focus for which the foundation was established. "The first and fundamental fact about foundations is that they do not start with a concept or an organization chart or a strategic plan. A foundation starts with a person, a donor" (Nielsen 1996, 10). The single donor's donation is the "fountainhead" for the future charitable acts and purpose of foundations.

All individual donors do not establish foundations. Thus, philanthropy, the act of donating money and/or property to others in need, is as much an individual's endeavor as it is an organization's one.

The Foundation Center defines a foundation as a nongovernmental, nonprofit organization that uses its own funds, usually from a single source such as an individual, family, or corporation. Funds are granted to other nonprofit organizations or individuals to support educational, social, charitable, or other such activities. Two types of foundations are (1) the independent foundation, which generally derives its funds from an individual, family, or group of individuals to aid social, educational, religious, or other charitable programs; and (2) the company-sponsored foundation, which obtains funds from profit-making corporations. The latter type is legally an independent entity with close relationships to the corporation funding the foundation. Generally funds are granted to areas related to corporate activities or in locations where corporations operate (Jacobs 2002).

HISTORICAL OVERVIEW

Philanthropy in the United States began with what some considered a "sentimental" notion of helping others and alleviating social ills. "The establishment of the General Education Board [GEB] in 1902 marked a new phase in foundation philanthropy. . . . The GEB was committed to an ideal of 'scientific and efficiently organized philanthropy' significantly different from the goals and organization of earlier donor groups. . . . These 'new philanthropists' believed that they could eliminate the root causes of social problems through research and the careful application of insights" (Anderson and Moss 1999, 4). Eventually the philosophy and operations of the GEB would dominate all foundations in the United States, including religious organizations.

Religious and secular philanthropy established and sustained many HBCUs in their early years. The missionary societies of the Baptist, Congregational, Methodist, and Presbyterian churches were the leading religious philanthropists. Included in the secular realm were the Peabody Fund, the Slater Fund, the Rockefeller Foundation, the Carnegie Foundation, the Rosenwald Fund, and the Phelps-Stokes Fund.

Although the religious organizations initially dominated the philanthropy for HBCUs, eventually they would be eclipsed by the secular organizations. In the early 1900s the missionary societies continued to provide more to HBCUs than the GEB. In 1915 the GEB held a conference on "Negro education" that excluded the leaders of the missionary societies. By the 1920s, "as GEB spending for black education dramatically increased, the board's support of particular schools or programs had become a kind of imprimatur, a warrant of worthiness for other givers interested in black education" (Anderson and Moss 1999, 5). The GEB supported the "idea that private education for Negroes should be replaced wherever possible by public schools, supported by taxation and controlled by whites" (5).

Private HBCUs had been established and supported primarily by the missionary societies. When the GEB took the vanguard in funding HBCUs, the American Missionary Association went from supporting forty schools to supporting one by 1950 (Anderson and Moss 1999).

Philanthropy for HBCUs was a double-edged sword. Although they gave money for the education of blacks, it also meant that the donors controlled the education of blacks. The GEB had substantial influence on philanthropy for HBCUs. Therefore, not only did philanthropy mean the demise of several HBCUs, it also meant that to receive funding the education of blacks was to have more of a vocational rather than liberal arts emphasis.

Evelyn C. J. Carroll as her dissertation in 1982 conducted one of the most extensive and inclusive studies on philanthropy and HBCUs. Her study focused on the years between 1930 and 1973, which was the period of greatest change in philanthropic organizations and their relation with HBCUs. Through excerpts from her dissertation the historical relationship between HBCUs and philanthropic organizations is provided. Following is her accounting:

> The establishment of the pioneer educational foundations between the years 1867 and 1917, and their contributions and work [is part of] the development of education for blacks. The five foundations: the Peabody Fund in 1867; the John F. Slater Fund in 1882; the General Education Board in 1903; the Anna T. Jeanne Fund in 1907; and the Rosenwald Fund in 1917 (Carroll 1982, 34–35). . . .
>
> The aims which [Booker T.] Washington held in his philosophy and approach to education for the black people were designed to: (1) secure opportunities for the full development of blacks; (2) improve relations between the whites and blacks through interracial cooperation; and (3) develop Tuskegee Institute [now Tuskegee University] as the supreme school for those ideals in black education. Washington concluded early in his career that to insure the success of Tuskegee, he must win the support of three groups—the "best class" of southern whites, northern whites with a philanthropic interest in the South, and members of his own race. Through his multitude of contacts with the great sources of wealth in America, at

Washington's death in 1915, Tuskegee had a permanent endowment of $2 [million], the largest of any black institution of higher education in the nation. By 1930, it had increased to $7 [million] (137–138). . . .

The new educational philanthropy, in the first three decades [of 1900] demonstrated unequivocally the possibilities and might of [the GEB's] financial control and influence in support of self-selected priorities, or those it was influenced to undertake. Toward the end of 1930, the General Education Board . . . with the largest financial assets, assumed the leadership in supporting a number of areas outside the parameters of teacher education in the private black colleges (138–139). . . .

The cause and effect paradigms of the dynamics of social change is present in the history of philanthropic support of the black institutions from a time of slavery through the Civil War years; the Reconstruction Period; the first and second World Wars; and the Civil Rights Movement. Philanthropic commitments and the development of the private black institutions in higher education are related significantly. Implications for change existed in the different emphases of activities and priorities; and the new roles in philanthropic support were adapted to meet changes within each period (140). . . .

The depression of the 1930s had a salutary effect on philanthropy and the private black institutions of higher education, marking transitions and new roles for both during the decade of the 1930s. The modern professional philanthropic foundation came into existence. A period of self-determination for the private black institutions commenced, stemming from the relaxing of church control and diminishing support from private philanthropy imposed by the long economic recession. A trend of interest in black higher education was indicated (141). . . .

The changes in the structure and organization of philanthropy were comprehensive in scope after 1930. . . . The reorganization in most of the foundations was based on careful appraisal as to the limitations and opportunities for the distribution and dissemination of funds. . . . The change of approach meant that the more effective philanthropic agency would limit its work to a few definite programs. . . . The establishments of a "program" and "project" approach was aimed at the development of specific priorities of support and toward facilitating a more judicious, equitable and effective system of grant-making in a number of fields. . . . It sought to eliminate the "direct contact," and the "personal" and "patron" relationship between the donor and the recipient which typically had characterized the relation between early philanthropy and black higher education for more than [50] years. The new policies and procedures implemented a more systematic procedure for evaluation requests for funds and the appropriation of gifts and grants for all purposes (142–144). . . .

The parallel period of change in philanthropy and the private black institutions of higher education in the 1930s focuses upon two important considerations: (1) the extent to which the transition in philanthropy would have significant meaning and the implications for the private black institutions of higher education in a period of change; and (2) from a larger and more prosperous range of philanthropic foundations, the potentiality of new roles and greater responsibilities in support of the black institutions of higher education (146–147). . . .

The needs were critical for all private black colleges and universities in the 1930s. The institutions entered the initial phase of self-development and goal-setting to achieve independence, autonomy and recognition in an effort to chart the course for their future toward becoming creditable institutions of higher education. Few approached financial adequacy; none was a recognized four-year college by national or regional professional or accrediting agencies in 1930. The situation was a compelling one for philanthropic support (147).

Limitations with regard to the new organization of the philanthropic agencies could affect the newly projected leadership roles of the increasing number of black administrators of the colleges, who, as chief negotiators and liaison between the institutions and the philanthropic organizations, would be called upon to utilize different insights, expertise and strategies now in seeking, successfully negotiating and acquiring financial support from the foundations. The adjustment from the personal contact approach, which was best known and followed in securing funds, to one which was impersonal and program oriented, presented a challenge for which there had been virtually no prior experience or preparation of black college administrators to assist the successful transfer. The critical responsibility lay in their ability to translate and channel the needs of the institutions into the programmatic scheme of the foundations (148). . . .

A further option apparent in the possible outcomes of the changes in foundation organization was that no significant change would occur in the relation to the black colleges. The practiced role of paternalistic, sporadic giving in the past would persist in the present. This could imply a dual standard by the foundations in the establishment of programs, especially designed and organized for black higher education based on the perceptions of needs in support, which in earlier times had deterred rather than assisted their growth and development (149). . . .

The significant outcome from the reorganization of philanthropic foundations in the 1930s to black education in the nation was the emergence of black higher education as an area of emphasis and concentration in three of the earlier and larger general purpose philanthropic foundations and the more recently organized foundations between 1930 and 1960 (152). . . .

Support to the black private institutions was based on the needs of the institutions at a particular time, as they were perceived by the foundations and within the purview of interests of funding, or as needs were interpreted to them by the administrators, trustees or other interested individuals of the institutions. In most cases, the priorities of support were within the context of the board programs the foundations adopted in their reorganization. In few exceptions were programs or priorities special or separate, which applied solely to the black institutions between the decades of 1930 and 1960 (153–154). . . .

The general plans for activities in black higher education included support and cooperation in the following priorities: (a) developing university centers, including professional schools, (b) promoting medical education and nurse training at a few centers, (c) in aiding a selected group of denominational colleges and also certain state-supported institutions, (d) in developing teacher-training facilities, especially in state normal schools and state agricultural and mechanical colleges, (e) in providing additional training for those engaged in the field of black education, and (f) in improving accounting systems of institutions. From 1940, general-purpose philanthropic foundations and corporation foundations added their strength to the support of specific priorities (155). . . .

After the 1954 Supreme Court [*Brown*] decision and subsequent rulings on the desegregation of schools, the larger foundations [gave] funds for specific programs to the black colleges and universities. . . . Several Southern foundations which had not contributed previously to the black institutions and the smaller and younger foundations joined the special interest groups and provided new sources of financial assistance to the private institutions of higher education for blacks (156–157). . . .

The Supreme Court decision in 1954 . . . and the civil rights legislation in 1964 were the historic events . . . which led to the infusion of the ideals of egalitarianism in education. . . . During these years [foundations] provided funds for the widest diversity of priorities in the history of [HBCUs]. Priorities which prior to this era had received little or no support in the private black institutions were established in an effort to equalize education opportunities, at college, graduate and professional levels of minority students. In addition, programs sought to counter the inequities in the black institutions in faculty development, administration and education program, critical areas which would enable them to compete in the transition to integrated education and the mainstream of American higher education (422). . . .

One of the most controversial problems in the development of the private black institutions and one fundamental to all other areas of growth and status has been the slow growth or inadequacy of permanent endowment. Endowment as a self-perpetuating and productive source of capital funds has had no continuing, historical precedence in philanthropic giving to the black private institutions. The endowments provided were usually in the form of annual gifts or support for restricted purposes, such as buildings, salaries, current expenses, financial emergencies or the basic needs in other areas of the institutions (161). . . .

After the emergency endowments grants in 1935, the General Education Board fully implemented an effective program of "conditional" or "matching" grant-making. This approach was used primarily to build and secure endowments for the private black colleges. Its special role was that of a "pump-priming" nature and operation. In the "conditional" or "matching" giving, the gift is contingent upon being matched by the recipient, with a definite share or sum, often less, equal to, or larger than the designated amount by the donor, with a specific time agreed upon for raising all or partial pledges. . . . The primary objective in this process was that of stimulating institutions to assume the responsibility for endowment and other needed funds, and to encourage giving from other sources also. Endowment in the [1930s and 1940s] were given mainly for buildings, improved salaries for teachers and general funds, drawn from the interest and used for the general operation and expenditures of the institutions. The options for meeting the "match obligation" were few in the black community. Limited resources for raising funds were available to the black colleges, which as a whole were dependent upon a constituency economically less capable of meeting the financial commitments and prospects of only nominal support from the small and ineffective support organizations and the professional and business segments. As mitigating as these factors may have been in meeting the obligations under this method of fund-raising, the institutions often were able to meet the stipulations of the agreement with the foundations; particularly the larger, private independent black colleges and several of the church-controlled black institutions. In other cases, it became necessary for the foundation to extend the time for the consummation of the conditional grant in several years and make a contingent appropriation against the original pledge, or even relinquish the contract, granting an outright gift finally (162–163). . . .

After 1940, grants for endowment to the private black colleges and universities as a priority of foundation contributions declined generally. . . . The 1972 [United Negro College Fund] survey of private foundations' interest in providing support to black colleges for endowment, in its summary of responses to specific fields of interest, revealed that "No foundation indicated an interest in contributing to an endowment" (167, 175). . . .

Though the conscience and interest of the foundations were raised to a very high level regarding the development of private institutions of higher education for blacks after 1930, the outstanding problems in support were the attainment of recognition of the schools as creditable and qualified four-year colleges and professional schools, capable of meeting the standards and aims of higher education in America. At this time, no black college or university, private or public, was recognized by state or regional accrediting agencies or professional education organizations. If foundations monies and support from other philanthropic sources were to be continued, the institutions must be able to justify their existence in terms of their strengths in financial security, educational programs and the ability to develop qualified and finished graduates, prepared to serve community needs and those of the nation. The apparent concentration of priorities in the foundations should have been in those areas of support which would increase the capital funds, student aid, strengthen curriculum and instruction, provide for faculty development, improve library resources, laboratory equipment, faculty salaries, and the physical plant, in order to assist the institutions to meet accreditation requisites. The high standards of admission to college and requirements for the educational program established by the Carnegie Foundation for the Advancement of Teaching in 1916 were deterrents to the accreditation of the black colleges; and the financial status of most was also a prohibitive factor in the process of self-study, required by the regional accrediting association for all institutions seeking approval of their status and membership. For these purposes, the General Education Board and the Carnegie Foundation for the Advancement of Teaching made periodic grants to the associations involved in accrediting the institutions. Larger grants were made directly to the regional accrediting agencies (the Southern Association of Colleges and Secondary Schools and the Middle States Association of Colleges and Secondary Schools) and were available to the institutions to assist them with the costs involved in conducting a year-long, and even longer time, period of self-examination and the production of self-studies reports and sponsoring the final protocol conferences. Grants were made to the Southern Association of Colleges and Secondary Schools and to its affiliate, the Association of Negro Colleges and Second Schools. Support for accreditation was not viewed as a major and sustaining priority of itself by the foundations; rather a necessary or temporal need against the time when the private black colleges would be sufficiently self-supporting so that such functions could be written into their budgets at appropriate intervals of review and study (185–186). . . . .

The early foundations gave generally and consistently for capital funds or current expenses between 1920 and 1960, for the majority of the private black schools existed at the basic needs levels. . . . Grants for capital funds from 1960 to 1972 have ranked highest as the selected interest of foundation in support of the institutions (189). . . .

The lack of capital funds in the private black colleges and universities during the Second World War years challenged the creative initiative of the administrators in the black institutions. From this situation, the first black philanthropic corporation was chartered to alleviate the problem of maintaining capital funds for the black institutions. The establishment of the United Negro College Fund had greater implications for impact upon the black community and the nation than simply fund-raising. It was envisioned as a pioneer in high-level practices of financing educational institutions by black leadership. Corporate contributions in support of the private black institutions had not occurred prior to 1944 [the year the United Negro College Fund was founded] (189–191). . . .

Although the greatest support [from foundations] was directed to developing the private institutions to the competitive level, they have not achieved this pinnacle of status generally. Mainly the priorities of foundations have brought a very small group of private colleges and institutions to the farthermost point in the development level, and only to the threshold of the competitive level. The greater proportion of institutions remain at the developmental level, and only the extended support of philanthropic priorities in the future can provide for continuing their development toward the competitive level (458). . . .

There has been a gradual attenuation of support from philanthropy to the private black institutions. In 1900 philanthropic organizations provide 100 percent of the support; 50 percent by 1930; 25 percent in 1960; and 17 percent in 1970 (460).

CONTEMPORARY PHILANTHROPY

How does an American university increase its reputation and esteem? According to Henry Rosovsky (1990), money is the sine qua non, and for private universities the size of the endowment is a fairly reliable indicator. A more dependable indicator of university status is the academic degree of excellence, which ultimately suggests that a capable faculty will attract good students, grants, and alumni in addition to public support and global recognition. However, for this to become a reality, HBCUs like all educational institutions must cultivate the art of asking for money. Fundraising will always be the recurring theme of academic life. There is never enough money to go around. Thus, like a good sales person, HBCUs must learn to become "closers," organizations that can move from polite preliminaries to asking for a seven-figure gift. Learn to think big—it only gets better with numerous opportunities.

The endowment of HBCUs have grown much slower than the nation's larger and more wealthy historically white institutions. Generally blacks are not as affluent as whites, and they therefore contribute less to their alma maters.

In an article by Sullivan (2000, on-line), over the past thirty years, black America has experienced phenomenal growth in both its business leadership class and its number of millionaires. To date the most notable beneficiaries have been HBCUs along with traditional civil rights organizations and the black church. However, it appears as though the young black artists and athletes have been unable to conceptualize the social impact they could have on black America if only they could structure a small percentage of their portfolio to invest in social change. Although many may not have attended an HBCU, few that did have demonstrated a desire to concern themselves with the wealth gap or racial disparities in education.

A larger question is what legacy will the black millionaires focus upon? Will they endow HBCUs for posterity? Unfortunately it is still not quite clear what they will do as leaders in the black community. Yet these artists, entrepreneurs, business executives, and athletes represent the new wealth and a potential foundation for sustaining HBCUs as well as black institutional life and social justice in twenty-first-century America. What are HBCUs doing to embrace and encourage this new surge of potential funders?

Although the HBCU with the top endowment in 2001 was Howard University (D.C.)—$324 million—a recent article in *Ebony* magazine declared Spelman College (Ga.) to be the richest black college in the country, with an average endowment per student of $114,500. Spelman's endowment was $229 million, second only to Howard University. Hampton University's (Va.) endowment was $175 million, and Morehouse College (Ga.) was $101 million (Davis 2002).

The endowments are outstanding fundraising efforts for HBCUs. Neither economic challenges, decreasing endowment funds, nor domestic and international turmoil could divert the attention of competent, visionary HBCU leaders from their pursuit of funds for academic survival and institutional competitiveness in a global society. For example, Howard University has embarked upon a $250 million fund-raising campaign to occur over the next five years.

According to Howard's president, H. Patrick Swygert, "if you look at the larger HBCU community one would have to conclude that the impact of HBCUs in this nation, based on producing productive, engaged citizens and leaders, far outweighs the investment that the nation has made in these institutions"(Smiles 2002, 16–17).

How have some institutions succeeded in overcoming the challenges of fundraising? Although the answers may be complex and varied, they center on leadership, relationships, and partnerships. It is also strategically important to engage, not alienate, the alumni and friends of HBCUs. Presidents must market the successes of the institution and learn to enjoy telling and sharing their institutional stories.

Blacks and those interested in promoting HBCUs must become positive public relations advocates for these institutions. Both strengths and weaknesses of HBCUs must be recognized. However, expanded efforts must be concentrated on enhancing the positive, historical advantages that have been a tradition of these institutions and will continue to be as HBCUs jockey to position themselves in a competitive educational environment.

Foundations entered the twenty-first century faced with unprecedented competition for their grants due to the rapid growth of nonprofit organizations and the wide array of problems confronting the nation (McIlnay 1998). Administrative issues confronting many organizations have caused foundations to demand improved management and a greater return on philanthropic investments. In addition, U.S. Congress and state governments are cutting back or eliminating aid to numerous cultural, social, health, and educational institutions. All of these actions have caused more institutions of higher education to turn to foundation support. Increased competition should not deter HBCUs from seeking foundation support.

Some foundations are very interested in understanding the needs of, and thus supporting, communities of color. A study funded by the Kellogg Foundation with support from the Ford Foundation, the David and Lucile Packard Foundation, the Charles Stewart Mott Foundation, and the California Endowment was done to raise awareness of philanthropy among minorities and to increase support for nonprofit organizations in communities of color. They dismissed the stereotype that people of color when in need seek mainly white-run foundations. This report indicated that 53 percent of all black households give to charity and 59 percent of their donations go to church and other religious purposes. It is suggested in the report that many HBCUs continue to look to the church for support (W. W. Kellogg Foundation 2002, on-line).

The Foundation Center in 2002 (on-line) identified nine foundations as being the leading benefactors of HBCUs and that have specifically indicated an interest in giving to HBCUs. The foundations and their assets follow:

Bill and Melinda Gates Foundation (Wash.) $21,149,088,035
Lilly Endowment Inc. (N.Y.) $12,814,397,581

The Ford Foundation (N.Y.) $10,814,697,000
The David and Lucile Packard Foundation (Calif.)
    $9,793,212,529
The Robert Wood Johnson Foundation (N.J.) $9,044,511,000
W. W. Kellogg Foundation (Mich.) $5,719,735,520
Pew Charitable Trust (Penn.) $4,800,776,253
The Rockefeller Foundation (N.Y.) $3,211,126,100
Carnegie Corporation of New York (N.Y.) $1,711,510,640

Far too many HBCUs do not avail themselves of these philan-thropic opportunities.

INDIVIDUAL PHILANTHROPY

In the 1988 movie *School Daze,* directed by Spike Lee, one of the board of trustees for the fictitious HBCU Mission College states, "The Catholics alone support the Notre Dames. The Jews alone support the Yeshivas. The Mormons alone support the Brigham Youngs. Who supports the black colleges? I'll tell you. The federal government and philanthropists. Why can't blacks support Spelman, Tuskegee, Morehouse, or Howard?"

There is a bitter truth as well as an inaccuracy to this statement. The truth is that the greatest external funder today of HBCUs is the fed-eral government. The inaccuracy comes in considering philanthropists, as in foundations, on an equal level as the federal government; in truth, philanthropists do not support private HBCUs in the manner in which they once did.

The first level of control of any institution is who is financially supporting the institution. Black celebrities such as Bill and Camille Cosby and Oprah Winfrey, and black millionaires such as Herman Rus-sell, Willie Gary, and Franklin and Susie Powell have made substantial monetary contributions to selected HBCUs. Yet, the individual philan-thropic financial support of HBCUs should not be solely dependent on these types of individuals. The bitter truth is that far too many blacks do not exhibit a philanthropic spirit toward HBCUs. More specifically, HBCU alumni do not donate money to their alma maters as they should and could. Citing the *United Negro College Fund Statistical Re-port 1998,* Drewry and Doermann state "that for thirty-eight of its thirty-nine members, 11. 9 percent of living alumni gave a smaller per-centage to their colleges in 1996–1997 than they did twenty years ago" (2001, 279).

Given the length of time of operation and the graduation rate, a small private four-year HBCU with an enrollment of 1,000 or less would have an average living alumni pool of 4,000. If each alumnus donated a minimum of $200 a year, that would mean that the school could be assured of $800,000 a year. The larger the school, the more alumni. Thus a school with 10,000 graduates, which would be reasonable to assume for public HBCUs, could be assured $2 million a year.

"However much funding set an agenda, lack of funding set its own agenda as well" (Drewry and Doermann 2001, 69). Black philanthropy is not a new concept. Since the 1700s blacks have pooled their monetary resources to advance their common cause (Carson 1993). In 2000, the earned income in black households was $543 billion, a $176 billion increase from 1996. The median income in 1998 for all black Americans was $25,351. In that year, blacks spent $24.7 billion for apparel products and services, $4.8 billion for alcoholic and nonalcoholic beverages, $2.3 billion for entertainment and leisure, $392 million for sports and recreational equipment, and $2.7 billion for tobacco products and smoking supplies (Target Market News 2002, on-line). Little of their income was received by HBCUs. Alumni are the exclusive external funding domain of a school. Either they are not being approached in a manner that compels them to give or when approached they do not feel compelled to give. Despite indications of growing wealth among African Americans, many HBCUs do not appear to be reaching out to these potential donors. Clearly, the appeal could attract new donors based upon their ethnicity or cultural background (Kellogg Foundation 2002, on-line).

GOVERNMENT RELATIONS

State Government

The historical role of state governments in starting public HBCUs and a few private HBCUs is discussed in Chapter 1. The present section serves as an overview of the contemporary relationship between HBCUs and state governments.

It can be said that governments—federal, state, and local—are part owners of colleges and universities. The influence of legislatures and taxpayers is very strong at public educational institutions. However, even private institutions cannot function without federal support and, in many instances, without state support (Rosovsky 1990). The economic conditions of the early twenty-first century have resulted in much state-level discussion of potential decreases in spending for education. Although spending on education will continue to be an urgent fiscal topic, the protection of resources for HBCUs will no doubt require considerable discussions, debates, and difficult negotiations. In some states HBCUs fare well when compared to other higher education institutions. These states are Mississippi, Missouri, North Carolina, Oklahoma, Tennessee, and Texas. In most of these states, as discussed in Chapter 3 concerning the *Fordice* case, this is a one-time opportunity with many strings attached. In other states, HBCUs were found not to be significantly better- or worse-funded than other institutions. However, one tends to overlook the fact that whatever the economic times, HBCUs are still trying to catch up to historically white colleges and universities.

Of the seven states that provided direct tax dollars to private colleges and universities, these institutions fared worse than public-sector institutions. For example, in Alabama and Louisiana, where HBCUs are located, a 7.3 percent decrease in state funding to private institutions was noted in 2000; simultaneously, more than a 3 percent increase was made to public institutions in Alabama. In Louisiana no increase in spending to private institutions was made, yet an average increase of 13 percent was made to public institutions. However, Louisiana's public HBCU, Grambling University, received only an 8.5 percent increase (Schmidt 2002, on-line).

Clearly, many states could use assistance in crafting appropriate educational funding strategies. The National Conference of State Legislatures with support from the Lumina Foundation for Education embarked in April 2002 on an eighteen-month project to assist state legislatures in making informed, long-term decisions on college affordability and access. Since the start of the 2002 fiscal year most states have reported that budgets did not meet projections, thus leaving them with very uncertain economic futures. During such times, higher education budgets are generally targeted for budget decreases or minimal increases. For HBCUs these times are critical for their future academic survival.

Callan and Finney (1997) suggest that during hard economic times when budgets are cut, a principle of shared responsibility is favored. Educational institutions should expect to absorb their share of budget shortfalls in such a way as to incur the least impact on educational effectiveness. College presidents and boards should have some flexibility in allocating reductions within these parameters. Increased tuitions should consider economic status of state residents and the relationship of tuition level to family income. When tuitions increase, states should exempt need-based student financial aid programs from reductions in state appropriations; this could further aid the impact of tuition increases on the students with the most need. Long-term, affordable higher education will require more, not less, investment by the states. In many instances HBCUs continue to be allocated less than other institutions. Funding equity must continue to be challenged by legislators, even in a tight economic market. Well-educated citizens are critical to the development of a state's economic and social potential. HBCUs have a track record of successfully educating productive citizens and must continue to do so with the support of the states.

Most people believe that state government provides the total funding for public higher education institutions. This is not accurate. For public HBCUs, state funding is less than half, usually about 30 percent to 40 percent of an institution's budget (Yates 2002). The other 60 percent to 70 percent is from tuition, grants, contracts, gifts, and foundations.

Lack of equitable state funding to public HBCUs, as opposed to the funding of historically white institutions, is at the heart of the initial complaints of the *Adams* and *Fordice* cases, discussed in Chapter 3. The plaintiffs, who were blacks or organizations representing blacks, realized that the states were not giving HBCUs an appropriate portion of the state funds for higher education for their sustainability and continued development. It appeared to them that the public HBCUs were being systematically starved.

Federal Government

Federal funding to all higher education occurs through grants, contracts, student financial assistance, and other agreements (Jackson 2001). The federal government has repeatedly come to the aid of education. Initially, federal dealings with education received the greatest attention through the judicial department. This was partly due to the result of the *Brown* decision on school desegregation and in other decisions in cases in which the Supreme Court had been engaged (Good and Teller 1973).

Wars, economic instability, and political and security uncertainties are just a few concerns that will force state and federal governments to play a more active role in education. Historically, whenever education was viewed as significant to the national defense or general welfare of the nation, the U.S. Congress has not refrained from supporting higher education. Thus World War II led to expansion of support for education. In 1944 the GI Bill authorized postsecondary educational aid that would enable millions of World War II veterans to attend college. The Cold War stimulated comprehensive federal education legislation with the passing of the National Defense Education Act (NDEA) in 1958 in response to the launching of the Sputnik satellite by Russia. To ensure that highly trained individuals would be available to help this nation compete in science and technology, funds were included to provide loans to college students. The passage of antipoverty and civil rights laws in the 1960s and 1970s focused on equal access and provided aid to needy college students. In 1980 Congress established the Department of Education as a cabinet-level agency.

Yet despite the growth of the federal role in education, HBCUs and minorities are still confronted with numerous challenges in their quest to engage in sound higher education in the twenty-first century. In 2002 federal aid to HBCUs was modest compared to the billions of dollars spent on international turmoil.

The initial response of the federal government to establish higher education institutions for blacks through agencies and the Freedmen's Bureau is discussed in Chapter 1. One is the money designated through the White House Initiative on HBCUs from the thirty U.S. departments listed in Chapter 7. The other is through student loans and grants.

Federal Grants, Contracts, and Other Agreements

In 1999 HBCUs received "less than 1 percent of the $14 billion the federal government awarded to all colleges and universities that year" (Dervarics 2001, 8). The National Science Foundation (NSF) reported that $164 million HBCUs received in 1999 was down "from the $202 million and $188 million that black colleges received in 1995 and 1996 respectively" (Dervarics 2001, 8). Additionally, the NSF awarded HBCUs "$43 million in 1998, about 2.2 percent of the $1.9 billion the agency awarded to higher education that year." Comparatively speaking the "average HBCU received just $400,000 from NSF that year, compared to an average of $19 million for top 100 colleges and universities" (Dervarics 2001, 8).

In the Higher Education Act of 1965, which was amended in 1998, Congress acknowledged the significant contribution that HBCUs have made in the postsecondary education of African Americans. Congress recognized the unequal manner in which funds have been dispersed to white institutions and to HBCUs by the states and the federal government and admits the role the state and federal governments, because of these discriminatory actions toward HBCUs, played in creating the current precarious state of a large number of HBCUs. In Title III of the Higher Education Act, three sections focus on remedying the discriminatory practices. These sections are "Strengthening HBCUs," "HBCU Capital Financing," and the "Minority Science and Engineering Improvement Program" (Jackson 2001, 176–177).

The Higher Education Act is the primary federal law that authorizes a series of basic higher education programs including aid to historically black colleges and universities. Title III of this act, passed in 1986, came at a very critical time for HBCUs—when many of these institutions would have closed if not for the work of the Congressional Black Caucus members and William Gray, then chairman of the House Budget Committee and now the CEO of the United Negro College Fund, who worked strategically to have Title III crafted and included in the Higher Education Act. Title III provided funds to HBCUs that needed and deserved this assistance.

The purposes for each Title III program are discussed in Chapter 3. Following is a summary of the status of each program.

- The Strengthening Historically Black Colleges and Universities Program provides funds to establish or enhance physical facilities in addition to providing resources for academics, financial management, and endowments. This program also provides funds to HBCUs with graduate programs that are contributing to the legal, medical, dental, and veterinary educational opportunities of blacks. Although funds for higher education were less in 2003 due to the "wartime budget," HBCUs were among the projected winners. The Strengthening HBCUs Program will increase from $206 million in 2002 to a requested $213 million in 2003, and the graduate program will go from $49 million in 2002 to a requested $51 million in 2003. Although the George W. Bush administration is focused on new spending for defense and antiterrorism, HBCUs will not likely loose programs or funds.
- The HBCU Capital Financing Program provides financial insurance for up to $375 million in bonds to make loans to qualifying HBCUs. A private investment-banking firm was selected as the Designated Bonding Authority (DBA) to make loans to HBCUs for a wide array of capital projects from classrooms to research to housing for students

and faculty. In addition an HBCU Capital Financing Advisory Board was established to advise the secretary of education and the DBA on the most efficient means for implementing the program to ensure that capital needs of HBCUs were appropriately facilitated via this program. H. Patrick Swygert, president of Howard University who was appointed by Roderick Paige, U.S. secretary of education, chairs this nine-member board. Over $80 million in bonds were awarded to HBCUs for capital projects in 2002.

- The Minority Science and Engineering Improvement Program (MSEIP) has two main objectives. One is to provide long-term enhancements of science and engineering education at HBCUs and other predominantly minority-serving institutions (i.e., their minority enrollment is 50 percent or more black, American Indian, Asian/Pacific Islander, or Hispanic). The other is to increase the participation of underrepresented minorities in science and technology. It is appropriate to fund HBCUs in their quest to strengthen minorities in science and engineering. The Educational Testing Service (ETS) issued a study that suggested HBCUs did a much better job than historically white institutions in steering black students into engineering and the sciences, in addition to preparing them for graduate studies (Chenoweth 1997). The 2003 request for funding was $8.5 million, the same amount provided for 2002. Funds are awarded annually for one to three years. For 2001 the average new award was $120,000.

With the signing of Executive Order 12232, President Jimmy Carter established the White House Initiative on HBCUs. As noted previously, the initiative is a federal program to support and increase the participation of HBCUs in federally funded programs. "Thirty U.S. departments participate through grants, contracts, and other agreements with HBCUs. Annually, each department is required to present a federal plan and report on how it assisted HBCUs" (Jackson 2001, 136).

In 1999, historically black colleges and universities received the following percentages of federal department budgets: The Agency for International Development, which sponsors programs overseas, 7 percent; Department of Agriculture, 9 percent; Department of Defense, 3 percent; Department of Education, 7 percent; Department of Energy, 3 percent; Depart of Health and Human Services, 2 percent; Department of Housing and Urban Development, 18 percent; U.S. Information Agency, 3 percent; Justice Department, 3 percent; Department of the Interior, 20 percent; Labor Department, 47 percent; National Aeronautics and Space Administration, 6 percent; National Credit Union Administration, 19 percent; National Endowment for the Arts, 1 percent; National Science Foundation, 1 percent; U.S. Nuclear Regulatory Commission, 6 percent; U.S. Small Business Administration, 4 percent; Social Security Administration, 32 percent; U.S. Department of State, 4 percent; U.S. Department of Veteran Affairs, 2 percent; Department of Commerce, 1 percent; Department of Transportation, 8 percent; and Department of the Treasury, 20 percent. The total awards of federal money to white schools in 1999 was $32,406,669,831. Black schools received $1,344,697,091, or 4 percent of the total awards of federal money to postsecondary institutions (Jackson 2001, 141).

Federal Student Assistance (FSA)

The federal student loan program had its beginning in the Higher Education Act of 1965. Guaranteed student loan programs provided many U.S. students with the money needed for education. However, the program was inundated with problems including fraud, abuse, mismanagement, and high default rates. The Credit Reform Act of 1990 gave the U.S. Congress the ability to intervene in correcting the problems. The 1992 amendment to the Higher Education Act of 1965 created the Federal Direct Student Loan Program, which was designed to make the federal education loan process less complex.

There are seven programs under the umbrella of the FSA office, which itself falls under the auspices of the U.S. Department of Education. They are federal Pell grants, Stafford loans, PLUS loans, consolidation loans, federal Supplemental Education Opportunity grants, federal work-study, and federal Perkins loans. All of these programs have specific eligibility requirements. Some can be obtained in combination. All are available to undergraduate and graduate students except for Pell grants, which are only available to undergraduate students.

Grants and work-study funding do not have to be repaid, whereas student loans must be repaid. The lack of repayment, or default, by former students causes disquiet for many colleges in the United States, especially small ones.

Loan repayment is deferred while a person is in school. Once a person leaves school, either because of graduating or an early exit, loan payments are required to begin. A person is considered to be in default when a payment is not made for 270 days (U.S. Department of Education 2002, on-line).

The federal government allows up to 25 percent, or one out of four loans, of a particular institution to be in default for three consecutive years. If this is exceeded, the institution loses eligibility for students to receive loans. In short, the repayment or lack of repayment of those who have left the school effects the availability of loans for current and future students (U.S. Department of Education 2000, on-line).

For a number of HBCUs, especially the small ones with yearly enrollments of less than 1,000, student loan default can mean the difference in keeping the school open or having to close it. Approximately 50 percent of students attending HBCUs receive student loans (U.S. Department of Education 2000, on-line).

By 1998, thirteen HBCUs had maintained the 25 percent default rate for more than three consecutive years and were thus on the brink of closing. These schools were Allen University (S.C.); Arkansas Baptist College; Barber-Scotia College (N.C.); Central State University (Ohio); Houston-Tillotson College (Tex.); Lane College (Tenn.); Mary Holmes College (Miss.); Miles College (Ala.); Paul Quinn College (Tex.); Texas College; Texas Southern University; and Wiley College (Tex.) (U.S. Department of Education 2000, on-line).

For some years HBCUs were exempt from the 25 percent, three-consecutive-years rule. Effective July 1, 1999, this exemption was ended by a provision of the Higher Education Amendment of 1998. By 2000 the thirteen schools listed above were working with the FSA and others to develop a plan to address the student loan defaults and were able to maintain their eligibility for federal student financial assistance (U.S. Department of Education 2000, on-line).

CONCLUSION

The economic independence and solvency of HBCUs is dependent on developing and sustaining permanent endowments. This is especially true for private HBCUs. As long as HBCUs remain greatly dependent on external funds such as foundations and governments, their ability to create educational programs that are relevant to their constituency is limited. As long as HBCUs' primary funding is based on the inclinations of foundations and the politics of governments, they remain at the mercy of others. Endowments, especially for private institutions, enable institutions to determine and establish their educational programs and seek external funding that enhances and enriches their programs. In short, endowments put institutions in a position of control of their destinies.

Central to a permanent endowment is the institution's president. He or she must have—or acquire—the skills for fundraising as well as institutional development staff with the necessary skills. It is not by accident or chance that Patrick Swygert, president of Howard University; Donald Stewart, former president of Spelman College who began the capital campaign in the 1970s on which Spelman's endowment is based; or William Harvey, president of Hampton University were able to achieve outstanding endowments for their institutions. These men honed their fund-raising skills, surrounded themselves with competent institutional development staff, and *planned* the acquiring of an endowment. The plans were for extended periods of time, often up to ten years.

And where did they begin to develop endowments? They began within the institutions' family—the alumni. Having acquired an endowment foundation, they were in the position to negotiate with foundations and governments to secure funds that met their needs rather than foundations and government fully dictating what their needs should be. Presidents such as Swygert, Stewart, and Harvey built the foundation for endowments first from within. By doing so, they were able to greatly remove their institutions from patriarchic relationships with external funders.

In the twenty-first century, foundations and the federal government choose to work with higher education institutions that have evidence that they (1) are or have the potential to be self-sustaining, (2) have shown an ability for accountability for the management, investment, and expenditure of the institution's funds, and (3) can demonstrate growth and productivity. These expectations are no different for HBCUs. Ultimately, as resources continue to become more competitive, historically black colleges and universities must develop procedures to value and communicate the receipt of all dollars, great and small.

REFERENCES

Anderson, Eric, and Alfred A. Moss Jr. 1999. *Dangerous Donations: Northern Philanthropy and Southern Black Education, 1902–1930.* Columbia, MO: University of Missouri Press.

Callan, Patrick M., and Joni E. Finney. 1997. *Public and Private Financing of Higher Education: American Council on Higher Education.* Phoenix, AZ: Oryx Press.

Carroll, Evelyn C. J. 1982. "Priorities in Philanthropic Support for Private Negro Colleges and Universities, 1930–1973." Ph.D. diss., University of Michigan (UMI No. 8214970).

Carson, Emmet D. 1993. *A Hand Up: Black Philanthropy and Self-Help in America.* Lanham, MD: University Press of America/Joint Center for Political and Economic Studies Press.

Chenoweth, Karin. 1997. "Forthcoming ETS Report Proclaims the Importance of HBCUs." *Black Issues in Higher Education* 14, 16: 16–18.

Davis, Kimberly. 2002. "The Richest Black College." *Ebony* 62, 11: 84–94.

Dervarics, Charles. 2001. "Black Colleges' Slice of Federal Research Pie Getting Smaller." *Black Issues in Higher Education* 18, 7: 8.

———. 2002. " Wartime Budget Has Few Higher Education Increases." *Black Issues in Higher Education* 19, 1: 8.

Drewry, Henry N., and Humphrey Doermann. 2001. *Stand and Prosper: Private Black Colleges and Their Students.* Princeton, NJ: Princeton University Press.

The Foundation Center. 2002. "Researching Philanthropy." http://fdncenter.org/research/trends.html (cited August 10, 2002).

Good, Harry G., and James D. Teller. 1973. *A History of American Education.* New York: Macmillan.

Jackson, Cynthia L. 2001. *African American Education: A Reference Handbook.* Santa Barbara, CA: ABC-CLIO.

Jacobs, David G., ed. 2002. *The Foundation Directory.* New York: Foundation Center.

Kellogg Foundation. 2002. "Emerging Philanthropy in Communities of Color: A Report on Current Trends." http://www.wkkf.org/documents/phi/vol.efcc/emergingphilantyhropyincommunities of color.asp (cited August 19, 2002).

Nielsen, Waldemar A. 1996. *Inside American Philanthropy: The Drama of Donorship.* Norman, OK: University of Oklahoma Press.

Rosovsky, Henry. 1990. *The University: An Owner's Manual.* New York: Norton & Co.

Schmidt, Peter. 2002. "State Spending on Higher Education Grows by Smallest Rate in 5 Years." *The Chronicle of Higher Education,* http://chronicle.com/v48/i19/19a.2001.htm. (cited August 20, 2002).

Smiles, Robin V. 2002. "Howard Launches $250 Million Fund-Raising Campaign." *Black Issues in Higher Education* 19, 2: 16–17.

Sullivan, Lisa Y. 2002. "The New Black Millionaires and Black Philanthropy in the 21st Century." http://www.charityvillage.com/research/rphl.html (cited August 19, 2002).

Target Market News. 2002. "Buying Power of Black America 2000." http://www.targetmarketnews.com/numbers/index.htm (cited May 17, 2002).

U.S. Department of Education. 2000. "HBCUs to Remain in Federal Student Aid Programs." http://www.ed.gov/PressReleases/03–2000/314.html (cited May 18, 2002).

———. 2002. "Direct Loans FAQ." http://www.ed.gov/DirectLoan/faqlist.html (cited May 18, 2002).

Yates, Eleanor Lee. 2001. "Capital Campaigns." *Black Issues in Higher Education* 18, 10: 18–25.

Chapter Five

Historically Minority Universities Bioscience and Biotechnology Program Initiative

This chapter will detail the innovative Historically Minority Universities (HMU) Bioscience and Biotechnology Program Initiative established in North Carolina in 1993. North Carolina has a sixteen-campus public university system. Of those campuses, five are historically black universities: North Carolina A&T State University, North Carolina Central University, Winston-Salem State University, Elizabeth City State University, and Fayetteville State University. The state also is home to six private HBCUs: Barber-Scotia College, Bennett College, Johnson C. Smith University, Livingston College, Saint Augustine's College, and Shaw University. These five public HBCUs and six private HBCUs together make North Carolina the state with the most HBCUs. These colleges and universities offer bachelor to doctorate degrees, including degrees in science and engineering. The institutions participating in North Carolina's Historically Minority Universities Bioscience and Biotechnology Program Initiative discussed in this chapter were the state's five public HBCUs and the University of North Carolina at Pembroke, a historically Native American institution that was established for the education of Native Americans.

Eleanor F. Nunn was the director of the HMU Bioscience and Biotechnology Program Initiative at the North Carolina Biotechnology Center. In this chapter Nunn describes a model developed in North Carolina, which was a collaboration of the public minority higher education institutions, state government, and a private nonprofit corporation, the North Carolina Biotechnology Center.

In addition, this project consisted of an enthusiastic group of science educators; corporate, nonprofit, governmental participants; and legislators who were committed to supporting HBCUs in their quest to continue or to establish scientific programs for the growing number of students interested in obtaining degrees in science from these universities. Although this program focused on the enhancement of HBCUs in bioscience/biotechnology, it was economically based. The ultimate goal was to increase the number of minorities graduating in the sciences as an initial step toward providing a competitive potential recruitment and employment pool for bioscience corporations in North Carolina. To successfully participate in the project, strong emphasis was given to the need to establish sound planning, appropriate collaborations, communications, and effective implementation practices and procedures. This HMU Initiative reflected what Robert Hargrove (1998) defines as essential to successful collaboration: The initiative was not based on the extraordinary individuals who participated in the project but on the extraordinary *combinations* of people, or perhaps even ordinary people who had the vision to see exciting new possibilities, with the compassion and desire to make it a reality.

The voluntary group of active individuals became immersed in the project without knowing the impact such plans, collaborations, and communication would have on their future life, occupations, or the future roles of biotechnology/bioscience programs at the six participating universities. Yet armed with a series of new and additional time-sensitive project tasks and responsibilities, the individual institution program leaders enthusiastically accepted the challenge of developing a biotechnology/bioscience program plan in an effort to prepare students for an enhanced scientific career.

One might understandably ask the question, Why focus on the science programs at public minority institutions? The answer is that HBCUs are the logical starting point if action was to be taken toward resolving the issue of underrepresentation of minorities in science. HBCUs continue to attract large numbers of minority students. In 1995 HBCUs enrolled 16 percent of all African American students in higher education nationally, although the institutions constitute only 3 percent of the nation's more than 3,700 institutions of higher education. In 1995 these institutions graduated 26 percent of all African Americans enrolled in four-year colleges (National Center for Education Statistics 1997).

In 1994, all states enrolling more than 5,000 Native Americans in higher education institutions were west of the Mississippi River. However, states enrolling 1,000 to 5,000 Native American students were generally distributed on both sides of the Mississippi River. In that same year, about 8 percent of all Native American students attended tribally controlled colleges. With the exception of Minnesota, Maine, and North Carolina, all states where Native Americans consisted of at least 1 percent of the total state enrollments were in the western half of the United States. The largest number of Native American students was concentrated in states where they most commonly resided (National Center for Education Statistics 1998). However, in North Carolina, the majority of African Americans and Native Americans who graduated from high school enrolled in HBCUs or at the University of North Carolina at Pembroke (formerly Pembroke State College).

North Carolina's minority colleges and universities have the capacity to provide a trained workforce for the state's future biotechnology/bioscience needs. The six public HMUs that participated in the biotechnology/bioscience initiative educated more than 26,000 students a year (University of North Carolina 1998, on-line).

IMPETUS FOR THE MODEL

As is evidenced in much of the United States and throughout the world, in North Carolina it was evident that the growing role of science and technology was having an increasing impact on education and training at all levels. Many educators, employers, and organizations sponsoring scientific research and development activities have viewed the underrepresentation of minorities in most scientific and technological fields as an issue of continuing concern. More than twenty years ago, the National Science Foundation (NSF) provided a report on the status of minorities in science and engineering. It is disturbing that some of the findings from that initial NSF report continue today. Although women have made substantial progress in science and engineering over the past thirty-five years, increasing their percentage of earned bachelor degrees from 23 percent in 1966 to 29 percent in 2000, blacks and Native Americans have not seen as significant an increase. The Commission on Professionals in Science and Technology Compendium Report from Professional Women and Minorities indicated that blacks earned 8.3 percent of the nation's science and engineering bachelor's degrees in 2000. Yet progress has occurred: For example, the number and percentage of black and Native Americans enrolling in college and completing bachelor, masters, and doctoral degrees in science have increased (National Science Foundation 2000). The National Council for Minorities in Engineering reported that enrollment of blacks in engineering programs has increased, though the same report states that enrollment of Native Americans in these programs has stagnated (*Black Engineer* 2003, on-line).

Sandra Harding (1993) suggests that science education has suffered from a lack of attention to a concern called the "racial" economy of science. This phenomenon has also been addressed by others who view the underrepresentation of minorities in science as an issue that might be more appropriately overcome by placing greater emphasis on the economic advantages of science and technology. Even in the twenty-first century, the limited number of minorities in science and technology precludes an increased presence for future opportunities in these fields. Those involved in the initiative were cognizant of this concern and chose to pursue some action toward increasing the number of minority graduates in the sciences. Although the model was to enhance biotechnology/bioscience at HBCUs, perhaps its most significant goal was to provide a larger minority recruitment pool of competitive graduates in science and technology for future employment in North Carolina biotechnology/bioscience companies.

Biotechnology is a group of new technologies that use living cells to make new products, improve existing products, and solve problems. Carl Feldbaum states that over twenty years ago the U.S. Food and Drug Administration approved the first biotechnology drug, Genentech, and Eli Lilly's recombinant human insulin for diabetics. To be sure, biotechnology has had a major impact on mainstream medicine. Millions of people worldwide have benefited from the approved medicines and vaccines, which increased from twenty-two in 1993 to 155 in 2002. (Feldbaum 2002, on-line). These technological advances have been ideally suited to North Carolina, with its quality educational institutions coupled with the state's traditional industries such as agriculture, food processing, forestry, health, and medicine, all of which can be greatly enhanced by biotechnology.

North Carolina is among the top five biotechnology regions in the country. The number of companies involved with biotechnology in North Carolina has grown consistently, from thirty in 1982 to 155 in 2003, employing approximately 17,000 residents and representing an annual payroll of over $850 million. About one-third of these companies are major international players, such as Ajinomoto, BASF, Bayer, Becton Dickinson, Biogen, GlaxoSmithKline, Syngenta, Nova Nordisk Pharmaceutical Industries, bioMerieux, Sphinx Labs, and Wyeth Vaccines (North Carolina Biotechnology Center 2003, on-line).

Like many other companies, biotechnology firms are experiencing somewhat of a financial slump. Yet despite the recent downturn, the

overarching trend has been continued growth. In terms of future employment, the North Carolina biotechnology industry is increasing 10 to
15 percent a year. It is projected that by 2025 as many as 125,000 North
Carolinians will be working in biotechnology with annual revenues of
$24 billion. Many of these new jobs will be ideally suited to college grad-
uates. They will be in biomanufacturing—the production of biological
products such as drugs, vaccines, vitamins, amino acids, and enzymes.
Some of these jobs currently pay an average of $40,000 per year (North
Carolina Biotechnology Center 2003, on-line). As the need continues for
a trained, technically skilled workforce, North Carolina must consistently build upon the solid foundation it has established to retain and
recruit biotechnology/bioscience companies. In addition, if the state is
to receive the greatest return on its investment in biotechnology, it must
continue to ensure that the state's labor force is prepared for the jobs
created by advancing technologies.

Today, more than ever before, it is essential for government as
well as private and nonprofit corporations to recognize the significant
potential role that minority colleges and universities can have on the
state's future workforce. Neither the state nor the nation can afford to
negate the knowledge and abilities of almost 30 percent of its people
and continue to be a thriving, successful, and productive technological
society. In a report titled "Workforce 2000: Work and Workers for the
Twenty-First Century," Johnson and Packer (1987) remind us that the
ability of the United States to remain competitive in a global economy is
directly related to the educational opportunities and training provided
to those groups that have been historically underrepresented and underserved. It is evident that HBCUs are attracting a large number of
blacks as well as other minority students who are graduating. Though
HBCUs have traditionally enrolled more African Americans and American Indians than other colleges and universities, funding to these institutions to enhance bioscience/biotechnology has been limited. The five
traditionally black universities and one Native American institution in
the initiative program needed more funding and resources to prepare
their students for jobs being created by biotechnology and related technology companies in the state.

Continuous funds are critical for the successful enhancement of
scientific advancements required for the development of competitive
knowledge-based skills of students attending HBCUs. It is therefore even
more essential today that HBCUs develop a strong leadership consortium, capable of locating and obtaining resources from a variety of entities such as government, private, and nonprofit groups as well as private

citizens. Why is this significant? When President George W. Bush unveiled a $2.2 trillion budget proposal for fiscal year 2004, with more than $3.5 billion to fight terrorism, he put into motion the need for even greater biotechnology research and development. Highly trained science and engineering graduates from HBCUs make up a growing part of the defense and security workforce, which affects the economic development of the nation. HBCUs like Hampton University's Northrop Grunman Fiber Optic Sensors Lab, Tennessee State University's Direct Methodologies Laboratory, Howard University's Material Science Research Center of Excellence, and North Carolina A&T State University's Center for Advance Materials and Smart Structures are currently involved in strategically important research. A variety of sensors are being developed, some of which can detect agents like anthrax. Another type of biometric sensor, retina scanners, can identify a person's eyes similar to fingerprints. The research laboratories of historically black colleges and universities are involved in many advanced technologies at a time when diverse collaboration from educational, scientific, and technical resources is critical. The nation's historically black colleges and universities are distinguishing themselves in these endeavors (Deen 2003, on-line).

In spite of these accomplishments, even U.S. Secretary of Education Roderick R. Paige, an HBCU graduate, feels that student aid will again face another tight year (Burd 2003). This will surely have an influence on minority students who are interested in attending postsecondary institutions, which include HBCUs. However, aid to historically black colleges and universities should increase from $255 million in 2002 to $277 million requested for fiscal year 2004, an increase of 8.8 percent (Brainard and Borrego 2003). Bush's proposed 2004 budget offers modest to no change for most science programs. The NSF and the National Institutes of Health (NIH) should both realize proposed increases in the 2004 budget. However, much of the research to be funded likely will involve the study of bioterrorism.

George Hill, a biomedical science professor at Meharry Medical College (Tenn.), notes three reasons why biotechnology research at HBCUs should not be overlooked. First, most of the research focuses on diseases that disproportionately affect blacks and other people of color such as diabetes, hypertension, stroke, and prostate cancer. Second, many African Americans students still prefer to obtain their degree "in an environment in which they can relate to a professor or scientist on the faculty. Students feel they have a better chance of getting a good education and training at such institutions." The HBCU environment maintains certain subliminal signals that must be understood by faculty. There is a strong sense of tradition and heritage at these institutions that is the product of their struggles; there is a unique experience of being in a majority status that enhances the comprehension of the majority versus minority state in the larger society; there is a unique experience of leadership and role models; and there are academic support programs that are often not offered at other institutions. Third, support for historically black colleges and universities increases the potential employment pipeline (Nunn 2001).

A majority of the federal funds for basic research goes to institutions classified as "research universities"; because most HBCUs are not classified as research institutions and many do not have the resources to accommodate extensive research, they receive little funding. Yet an article in *The Scientist* by Steven Benowitz suggested that the goal of science programs at HBCUs was to afford undergraduate African Americans the opportunity to do state-of-the-art research that would allow them to continue their education at major research institutions and become scientists (1997, on-line). Sebetha Jenkins, president of Jarvis Christian College in Texas, an HBCU, in 2002 spoke before the House Science Subcommittee on Research. She suggested that when compared to research institutions, HBCUs were grossly lacking the required research infrastructure. Such limitations stalled faculty members' opportunities to conduct state-of-the-art research within their field (U.S. House of Representatives Science Committee's Subcommittee on Research 2002, on-line).

The NSF recognized in 1998 that HBCUs accounted for about 80 percent of projects in science deferred due to a lack of funds. Without adequate funds, scientific programs at all HBCUs are potentially compromised. Basic scientific equipment, materials, and appropriate space are a challenge for many HBCUs. Based on data reviewed by the United Negro College Fund, of more than $2.7 billion in NSF funds for institutions of higher education, HBCUs received only 1 percent of these funds. Congresswoman Eddie Bernice Johnson (D-Tex.), member of the House Science Subcommittee on Research, has been a strong supporter of more funds to the NSF. It is her hope that additional funds would enhance the quality of undergraduates in science, mathematics, and engineering education (Phillips 2003, on-line).

One would also hope that increased funds to the NSF would translate to greater funding opportunities to minority institutions. However, even with the support extended to HBCUs, such omission represents a huge missed opportunity for the untapped student resources at HBCUs to receive an enhanced science curriculum. Can this nation continue to remain a competitive science and technology society, with an effective workforce, if it does not address the need to increase the minority presence in science, mathematics, engineering, and technology? What better place to start than at HBCUs. Dr. Rita Colwell, director of NSF, has suggested that if women and minorities were afforded greater opportunities to move into these fields, there would be no shortage of scientists and engineers in the United States (House Science Committee 2002, on-line).

Lack of or inadequate funding is a threat to the ability of HBCUs to competitively train the vast untapped sources of future scientists. In addition, this continues to be a struggle for HBCUs to maintain their historical record in training and graduating teachers and scientists in today's advanced technologies. Even so, the programs designed to aid minority institutions in improving science and engineering did not receive a proposed increase in 2004. The agreed upon amount remained the same as it was in 2002, which was $8.5 million.

For historically minority colleges and universities, the underrepresentation of African Americans and Native Americans in science and technology represents a national disaster, requiring urgent and immediate planning and resource allocation. Although most experts agree that quality and delivery of science education must continue to be improved, it is also imperative that if the United States—and North Carolina specifically—desires to remain scientifically and technologically competitive, science education must be more relevant and available to all students, not just a few.

THE MODEL

If North Carolina's minority institutions were going to be successful participants in the HMU Bioscience and Biotechnology Program Initiative, they had to be prepared for change. Yet change in education, particularly higher education, comes slowly. Therefore, the initiative assisted the universities in preparing for change by providing appropriate resources, administrative management, communication, and collaboration for each institution to develop individual, institutional, and bioscience/biotechnology plans.

Several individuals, organizations, and the state legislature contributed to the initiation of a concept that gave public minority institutions the opportunity to enhance their bioscience/biotechnology programs. Many people collaborated and negotiated the initiation of the program initiative. Participants included, but are not limited to, the members of the North Carolina General Assembly, Speaker Daniel T. Blue of the North Carolina House of Representatives, Representative Howard Hunter, Representative H. M. "Mickey" Michaux, Senator William Martin, and all members of the North Carolina Black Legislative Caucus, along with Lenwood Long, Arche McAdoo, Andrea L. Harris, and Charles E. Hamner.

The idea to aid HBCUs in their quest to enhance their science programs was in large measure due to the progressive leadership, strategic creative wisdom, and economic and educational vision of corporate leaders, legislators, and others. The success of such a program is ultimately based upon the interdisciplinary team assembled to administer, manage, and support the universities. Thus was born a "model" that was successful in enhancing bioscience/biotechnology at North Carolina's public minority universities. The North Carolina General Assembly began the process in July 1993 by appropriating $1 million to establish a biotechnology program initiative for the state's five public HBCUs and one Native American university as a first major effort toward providing resources for planning.

House Bill 229, Sec. 25.8, established the Bioscience/Biotechnology Initiative: Biotechnology Funds for Minority Universities. Funds appropriated for this act came from the general fund and went to the North Carolina Biotechnology Center, an educational-based, economically focused bioscience/biotechnology program for public minority higher education institutions (Nunn 2001).

The North Carolina Biotechnology Center was established in 1981 with funding from the North Carolina General Assembly, and since it was established, it has been the primary organization promoting biotechnology in the state. The center was the first state-sponsored biotechnology initiative in the United States. When it was established, the center functioned as a part of the state government. However, in 1984 the center became a private, nonprofit corporation, which afforded it a greater opportunity to operate in a more creative and nonpartisan way. In 1993, when the HMU initiative was established, Dr. Charles E. Hamner was the president and CEO of the North Carolina Biotechnology Center. Although the center was a practical, experienced organization ideally suited for the programmatic site and establishment of the HMU biotechnology/bioscience initiative, it was Hamner's leadership and continuous support that specifically represented a significant catalyst for the success of the program.

Likewise, in the General Assembly, a minority legislator who served as the first African American Speaker of the North Carolina

House of Representatives, Daniel T. Blue, also an HBCU graduate, was a notable advocate of the initiative. Other black legislators who were active participants on various HBCU initiative committees were Representative Howard J. Hunter Jr., Representative Henry M. Michaux Jr., and Senator William N. Martin, all graduates of HBCUs. However, stating the names of these legislators should not imply that support for the initiative was not received from all legislators. Support from both the General Assembly as a whole and key legislators was critical to the fiscal continuation of the program.

North Carolina has a history of supporting creative endeavors, as indicated by the earlier funding of the North Carolina Biotechnology Center. Thus it was only natural that the legislative body would be receptive to the funding of the HMU Bioscience and Biotechnology Program Initiative, a program that would represent another creative education concept with potential economic opportunities for the state's public education institutions and North Carolina in general.

During the nine years that the HMU initiative was in effect at the North Carolina Biotechnology Center, executive leadership changed at each of the six participating institutions. Fortunately, this did not detract from the implementation of the initiative, in part because the program administrators maintained frequent communications with chancellors and other appropriate administrators in addition to science faculty and staff. Institutionally, chancellors, deans, division or department chairpersons, faculty, staff, and students had to devise an individual process for planning, communicating, and collaborating. This process was lead by at least two persons from each of the six institutions; they in turn became the lead representatives of the program initiative at their university. The North Carolina Biotechnology Center formed committees to support program plans and development, infrastructure needs, and proposal review to further enhance each institution's program. Another significant reason for the program's success was its chairperson, Andrea L. Harris, president of the Institute for Minority Economic Development, who served in that role for the entire nine years of the initiative.

Each of the participating institutions was enthusiastic for a variety of reasons. First, the program was entirely voluntary. Second, universities did not have to compete for funds or compete with each other. Each university received the same amount of funds. Third, the funds could be used to enhance university biotechnology/bioscience programs based on plans developed and submitted by each institution. Although the institutions agreed on basic needs, the center did not specify how they were to address the needs. Fourth, annual proposals, reviewed by an external support team, were submitted indicating the use and reasons for the requested funds, and each university received its chancellor's support. Perhaps more important was the evolving establishment of a new type of support and collaboration within campus departments as well as collaborations between institutions. The communication and collaboration among the universities served to collectively enhance the institutions, faculty, and students.

The interdisciplinary nature of biotechnology demanded a type of teamwork or collaboration critical to the success of the initiative. In essence, the professors who were designated the initiative leaders at their respective universities had to assume a new working relationship with colleagues. All participants were learning to adapt to the changing dynamics of twenty-first-century science education and research. They were now in charge of developing institutional purposes, objectives, and responsibilities for the university's biotechnology/bioscience program. However, to successfully implement the universities' biotechnology/bioscience plans, several essential resource needs had to be met. They were identified as curriculum development, faculty development, student recruitment, support staff, facilities, equipment, and supplies (Nunn 2001).

THE MODEL OUTCOMES

Curriculum Development

The six institutions proposed new curricula and modified existing ones to more adequately provide the skills, training, and courses required for a quality education in biotechnology. The universities recognized the need to incorporate new techniques and topics into the science curriculum. Some core courses for science majors remained the same while others were changed to include hands-on biotechnology techniques and laboratory exercises that emphasize such topics as nucleic acid and protein purification, low- and medium-pressure and high-performance liquid chromatography, gel electrophoresis, hybridization, DNA sequencing, and cloning. Interdisciplinary courses in chemistry and biology also were modified to include more techniques relevant to bioprocessing. New and enhanced courses include molecular biology, biotechnological techniques, and biochemistry, as well as research and internships as a major component of the curriculum. To strengthen current bachelor of science degree programs, minors in biotechnology were also proposed by several of the participating universities. In addition, one institution developed a certificate program in biotechnology. With strong support from Dr. Wilveria B. Atkins, who served as the first chairperson of the initiative at Winston-Salem University, along with others, this university developed the first undergraduate major in molecular biology in the public university system in North Carolina. Because all of the participating universities offer baccalaureate programs in biological and physical sciences, initial course enhancement focused on these areas.

Although four of the participating institutions were already committed to graduate education through the master's degree level and one institution offered a doctorate in engineering, with the exception of engineering graduates, the pool in science remained small. None of the six schools was classified as a research university. Thus, with limited research undertaken, curricula were based on science education and training, with evolving programs designed to enhance laboratory techniques and skill development. The initiative's objective to enhance or modify the existing curricula with enhanced laboratory techniques to include biotechnology was achieved by each of the participating universities.

Faculty Development

Faculty and staff development was a major component of the initiative. Some participant training included Cold Spring Harbor workshops; computational genomic, combinatorial antibody libraries; bioinformatics workshops; training in recent advances in gene expressions technology; and attendance at the National Minority Research Symposium.

Although funds were available to support faculty training and development, release time for faculty to participate in this training was limited and often uncertain. Because the six institutions were primarily undergraduate in their focus, there was only a limited pool of graduate students who could be used as temporary replacement instructors. Despite some staffing challenges, each institution's faculty and staff were able to participate in educational training and development programs. However, this is an area that requires additional support from the institutional leadership, such that a more useful procedure to engage faculty and staff in the plethora of educational training and research opportunities is developed (Nunn 2001).

Science faculty recruitment continues to be a challenge for minority institutions. The faculty shortage in certain fields and particularly among black faculty is real. The reasons for the faculty shortage are many and varied. Although some postsecondary institutions have resources that are more attractive to science faculty, in some instances faculty salaries in HBCUs have not kept pace with the competition. In other cases the advancing age of current faculty has been a reason for shortage (Nunn 2001).

Chancellor Harold Martin of Winston-Salem State University, an HBCU, indicates that to recruit and to retain the very best faculty requires not only providing competitive compensations but having the very best facilities, classrooms, research facilities, and office space for faculty to do their very best (*UNC-TV Black Issues Forum* 1999, on-line). The prospect of significantly improving upon the underrepresentation of black and Native American science faculty is not proceeding at the rate needed. Although most faculty of color work primarily at historically black colleges and universities, the competition is keen throughout the professional labor force for well-educated ethnic minority personnel. As the technological era demands an increasing number of skilled professionals, the competition will continue. Each of the universities in the HMU initiative indicated a need for additional faculty. At these institutions, full-time faculty members were often involved in a variety of activities in addition to their assigned teaching responsibilities: mentoring students, writing proposals, and working on administrative and organization activities. The institutions must develop new plans to alleviate the faculty shortage. Specific strategic efforts must be designed to recruit and retain talented faculty, especially African Americans and Native Americans, for teaching careers in the sciences. The challenge confronting higher education institutions and especially HBCUs will be the recruitment, retention, and renewal of vital science faculty members. A faculty and staff skilled in techonology may influence many areas, including the ability to attract and recruit new faculty as well as students.

Student Recruitment

Each of the six participating universities indicated increases in the number of undergraduate students enrolled in biotechnology/bioscience-related courses from over 750 in 1993 to over 3,000 in 1999. The development of new and modified courses at each university, enhanced faculty and staff development, and an increased awareness of biotechnology and related opportunities were some factors contributing to the increase in student enrollment in the sciences. In addition, four of the six universities were providing opportunities for students to obtain science internships internal and external to the universities.

Facilities, Equipment, and Supplies

Although enrollments are increasing, along with the interest of students in biotechnology-related courses, the problems of science and technology programs and science departments at historically minority colleges and universities are the triad of equipment, supplies, and appropriate facilities. No institution can effectively engage in competitive science programs if this triad is inadequate, even if faculty and students are interested, enthusiastic, and committed to matriculating in the sciences.

With the HMU initiative there was a marked increase in the purchase of supplies and state-of-the-art equipment to accommodate hands-on laboratory experiences of students and faculty. Chemical reagents, antibodies, cell cultures, bacterial stock culture, pipet tips, petri dishes, restriction enzymes, and other supplies are required to conduct biotechnology experiments and procedures, and their purchase was covered by initiative funding. Equipment purchases included electrophoresis systems; spectrophotometers with computer attachments that may be used in instrumental analysis; gene guns, used to enhance laboratory exercises in gene transfer in plant biotechnology courses; light compound microscopes, for use in general microbiology laboratories; gradient HPLCs, used for protein purification; and solid phase synthesizers, used for protein modeling studies (Nunn 2001).

Although all the participating schools were pleased to have the opportunity to purchase state-of-the-art equipment to meet the needs of their individual programs, each university felt that student enrollment in science courses could not grow in the absence of new and larger facilities to accommodate a changing science education curriculum, a curriculum that ultimately includes increased research opportunities. The HMU Bioscience and Biotechnology Program Initiative provided funds for equipment and supplies but could not provide funds for facilities or capital improvement. A need for renovated or new facilities was observed during the annual campus site visits. However, when a $31 billion bond for education passed in North Carolina in 2000, many of the universities will in the future build new science facilities.

CONCLUSION

The initiative resulted in a tripling of enrollment in biological and physical sciences. Increased enrollment at the participating institutions was a product of curriculum development, faculty training, acquisition of equipment and supplies, and improvements to facilities, but perhaps the greatest catalyst for enrollment increase was the *changing opportunities* presented to students. Students at the six universities are now actively engaged in biotechnology courses, programs, activities, and research experiences on and off campus. The students have had research experiences in universities and laboratories within the United States and abroad. Graduates of the universities' programs have begun to seek graduate programs for advanced training or employment options at major technology companies and federal agencies. Students are participants in various facets of technology from presenting research papers and working in laboratories with research scientists to meeting Nobel Prize winners. All of these factors have contributed to the interest and motivation of students to biotechnology/bioscience (Nunn 2001).

As a result of the HMU Bioscience and Biotechnology Program Initiative, the illusion that minorities, especially those trained at historically minority colleges and universities, are not capable of being successful in the sciences was dispelled. Increasing enrollments in biological and physical sciences, students collaborating with research scientists, graduates entering graduate schools for advanced study and training, and students being hired by technology companies and agencies are just some illustrations of the progress made by an action-oriented minority university biotechnology/bioscience initiative. Evolving technology suggests that these resources must continue to be provided to HBCUs if competitive educational training and research opportunities are to continue for students and faculty.

In September 2001 the North Carolina General Assembly formally declared the initiative a success and established a permanent appropriation for the HMU Bioscience and Biotechnology Program Initiative (Nunn 2001). The North Carolina Biotechnology Center had administered the initiative for eight years as universities developed individual plans and implementation methods. To assist in the continuation of this program a $60,000 Eleanor Nunn Lectureship in Biotechnology Grant was established by the North Carolina Biotechnology Center, which in turn awarded $10,000 to each of the six participating universities. The state continues to fund the program through the North Carolina General Administration for Higher Education.

REFERENCES

Benowitz, Steven. 1997. "Historically Black Colleges Combine Research, Education." *The Scientist.* http://www/thescientist.com/yr1997/feb/research_970217.html (cited March 1, 2003).

Black Engineer. 2003. "Setbacks in Engineering." http://www.blackengineer.com/artman/publish/article–29.shtml (cited March 1, 2003).

Brainard, Jeffrey, and Anne Marie Borrego. 2003. "Bush Budget Offers Small Increases for Most Science Programs." *The Chronicle of Higher Education* 46, 23: A23.

Burd, Stephen. 2003 "Another Tight Year for Student Aid." *The Chronicle of Higher Education* 46, 23: A21.

Deen, Lango. 2003. "Who's Protecting America?: The Black Colleges' Role." http://www.blackengineer.com/artman/publish/article–24.shtml (cited March 1, 2003).

Feldbaum, Carl B. 2002. "It Was 20 Years Ago Today . . ." *U.S. Biotechnology Trends* (Fall 2002), http://www.bio.org/news/speeches/20021114.asp (cited March 1, 2003).

Harding, Sandra. 1993. *"Racial" Economy of Science.* Bloomington, IN: Indiana University Press.

Hargrove, Robert. 1998. *Mastering the Art of Creative Collaboration.* New York: McGraw-Hill.

Johnson, William B., and Arnold E. Packer. 1987. *Workforce 2000: Work and Workers for the Twenty-First Century.* Indianapolis, IN: Hudson Institute.

National Center for Education Statistics. 1997. *Digest of Education Statistics, 1997.* Washington, DC: U.S. Department of Education.

———. 1998. *American Indians and Alaska Natives in Post Secondary Education (Technical Report).* Washington, DC: U.S. Department of Education.

National Science Foundation. 2000. *Women, Minorities, and Persons with Disabilities in Science and Engineering.* Arlington, VA: National Science Foundation.

North Carolina Biotechnology Center. 2003. *Quick Facts: North Carolina's Biotechnology Industry.* http://www.ncbiotech.org/ncindustry/quickfacts.cfm (cited March 1, 2003).

Nunn, Eleanor F. 2001. *Biotechnology Education and Training in North Carolina Public Historically Minority Universities: A Five-Year Evaluation.* Ph.D. diss., Cincinnati, OH: The Union Institute.

Phillips, Bruce. 2003. "U.S. Rep. Johnson Wins Support for NSF Funding." http://www.blackengineer.com/artman/publish/article–36.shtml (cited March 1, 2003).

UNC-TV Black Issues Forum. 1999. http://www.unctv.org/bif/transcript/1999/bif1525.html (cited March 1, 2003).

University of North Carolina. 1998. *Statistical Abstract of Higher Education in North Carolina, 1997–1998.* http://www.ga.unc.edu/publications (cited March 1, 2003).

U.S. House of Representatives Science Committee's Subcommittee on Research. 2002. *Preparing a 21ˢᵗ Century Workforce: Strengthening and Improving K-Undergraduate Science, Math, and Engineering Education.* http://www.house.gov/science/hearings/research02/apr22/jenkins.htm (cited March 1, 2003).

Chapter Six

⚫⚫ Research Agenda for the Twenty-First Century

While we were writing the first five chapters of this book, research gaps on HBCUs became apparent. There are two aspects to the nature of the gaps. One is a lack of a continuum on research topics. This appears to be due in large part to the fact that most research on HBCUs are dissertations. Dissertation research topics tend to be identified based on the specific interests of doctoral students rather than in a context of developing a systematic research agenda on HBCUs. The other aspect of the gaps is that the majority of the accessible and reputable research conducted focuses on the history of HBCUs; only a few give attention to the current status of HBCUs. Reporting the current status of historically black colleges and universities is needed. However, our concern is that very little of the reporting lends itself to an analysis, synthesis, and evaluation of the current status in a way that HBCUs can use in their given settings and situations, and project into their future sustainability.

Now, perhaps, more than ever before in their existence, HBCUs need to be proactive rather than reactive. They need research that is used as the base for strategic planning on all fronts. Pragmatic research studies to calculate the future for policies and practices of these non-monolithic institutions are needed. Related to the need for pragmatic research is the lack of an apparatus to transmit the research to HBCUs so it can influence planning.

The purpose of this chapter is to suggest research topics that need to be conducted on HBCUs. It is anticipated that the suggested topics will serve as a futuristic, proactive knowledge foundation for HBCUs. Researchers working collaboratively with people in HBCUs are needed.

Research on HBCUs is interdisciplinary. This means that the knowledge base of disciplines and fields of study other than higher education must be incorporated in the research to produce meaningful research about HBCUs. Therefore, it is neither possible nor necessary to place the research suggestions into discrete categories. The suggestions are headed with the chapter or chapters in which related topics are discussed. The suggestions are not considered exhaustive.

CHAPTER 1

As of 2002, 50 percent or more of the student enrollment at five HBCUs is nonblack. These institutions continue to be identified as HBCUs and receive the federal funding for HBCUs. Another five have student enrollments that are 30 percent to 49 percent nonblack, with the majority of the nonblack percentage being white. Such demographic shifts alter the mission, curriculum, and social context of the institutions, covertly or overtly. Research suggestions: In the twenty-first century, what constitutes an HBCU? When is an HBCU no longer an HBCU? What is the role of the history of an institution if most of the student enrollment is not a member of the population for which the institution was established to serve? How is institutional mission changed, explicitly and implicitly, due to the shift in student enrollment demographics?

Doctorates in Black Studies are only offered at Harvard University, the University of Massachusetts, Temple University, Yale University, and the University of California–Berkeley. The University of North Carolina–Chapel Hill is the only institution that offers a doctorate in African American Literature. Given that doctoral degrees programs centered on blacks are based at historically white institutions, it is not surprising that the majority of the dissertation research conducted on HBCUs is also done at non-HBCU doctoral-granting institutions. Although the data do not indicate an inherit bias in the research, it seems reasonable to anticipate that those pursing doctorates at HBCUs would conduct the majority of the research on HBCUs. Research suggestions: What role and responsibility do doctoral-degree–granting HBCUs have in generating research on HBCUs? What pathways exist or are being created for doctoral students at HBCUs to conduct practice and policy research on HBCUs?

HBCUs have an historical and contemporary legacy of providing education opportunities for the African diaspora. The primary focus is in the Caribbean and the African continent, and a few HBCUs are involved with Latin America. Although most HBCUs require foreign students to attend classes in the United States, several HBCUs are establishing a physical presence outside of the United States to offer their degrees. Research suggestions: Which HBCUs have a physical presence outside of the United States? How is the outside presence view compatible with the institution's mission? What degrees are offered outside of the United States? What are the program designs and delivery systems, including institutional oversight? How do the outside programs align with regional accreditation? What are the successes and challenges of the programs offered outside of the United States? Should and what role can HBCUs serve in digitizing the African diaspora for education purposes?

The integration of technology in teaching and learning only recently has become an acceptable tool in higher education. Research on its use and the issues concerning technology-based education is just becoming readily accessible. The majority of the research focuses on higher education generally or specifically on historically white institutions. In a 2000 study conducted by the National Association for Equal Opportunity in Higher Education, 58 percent of HBCUs offered distance education and 15 percent were offering degrees through distance education. This distance education is primarily occurring at public HBCUs and large private HBCUs. Small private HBCUs are focusing their technology infrastructure on campus-based concerns such as integrating technology in the classroom and library as well as some accessibility in dormitories. These HBCUs have generally concluded that distance education is not compatible with the institutional mission. It has been generally concluded that distance learning and e-learning erases disparity in learning opportunities and differences. HBCUs have a legacy of creating and providing education access and opportunities with very little resources. Research suggestions: What is the role of college or university websites in distance education and e-learning? What technology infrastructure management system, human and technological, is needed to address the rapid changes in technology? How is the Internet incorporated in distance education and e-learning? What are HBCUs' specific offerings through distance education, and what are the decision processes to determine the courses and degrees that are offered through distance learning? What are the program designs and delivery systems, including institutional oversight? How does distance education align with the institutional mission? How does distance education offerings align with regional accreditation? What are the successes and challenges of the distance education offerings? What markets are being attracted by HBCUs that use distance education? What is the relationship among learning styles, race, culture, and e-learning? What are culture-specific learning opportunities that need to be provided through distance education and e-learning? What training is faculty receiving to integrate technology in the curriculum? How can learning and research opportunities for HBCU students and faculty be broadened through technology?

Nationally, resignation of presidents of colleges and universities after a year or less in that position is becoming a frequent occurrence. The rapid turnover of presidents is occurring at HBCUs also. Additionally, some HBCUs are hiring presidents who have never had an affiliation with HBCUs as a student, faculty member, or administrator. Research has been conducted on the attributes of effective presidents at historically white institutions. Given the milieu of HBCUs there is no reason to conclude that the same effective attributes would be appropriate of HBCU presidents. The continued existence of HBCUs will depend on the leadership abilities and responsiveness of its presidents. Research suggestions: What are the attributes of effective presidents of HBCUs? What accounts for the effectiveness? How do the attributes vary based on institutional environments, size and organizational complexity, and professional tasks? How are HBCU presidents mentored? How do mentoring, personal attributes, and organizational factors vary and/or correspond to effectiveness based on gender? What role does experiential knowledge of HBCUs play in being an effective president? How are HBCU presidents determining and responding to institutional needs, adapting self and the institution to changing conditions in higher education generally and the education of blacks specifically? What are HBCU presidents' responses to new ideas, creativity, and possibilities?

College and university boards of trustees have fiduciary and policy responsibilities. Presidents report to the boards and are ultimately hired by them. Incompatible expectations between presidents and boards of trustees is reported as the main contributory factor to the rapid turnover of presidents in both HBCUs and historically white institutions. Presidents, however, can be influential in selecting the members of the boards of trustees. The mutually reciprocal relationship between presidents and boards of trustees requires cooperation and collaboration. Research suggestions: What are the attributes of effective HBCU board of trustee members, individually and collectively? What accounts for board effectiveness? How do the attributes vary based on institutional environments, size and organizational complexity, and professional tasks? What types of training do and/or should board members receive? What are patterns of effective interaction between board members and the president? What role does experiential knowledge of HBCUs play in being an effective president?

HIV/AIDS and substance abuse are critical social and health issues in the black community. HBCUs should feel an obligation to address these issues in the black community, and they can do this primarily by training professionals in these fields. In his 2001 study report for the National HBCU Consortium on Substance Abuse, Patrick Coggins states, "Students are less interested in the Substance Abuse field because it was thought to be low paying and unattractive" (6). The research suggestions for this topic are derived from Coggins's study. Research suggestions: What are HBCUs that are not part of the consortium doing in the field of substance abuse? To what extent are blacks able to attain the credentials as licensed substance abuse counselors? What is the rate of employment and position level of individuals who graduated from HBCUs with a major in Substance Abuse? What is the relation between same-race culture and ethnic background of practitioner and client to the effectiveness of treatment? What do HBCUs need to do to cultivate an interest in undergraduate students' level of interest in the substance abuse profession as a means to increase the number of black clinicians, researchers, and policymakers in the field?

CHAPTERS 1 AND 3

One of the contentions in the *Fordice* and the *Adams* cases was that HBCUs duplicated the curriculum of historically white institutions. Based on this contention, it is concluded that the need for HBCUs no longer exists. Benjamin E. Mays and Samuel DuBois Cook, presidents emeritus of Morehouse College and Dillard College, respectively, contend that HBCU curriculums both address Western (white) teachings *and* provide opportunity for analysis, evaluation, and synthesis of the black condition in relation to the Western emphasis. Research suggestions: What are the criteria used to determine whether HBCUs and historically white institutions' curriculum can be considered duplicates? What are the specific points of duplication and nonduplication in the curriculum? How do the points of duplication and nonduplication in the curriculum align with the institutional mission to justify the legal, political, and financial decisions made for and about HBCUs?

CHAPTERS 1 AND 4

Graduates of HBCUs have had pivotal roles in the development and advancement of HBCUs. Those roles can be external or internal. Externally, they have promoted the institutions by providing programmatic assistance. Internally, many made career choices to work in HBCUs. Research suggestions: What has been the role of HBCU graduates in institutional development? How has this role been exemplified in different eras?

Some states experienced major legal cases regarding the public HBCUs. These states recognized the role that HBCUs play in their higher education system and worked at redressing the discriminatory practices, mostly monetary. North Carolina is one example of such a state. Research suggestions: What is the political makeup of a state that recognizes the importance of HBCUs? What role does the state populace, and more specifically the black populace, play in the state affirming HBCUs?

CHAPTER 4

Little research has been conducted on HBCUs and philanthropy, more specifically foundations. The research that is available is historical in nature, generally focusing on the late 1860s through the early 1970s. Given HBCUs' reliance on external nongovernmental funding, extensive research on contemporary foundation giving and the politics of the decisions for giving is needed. Research suggestions: What is the nature of contemporary patterns of giving, relationships, and continuing commitment to HBCUs by foundations? How do the priorities of HBCUs relate to the priorities of foundations? What social and cultural events in the United States have globally facilitated or impeded foundation giving to HBCUs? What types of strategic planning are occurring between HBCUs and foundations? What has been the result of the strategic planning? What are the positions and roles of blacks in foundation administration and on executive boards?

The continued existence of HBCUs is dependent in large part on the political and economic support of blacks. Philanthropy is not a new phenomenon for blacks. Grassroots philanthropy can be traced throughout the history of African Americans. The major philanthropic organization for blacks is the church. HBCU graduates readily admit the educational, professional, and personal benefits they received by attending an HBCU. A few individual blacks have made major financial contributions to their alma maters or HBCUs with which they have a special interest. Yet, numerous HBCUs do not generally receive a significant level of financial support from alumni. Research suggestions: What are the enculturation methods used by HBCUs with current students on future alumni philanthropy? What are the models used by HBCUs with successful alumni donations? What attributes and/or factors contribute to alumni giving and not giving?

CHAPTER 5

Historically black colleges and universities can no longer afford to operate as isolates. Their existence is dependent on collaborations, with mutual benefits seen by all involved. The collaboration in North Carolina, discussed in Chapter 5, is one example of the types of relationships HBCUs can initiate. Information about this and other collaborations needs to be shared with HBCUs. Research suggestions: What are the successful models of collaboration designed to enhance HBCUs, especially in science and technology? How did they come into being? What were the challenges of creating these collaborations?

Technological advances have greatly influenced the educational system in the United States. One of the problems confronting the leaders of higher education is keeping pace with the sheer speed of change, especially in scientific and technological advances. Demographics, economic policies, political decisions, changing social mores, and advancing technological developments will continue to reshape the structure and substance of higher education in the decades to come. Although these are basic concerns for all higher education institutions, the concerns are more intense for the majority of historically black colleges and universities, which continue to operate primarily on tuition, have minimal resources for study in the sciences and technology, and have facilities for science and technology that need repair and/or renovations. In 1990, historically black colleges and universities graduated 44 percent of African Americans who received degrees in the sciences (*Academe* 1995). These numbers have not changed at the beginning of the twenty-first century. Research suggestions: What are the effects of demographics, economics policies, political decisions, changing social mores, and advancing technological developments on the underrepresentation of African Americans in science and technology? Although several groups have provided resources to historically black colleges and universities to address the issue of underrepresentation of African Americans in science and technology, what has been the value of the assistance and additions to addressing the underrepresentation issue? Most HBCUs provide basic research curricula in the sciences; what are the employment patterns of the graduates? Is there a difference in the employment, educational, and other patterns of science majors in historically black colleges and universities that benefited from programs specifically designed to enhance the underrepresentation of African Americans in science and technology and those who attended historically black colleges and universities that were not part of programs to address the underrepresentation?

REFERENCES

Coggins, Patrick. 2001. *Analysis of Substance Abuse Degree Program Offered by HBCUs.* Unpublished report, Stetson University, Deland, FL.
"The Historically Black Colleges and Universities: A Future in the Balance." 1995. *Academe* 81, 1: 51.

Chapter Seven

✍ Directory of Organizations and Print Resources

This chapter contains two types of information about HBCUs. First is presented a directory of organizations, associations, and governmental agencies that work with HBCUs; second, printed materials regarding HBCUs.

ORGANIZATIONS

Five organizational structures comprise the recognized system established specifically to promote, empower, and enhance the development and future of historically black colleges and universities. The structures are two not-for-profit national organizations, one federal program, one professional association's office, and a network organization for HBCU faculty. In addition, four other organizations specifically assist with the needs of HBCUs, their faculty, and their students.

Black College Communication Association
http://www.bccanews.org
The Black College Communication Association is a nonprofit national organization of administrators of HBCUs with communications programs. The organization identifies resources that can strengthen communications programs at HBCUs; provide technical assistance to HBCUs seeking accreditation; and assist in establishing advanced hardware systems, which can be used and shared by member institutions for the academic enhancement of communications programs.

Member institutions are Alabama A&M University, Alabama State University, Alcorn State University (Miss.), Bowie State University (Md.), Central State University (Ohio), Clark Atlanta University (Ga.), Coppin State College (Md.), Edward Waters College (Fla.), Florida A&M

University, Florida Memorial College, Fort Valley State College (Ga.), Grambling State University (La.), Hampton University (Va.), Howard University (D.C.), Jackson State University (Miss.), Lane College (Tenn.), Lincoln University–Missouri, Lincoln University–Pennsylvania, Morgan State University (Md.), Norfolk State University (Va.), North Carolina A&T State University, North Carolina Central University, Rust College (Miss.), Savannah State University (Ga.), Shaw University (N.C.), South Carolina State University, Southern University–Baton Rouge (La.), Southern University–New Orleans (La.), Tennessee State University, Texas Southern University, Tougaloo College (Miss.), University of the District of Columbia, Virginia State University, West Virginia State College, Wilberforce University (Ohio), Winston-Salem State University (N.C.), and Xavier University (La.).

HBCU Faculty Development Network

http://www.hbcufdn.org/

The HBCU Faculty Development Network began in 1994. Its goal is to create a collaborative spirit among HBCUs for the enhancement of teaching and learning. It also facilitates collaboration between faculty and administrators. The network identifies the following objectives:

1. To provide an avenue for support for sharing innovative instructional methods
2. To provide support in securing resources and information
3. To promote collaboration among faculty
4. To stimulate research, publication, and scholarly activities
5. To promote the connection between classroom and community service
6. To promote utilization of technology
7. To enhance communication among diverse peoples in a global society

Historically Black Colleges and Universities/Minority Institutions Research Alliance (HMIRA)

http://hmira.org/

HMIRA was established in 1998 as a collaboration of fourteen HBCUs and minority institutions for the purpose of providing quality research and development for government, industry, and academia. It enables more students from smaller colleges to participate in research projects.

The fourteen HBCUs in the alliance are Alabama A&M University, Bethune-Cookman College (Fla.), Claflin College (S.C.), Dillard University (La.), Edward Waters College (Fla.), Florida A&M University, Grambling University (La.), Langston University (Okla.), Morgan State University (Md.), Morris Brown College (Ga.), Oakwood College (Ala.), Prairie View A&M University (Tex.), Southern University (La.), and Tuskegee University (Ala.).

National Association for Equal Opportunity in Higher Education (NAFEO)

8701 Georgia Avenue, Suite 200
Silver Springs, MD 20910
(301) 650-2440
http://www.nafeo.org/
NAFEO, founded in 1969, was established to keep the interests, concerns, and needs of HBCUs and predominantly black postsecondary institutions on the national agendas of the executive, legislative, regulatory, and judicial branches of federal and state governments. It promotes the formulation and implementation of policies, programs, and practices to protect and amplify HBCUs. It accomplishes this through education and training, management consulting, evaluation and research studies, institutional development, and project management. An annual conference is held. Its 118 members include the 103 HBCUs as well as postsecondary institutions that are predominately black, regardless of regional accreditation status.

Office for the Advancement of Public Black Colleges

1307 New York Avenue NW, Suite 400
Washington, DC 20005-4701
(202) 478-6049
http://www/nasulgc.org/minority.htm
The Office for the Advancement of Public Black Colleges is part of the National Association of State Universities and Land-Grant Colleges (NASULGC). NASULGC was established in 1887 for the purpose of supporting and promoting historically white postsecondary land-grant institutions.

The Office for the Advancement of Public Black Colleges facilitates the association's work with the seventeen land-grant HBCUs. The HBCUs are collectively known as the "1890 Institutions" because 1890 is the year of the Second Morrill Act, which established black land-grant institutions.

The office in association with other "minority-related groups" endeavors to maintain visibility and support of public land-grant HBCUs through policy development and serving as a clearinghouse for HBCUs on information. The office identifies three ways it achieves it purpose:

1. Working to bring these institutions into more meaningful and productive relationships with federal agencies
2. Promoting research on the roles of public black universities in American society
3. Serving as a link between public black colleges and sources of financial support, such as foundations, corporations, and governmental agencies

N. Joyce Payne, director of the Office for the Advancement of Public Black Colleges, created the Thurgood Marshall Scholarship Fund with the Miller Brewing Company and the support of Supreme Court Justice Thurgood Marshall. The fund, which began in 1987, works in conjunction with the purpose of the office and provides scholarships to students attending one of its forty-five membership institutions.

As stated on the fund's website, http://www.thurgoodmarshall-fund.org/, in addition to the scholarships, "TMSF helps member schools increase their individual endowments through joint fund raising and marketing campaigns."

Science and Engineering Alliance (SEA)

http://www.llnl.gov/sea/
The Science and Engineering Alliance (SEA) is a nonprofit organization founded in 1990. It serves four state-supported historically black colleges and universities in partnership with Lawrence Livermore National Laboratory in California and in collaboration with other organizations. The HBCUs are Alabama A&M University, Jackson State University (Miss.), Prairie View A&M University (Tex.), and Southern University (La.).

SEA's purpose is to help ensure an adequate number of top-quality minority scientists while meeting the research and development needs of the public and private sectors. It achieves this purpose by serving as a "partnership broker." As such it provides services in technical marketing and community relations, development of training and experiential programs for faculty and students, and creations of partnership opportunities with public and private sectors.

Tom Joyner Foundation

http://www.tomjoyner.com/foundation/

Tom Joyner is a nationally recognized radio personality and a graduate of Tuskegee University (Ala.). The Tom Joyner Foundation provides scholarships to students at HBCUs who have financial difficulty staying in school. The funds are given directly to the HBCUs for the purpose of helping identified students complete their education. Each month an HBCU is selected as a recipient of the foundation.

United Negro College Fund (UNCF)

8260 Willow Oaks Corporate Drive

Fairfax, VA 22031

(800) 331-2244

http://www.uncf.org

UNCF was incorporated in 1944. It is the oldest organization in the United States that supports HBCUs. Member institutions of UNCF are regionally accredited, private four-year HBCUs. Currently, there are thirty-eight member institutions.

Dr. Frederick D. Patterson, president of Tuskegee Institute, now Tuskegee University, initiated the idea of private HBCUs "[pooling] their small monies and [making] a united appeal to the national conscience." This idea gave birth to UNCF.

UNCF realizes its mission by providing a variety of programs that provide member colleges and universities with financial assistance to their students, by raising operating funds, and by supplying technical assistance. Some UNCF programs are scholarships based on geography, academic majors, and merit and need. Among the other programs are the Infrastructure Development Assistance Program, Financial Aid for Graduate Study, Precollege Program, Study Abroad Programs, Curriculum Development and Teaching Program, and Faculty Development Programs and Fellowships.

White House Initiative on HBCUs

http://www.ed.gov/offices/OPE/hbcu

In 1980, President Jimmy Carter signed Executive Order 12232. This executive order established the White House Initiative on HBCUs. The executive order authorizes a federal program in support of HBCUs. Subsequent presidents signed similar executive orders.

With Executive Order 12677, President George H. W. Bush in 1989 established the President's Advisory Board on Historically Black

Colleges and Universities. The board advises the president and the secretary of education on these institutions. In addition, the board "issues an annual report to the President on HBCU participation in federal programs; advises the Secretary of Education on increasing the federal role in strengthening HBCUs; and reports to the President on how to increase the private sector role in strengthening these institutions."

In 1993, President William J. Clinton's Executive Order 12876 characterized the mission of the White House Initiative on HBCUs as a means "to advance the development of human potential, to strengthen the capacity of historically Black colleges and universities to provide quality education, and to increase opportunities to participate in and benefit from Federal programs."

Four-year, graduate, and professional HBCUs that are regionally accredited benefit from the White House Initiative. To increase the participation of HBCUs in federally funded programs, thirty United States departments participate through grants, contracts, and other arrangements. Annually, each department is required to present a federal plan and report on how it assisted HBCUs.

The departments are Agriculture, Agency for International Development, Appalachian Regional Commission, Commerce, Central Intelligence Agency, Corporation for National Service, Defense, Education, Energy, Environmental Protection Agency, Equal Employment Opportunity Commission, Health and Human Services, Housing and Urban Development, the Interior, Justice, Labor, National Aeronautics and Space Administration, National Credit Union Administration, National Endowment for the Arts, National Endowment for the Humanities, National Science Foundation, Nuclear Regulatory Commission, State, Transportation, and the Treasury.

The initiative promotes collaborative projects between HBCUs and the private sector. The projects are to further the career perspectives of HBCU graduates and assist in increasing HBCU graduates with degrees in science and technology.

PRINT RESOURCES

This section contains books, dissertations, journal articles, academic papers, and reports and ERIC materials about historically black colleges and universities. The resources focus on various aspects of, concerns about, and issues related to HBCUs. Books are divided into two categories: (1) books about specific HBCUs, and (2) monographs and dissertations about HBCUs. Brief summaries of the content of the scholarly books are provided. The "Periodical Articles" section includes reports from the federal government, research studies, and papers presented at professional association conferences.

The resources in this chapter are meant to complement the references at the end of each chapter. It is the intent of the authors to provide a cross section of print materials that are accessible and creditable for readers.

As noted earlier in this book, the most consistent research on historically black colleges and universities specifically has been done in dissertations. A review of the material amplifies the gaps in and shortage of research on HBCUs.

Books about Specific HBCUs

Bellamy, Donnie D. 1996. *Light in the Valley: A Pictorial History of the Fort Valley State College Since 1895.* Fort Valley, GA: Fort Valley State College.

Biggers, John Thomas, Carrol Simms, and John E. Weems. 1978. *Black Art in Houston: The Texas Southern University Experience.* College Station, TX: Texas A&M University Press.

Black-Patterson, Zella J. 1979. *Langston University: A History.* Norman, OK: University of Oklahoma Press.

Brooks, Lyman Beecher. 1983. *Upward: A History of Norfolk State University, 1935–1975.* Washington, DC: Howard University Press.

Carter, Wilmoth A. 1973. *Shaw's Universe: A Monument to Educational Innovation.* Rockville, MD: D.C. National Publishing.

Cohen, Rodney T. 2000. *The Black Colleges of Atlanta.* Scottsdale, AZ: Arcadia.

———. 2001. *Fisk University, TN.* Scottsdale, AZ: Arcadia.

Dawson, Martha E. 1995. *Hampton University: A National Treasure.* Silver Spring, MD: Beckham Publishing Group.

Flemming, Shelia Y. 1995. *Bethune-Cookman College, 1904–1994: The Answered Prayer to a Dream.* Daytona Beach, FL: Bethune-Cookman Bookstore.

Goggins, Lathardus. 1987. *Central State University: The First One Hundred Years, 1887–1987.* Wilberforce, OH: Central State University.

Guymon, Margaret F., and N. E. Wilson. 1990. *Century of Wisdom: Selected Speeches of Presidents of Florida A&M University.* Tallahassee, FL: Four-G Publishers.

Heintze, Michael R. 1985. *Private Black Colleges in Texas, 1865–1954.* College Station, TX: Texas A&M University Press.

Johnson, Charles W. 2000. *The Spirit of a Place Called Meharry: The Strength of Its Past to Shape the Future.* Franklin, TN: Hillsboro Press.

Jones, Maxine D., and Joe M. Richardson. 1990. *Talladega College: The First Century.* Tuscaloosa, AL: University of Alabama Press.

Lindsey, Donald. 1995. *Indians at Hampton Institute, 1877–1923: Blacks in the New World.* Champaign, IL: University of Illinois Press.

Manley, Albert E. 1997. *A Legacy Continues [Spelman College].* Lanham, MD: University Press of America.

Murphy, E. Louise, Frances Ross Coble, and Simona Atkins Allen. 1993. *The History of Winston-Salem State University, 1892–1992.* Virginia Beach, VA: Donning Co. Publishers.

Norrell, Robert. 1985. *Reaping the Whirlwind: The Civil Rights Movement in Tuskegee.* New York: Random House.

Posey, Josephine. 2000. *Alcorn State University.* Scottsdale, AZ: Arcadia.

Rhodes, Lelia G. 1979. *Jackson State University: The First Hundred Years, 1877–1977.* Jackson, MS: University Press of Mississippi.

Richardson, J. M. 1980. *A History of Fisk University, 1865–1946.* Montgomery: University of Alabama Press.

Smith, Gerald L. 1994. *A Black Educator in the Segregated South: Kentucky's Rufus B. Atwood.* Lexington, KY: University Press of Kentucky.

Spofford, Tim. 1988. *Lynch Street: The May 1970 Slayings at Jackson State.* Ashland, OH: Kent State University.

Thrasher, Max. 2000. *Tuskegee: Its Story and Its Works.* Manchester, NH: Ayer Company Publishers.

Williams, Lawrence H. 1987. *Black Higher Education in Kentucky, 1879–1930.* Lewiston, NY: Edwin Mellen Press.

Withrow, Dolly. 1993. *From the Grove to the Stars: West Virginia State College, 1891–1991*. Charleston: West Virginia State College Foundation/ Pictorial Histories Publishing Companies.

Dissertations

Aaron, Marvin Ray. "The Higher Education of African Americans in Kansas City, Missouri: A History of Lincoln Junior College, 1936–1954." Ph.D. diss., University of Missouri–Kansas City, 1999 (UMI No. 9957685).

Blackmon, Samantha. "Uplifting Education: A History of Writing Instruction at Two Historically Black Colleges and Universities." Ph.D. diss., Wayne State University, 2001 (UMI No. 3010069).

Brady, Kevin Patrick. "From Isolation to Ambiguity: Fiscal Equity, the Perpetuation of Past Discrimination, and the Status of the Public Historically Black College and University." Ph.D. diss., University of Illinois at Urbana-Champaign, 2001 (UMI No. 9996619).

Buford, Juanita Frye. "A Study of Faculty Development at a Historically Black Medical School." Ed.D. diss., Peabody College for Teachers of Vanderbilt University, 2000 (UMI No. 9964900).

Cathey, Mary Ann Newson. "A Comparative Analysis of Freshman Curricula at Four Historically Black Colleges." Ph.D. diss., University of Mississippi, 1998 (UMI No. 9842366).

Coaxum, James, III. "Classifying Historically Black Colleges and Universities: A Missing Link in Research." Ph.D. diss., Vanderbilt University, 1999 (UMI No. 9933234).

Cody-Mitchell, Emma Denise. "The Economic Health of Private Historically Black Colleges and Universities: 1986–1995." Ph.D. diss., University of Tennessee, 2000 (UMI No. 9985614).

Collins, Alicia Carol. "Socialization at Two Black Women's Colleges: Bennett College and Spelman College." Ed.D. diss., University of Pittsburgh, 2001 (UMI No. 3013254).

Eaves, John Henry. "Determining Which Factors Lead to the Academic Success of African-American College Students at the Nation's Only All-Male, Predominantly Black Post-Secondary Institution: 'Demystifying the Morehouse Mystique.'" Ph.D. diss., University of South Carolina, 1999 (UMI No. 9939172).

Fox, Linette Pratt. "A Study of the Existence of Selected Characteristics that May Be Necessary for Entrepreneurial Success Among African-American Business Majors at Johnson C. Smith University." Ph.D. diss., Union Institute, 1997 (UMI No. 9814752).

Hale, Joseph Alexander. "The Effects of Personal Background and Psychosocial Variables on Student-Athletes' Academic Performance and Retention at Black Private Colleges." Ed.D. diss., Grambling State University, 1998 (UMI No. 9920418).

Hill, Lillie Pearl. "A Study of the Impact of Title III Funds on Small Black Private Church-Related Colleges." Ed.D. diss., Grambling State University, 1998 (UMI No. 9920419).

Holmes, Gwendolyn Vinson. "A Descriptive Study of Reform in Teacher Education at Historically Black Colleges and Universities." Ed.D. diss., Virginia Polytechnic Institution and State University, 1997 (UMI No. 9829425).

Jackson, Winsome Elaine. "Success Factors for African-American Students at Two Historically Black Institutions of Higher Education." Ed.D. diss., University of San Francisco, 1999 (UMI No. 9933316).

James, Anne Deloris. "Attitudes of Technical Communication Faculty at Selected Historically Black Colleges and Universities Toward Teaching with Instructional Technology." Ph.D. diss., Indiana University of Pennsylvania, 2000 (UMI No. 30002448).

Johnson, Barbara Jean. "Nurtured or Neglected: An Analysis of African-American Faculty Socialization at Historical Black Colleges and Universities." Ph.D. diss., Vanderbilt University, 1999 (UMI No. 9933248).

Lawrence, Freda M. "Model Components of Program Services' Administration for Students with Disabilities in Historically Black United States Colleges and Universities: Deducing Proactive Sensitivity from Reactive Discrimination." Ed.D. diss., Northern Illinois University, 2000 (UMI No. 9976677).

Mangum, Elmira. "A Study of the Leadership Behavior of Public Four-Year Historically Black College and University Presidents as Perceived by the Presidents and Their Upper Echelon Administrators." Ph.D. diss., State University of New York at Buffalo, 1998 (UMI No. 9833620).

McGruder, Juan Andre. "The Impact of Institutional Collaboration on Mission, Character, and Financial Stability: The Case of the Atlanta University Center." Ph.D. diss., Vanderbilt University, 1999 (UMI No. 9958454).

Payne, Ilene D. "The Viewpoint of Historically Black Colleges/Universities (HBCU) Presidents: Four Viability Issues HBCUs in a Pluralistic Society." Ph.D. diss., Union Institute, 1995 (UMI No. 9602203).

Person, Carl S. "Revitalization of an Historically Black College: A Maryland Eastern Shore Case." Ed.D. diss., Virginia Polytechnic Institution and State University, 1998 (UMI No. 9911825).

Price, Sherrell M. "Black Students' Perceptions at Historically Black Colleges and Universities Concerning Faculty, Staff, and Various Aspects of the Institutions that Contribute to the Overall College Experience." Ed.D. diss., University of Alabama, 1995 (UMI No. 9616902).

Redmond, Walter J., Jr. "Strategies for the Development of Asia-America Outreach: Internalization in Historically Black Colleges and Universities in the United States." Ed.D. diss., George Washington University, 2000 (UMI No. 9973074).

Reese, Deitra Mechelle. "A Study of the Health Risk Behaviors of Students Attending Historically Black Colleges and Universities." Ph.D. diss., University of Tennessee, 1998 (UMI No. 9923321).

Robinson, Yolanda Anderson. "The Federal Commitment to Historically Black Colleges and Universities: The Dollars and Sense of Title III of the Higher Education Act of 1965." Ph.D. diss., Claremont Graduate School, 1997 (UMI No. 9724351).

Rowland, Terri Y. "Institutional Advancement Initiatives of Historically Black Colleges and Universities: A Multicase Study of African American Higher Education." Ed.D. diss., North Carolina State University, 1997 (UMI No. 9737668).

Roy, Jerrold Wimbish. "Student Activism and the Historically Black University: Hampton Institute and Howard University." Ed.D. diss., Harvard University, 2000 (UMI No. 9968323).

Royster, Vivian Joan Hall. "An Investigation of the Relationship of Selected Planning Strategies and Success in Funding Library Programs at Historically Black Colleges and Universities: 1982–1992." Ph.D. diss., Florida State University, 1998 (UMI No. 9905348).

Samuels, Albert Leon. "Schools Desegregation from *Brown* to *Fordice*, 1954–1992: A Case Study in American Individualism." Ph.D. diss.,

Louisiana State University and Agricultural and Mechanical College, 1998 (UMI No. 9902661).

Scott, LeKita Vaney. "A Description of Successful Fund-Raising Units at Public Historically Black Colleges and Universities." Ph.D. diss., Florida State University, 2001 (UMI No. 9994577).

Terrell, Hellenna Lolitha. "Faculty Involvement in Governance at an Historically Black College: A Case Study." Ed.D. diss., University of Alabama, 1999 (UMI No. 9949408).

Thomas, Idella Boone. "An Examination of How Eight Graduates of Historically Black Colleges/Universities Perceive the Writing Preparation They Received as Undergraduates: A Case Study Approach." Ph.D. diss., Indiana University of Pennsylvania, 1999 (UMI No. 9941889).

Thompson, Valerie Kizziah. "Increasing the Number of Women of Color for Executive-Level Administration in Higher Education: A Focus on Strategies Used at Selected Historically Black Colleges and Universities." Ph.D. diss., University of Minnesota, 1999 (UMI No. 9924689).

Wesley, Vinetta L. "Leadership at Historically Black Colleges and Universities: Impact on Student Outcomes." Ed.D. diss., Peabody College for Teachers of Vanderbilt University, 1997 (UMI No. 9729106).

White, Belinda Johnson. "A Descriptive Study into Factors of the First Job Choice for African American Male Undergraduate Business Students at Morehouse College." Ph.D. diss., Georgia State University, 2000 (UMI No. 9991813).

Wright-Tatum, Patricia. "Job Satisfaction of Academic Administrators at Historically Black Colleges and Universities." Ph.D. diss., University of Missouri–Columbia, 1999 (UMI No. 9946315).

Monographs

Christy, Ralph D., and Lionel Williamson (eds.). 1991. *A Century of Service: Land-Grant Colleges and Universities, 1890–1990.* New Brunswick, NJ: Transaction Publishers.

The historical and contemporary educational and service experiences of black land-grant institutions are examined. Chapter titles include A National Resource—A National Challenge: The 1890 Land-Grant Colleges and Universities; Policy Alternatives to Meet the Challenges of Institutional Design and Change; and Keeping the Land-Grant Tradition: The Future Roles of the 1890 Land-Grant Institutions.

Drewry, Henry N., and Humphrey Doermann. 2001. *Stand and Prosper: Private Black Colleges and Their Students.* Princeton, NJ: Princeton University Press.

The authors provide a broadly focused history of HBCUs as well as the recent progress of forty-five private HBCUs. Chapter titles include Major Historical Factors Influencing Black Higher Education; Faculty: Challenge and Response; External Sources of Support; and Leadership and Financial Independence.

Foster, Lenoar, Janet A. Guyden, and Andrea L. Miller (eds.). 1999. *Affirmed Action: Essays of the Academic and Social Lives of White Faculty Members at Historically Black Colleges and Universities.* Lanham, MD: Rowman & Littlefield Publishers, Inc.

This collection of essays describes the experiences of whites who are on the faculty of historically black colleges and universities. Chapter titles include White Faculty at Historically Black Colleges and Universities: A Historical Framework; The Academic Road Less Traveled: Challenges and Opportunities; and Building Conversations of Respect: The Voice of White Faculty at Black Colleges.

Freeman, Kassie (ed.). 1999. *African American Culture and Heritage in Higher Education Research and Practice.* Westport, CT: Greenwood Publishing Group.

The black contributors provide an examination of the influence that the African American culture should and does have on higher education research and policies. Chapter titles include African American Students and Self-Concept Development: Integrating Cultural Influences into Research and Practice; Cultural Capital and the Role of Historically Black Colleges and Universities in Educational Reproduction; and Policy, Practice, and Performance: Higher Education Policies and Professional Education in American Black Colleges.

Guthrie, Robert V. 1998. *Even the Rat Was White: A Historical View of Psychology.* 2d ed. Boston: Allyn and Bacon.

The author examines the emergence of psychology from a black perspective and the role of historically black colleges and universities in it. Chapter titles include The Psychology of Survival and Education; Black Psychologists: Training, Employment, and Organizations; and Production of Black Psychologists in America.

Hardin, John A. 1997. *Fifty Years of Segregation: Black Higher Education in Kentucky, 1904–1954.* Lexington, KY: University Press of Kentucky.

The author provides a fifty-year documented chronology of the systematic methods used by the white power system in Kentucky to keep black colleges without funds and academically challenged, and the response of blacks to the actions. Chapter titles include Acceptance of Civil Racism, 1910–1930; Hopes, Reforms, and Resistance, 1930–1939; and Desegregated But Still Separate, 1949–1954.

Powell, Richard J., and Jock Reynolds. 1999. *To Conserve a Legacy: American Art from Historically Black Colleges and Universities.* Cambridge, MA: MIT Press.

The book provides information on the art collections at six HBCUs as cultural repositories. Chapter titles include Profiles of the Participating Historically Black Colleges and Universities; Conserving a Legacy: Forging a Partnership; and Conservation and Photographic Archives.

Sims, Serbrenia J. 1994. *Diversifying Historically Black Colleges and Universities: A New Higher Education Paradigm.* Westport, CT: Greenwood Publishing Group.

The author presents a four-step model for HBCUs to diversify student populations. Chapter titles include Diversity and the Historically Black Colleges and Universities: Definitions, History, and Issues; Diversity Transition Model for Historically Black Colleges and Universities: Building Bridges Between Cultures; and The Role of Historically Black Colleges and Universities' Faculty in Teaching Diversity.

Periodical Articles

Allen, Walter R. 1988. "Improving Black Students Access and Achievement in Higher Education." *Review of Higher Education* 11: 403–416.

Allen, Walter R., and Joseph O. Jewell. 2002. "A Backward Glance Forward: Past, Present, and Future Perspective on Historically Black College and Universities." *Review of Higher Education* 25, 3: 241–261.

Berger, Joseph B., and Jeffrey F. Milem. 2000. "Exploring the Impact of Historically Black Colleges in Promoting the Development of Undergraduates' Self-Concept." *Journal of College Student Development* 41, 4: 381–394.

Blumenstyk, Goldie. 1997. "A Small Black College Uses Unconventional Means to Get Computers on its Campus." *Chronicle of Higher Education* 43, 27: A21–A22.

Borden, Victor H. 2000. "The Top 100: Interpreting the Data." *Black Issues in Higher Education* 18, 8: 40–48.

Brotherton, Phaedra. 2000. "Minority Bachelor's Degrees on the Rise." *Black Issues in Higher Education* 18, 8: 34–38.

Carson, Emmett D. 1994. "Diversity and Equity among Foundation Grantmakers." *Nonprofit Management & Leadership* 4, 3: 331–334.

Chenoweth, Karin. 1997. "Forthcoming ETS Reports Proclaims the Importance of HBCUs." *Black Issues in Higher Education* 14, 16: 16–19.

Cowan, T., and J. Maguire. 1995. "History's Milestones of African-American Higher Education." *Journal of Blacks in Higher Education* 7: 86–90.

Cross, Theodore L. (ed.) 1994–1995. "Hampton University: The New Breeding Ground for Black Physicists." *Journal of Blacks in Higher Education* 2: 6–8.

———. 1995. "The Resurrection of Paul Quinn College." *Journal of Blacks in Higher Education* 7: 35–36.

———. 1996. "Howard College of Medicine Honors a Distinguished Surgeon." *Journal of Blacks in Higher Education* 11: 44.

Cross, Theodore Robert Bruce Slater. 1998. "Marshalling Black Voting Power to Increase African-American Opportunities in Higher Education." *Journal of Blacks in Higher Education* 21: 94–101.

Davis, Leroy. 2001. "A Clashing of Soul: John Hope and the Dilemma of African-American Leadership and Black Higher Education in the Early Twentieth Century." *Peace Research Abstracts* 38, 4: 451–600.

Dervarics, Charles. 1997. "Dialing for Dollars." *Black Issues in Higher Education* 14, 13: 22–24.

Edelman, Marian Wright. 2000. "Spelman College: A Safe Haven for a Black Woman." *Journal of Blacks in Higher Education* 27: 118–123.

Fennell, Reginald. 1997. "Health Behaviors of Students Attending Historically Black Colleges and Universities: Results from the National College Health Risk Behavior Survey." *Journal of American College Health* 46: 109–117.

Fields, C. D. 1996. "Taking Care of Business (Schools): HBCUs Attracting 'Cream of the Cream.'" *Black Issues in Higher Education* 13, 21: 12–18.

Freeman, Kassie. 2002. "Black Colleges and College Choice: Characteristics of Students Who Choose HBCUs." *Review of Higher Education* 25, 3: 349–358.

Fullwood, Sam. 1998–1999. "The Travails of LeMoyne-Owen College." *Journal of Blacks in Higher Education* 15: 101–104.

Gray, William H., III. 1997. "The Case for All-Black Colleges." *The ERIC Review* 5, 3: 21–23.

Haynes, Leonard L., III. 1997. "A Century of Success: Historically Black Colleges and Universities, America's National Treasure—Annual Report/The African America Education Data Book. Volume I: Higher and Adult Education." *Journal of Negro Education* 66, 1: 94–96.

Hollis, Mike. 1997. "Overcoming Segregation in Alabama Becomes Responsibility of HBCUs." *Black Issues in Higher Education* 14, 4: 8, 10–11.

Jalata, Asafa. 2002. "Revisiting the Black Struggle: Lesson for the 21st Century." *Journal of Black Studies* 33, 1: 86–116.

Lords, Erik. 2001. "Philanthropic Forklift Driver Uplifts Through Giving." *Black Issues in Higher Education* 18, 6: 32–33.

Manzo, Kathleen Kennedy. 1994. "Database to Target HBCU Students: New Program Hopes to Increase Number of African American Ph.D.s." *Black Issues in Higher Education* 11, 5: 26.

Naughton, Jim. 1998. "Title IX Poses a Particular Challenge at Predominantly Black Institutions." *Chronicle of Higher Education* 44, 24: A55–A56.

Nettles, Michael, Ursula Wagener, Catherine Millett, and Ann Killenbeck. 1999. "Student Retention and Progress: A Special Challenge for Private Historically Black Colleges and Universities." *New Directions for Higher Education* 108: 51–68.

Perna, Laura W. 2001. "The Contribution of Historically Black Colleges and Universities to the Preparation of African Americans for Faculty Careers." *Research in Higher Education* 42, 3: 267–294.

Redd, Kenneth. 1998. "Historically Black Colleges and Universities: Making a Comeback." *New Directions for Higher Education* 102: 33–44.

Sav, Thomas. 1997. "Separate and Unequal: State Financing of Historically Black Colleges and Universities." *Journal of Blacks in Higher Education* 15: 101–104.

———. 2000. "Tests of Fiscal Discrimination in Higher Education Finance: Funding Historically Black Colleges and Universities." *Journal of Education Finance* 26, 2: 157–172.

Shaw, R. G. 1991. "Forging New Alliances with Historically Black Colleges." *Community, Technical, and Junior College Journal* 61, 6: 41–43.

Suggs, Ernie. 1997. "HBCUs Getting up to Speed on the Information Highway." *Black Issues in Higher Education* 14, 7: 22–23.

Wade, Bruce H. 2002. "How Does Racial Identity Affect Historically Black Colleges' and Universities' Student Perceptions of September 11, 2001?" *Journal of Black Studies* 33, 1: 25–43.

Wagerer, Ursula, and Michael T. Nettles. 1998. "It Takes a Community to Educate Students." *Change* 30, 2: 18–25.

Reports

Farmer, Vernon L., and Betty L. Farmer (comps.). 1993. *History of Black Higher Education in America: A Selected Bibliography.* ERIC ED 363247.

Frierson, Cynthia L. 1993. *Perceptions of African American Educators Towards Historically Black Colleges and Universities.* ERIC ED 375193.

Gill, W. E. 1992. *The History of Maryland's Historically Black Colleges.* ERIC ED 347887.

Historically Black Colleges and Universities for the 21st Century: Annual Report of the President's Board of Advisors on Historically Black Colleges and Universities. ERIC ED 428626.

Nazeri, Janet Lea, and Mehdi Nazeri. 2000. *Desegregation and Diversity: The Paradox of a Historically Black University's Successful Mission Refinement.* ERIC ED 446693.

Richmond, Peggy A., and Sheilah Maramark. 1996. *On the Road to Economic Development: A Guide for Continuing Education Programs at Historically Black Colleges and Universities.* Washington, DC: Research and Evaluation Associates, Inc. ERIC ED 406921.

Sallie Mae. 1999. *Supporting the Historically Black College and University Mission: The Sallie Mae HBCU Default Management Program.* Reston, VA: Sallie Mae. ERIC ED 434559.

Stephens, Lowndes F., et al. 1994. *Motivations for Enrollment in Graduate and Professional School among African American Students in HBCUs.* Clemson, SC: Clemson University, Houston Center for the Study of the Black Experience Affecting Higher Education. ERIC ED 371064.

Walker, C., O. Bandele, and D. Mellion. 1998. *Multicultural Education: Ways to Utilize the Historically Black Land-Grant Agricultural Programs.* ERIC ED 427097.

Wenglinsky, Harold. 1997. *Students at Historically Black Colleges and Universities: Their Aspirations and Accomplishments.* Princeton, NJ: Policy Information Center Educational Testing Service.

White House Initiative on Historically Black Colleges and Universities. 1999. *Historically Black Colleges and Universities for the 21st Century: Annual Report of the President's Board of Advisors of Historically Black Colleges and Universities.* ERIC ED 428626

Williams, Sharon. 2000. *How Did Howard University, One of the Leading Historically Black Colleges and Universities, Develop as an Academic Institution during the Period 1967 through 1997?* ERIC ED 446705.

‣ Appendix 1: HBCUs by State

Following is a list of the 103 institutions by state as well as general background information. Carnegie classifications for four HBCUs were not included (N/I) in the current "Carnegie Classification" report. Included are total student enrollment ranges and percentages. The total student enrollment ranges are from the National Association for Equal Opportunity in Higher Education (NAFEO) (1999). The percentages on nonblack student and nonresident alien enrollment are the most recent data from the United States Department of Education (1996). Nonblack enrollment consists of United States citizens who are not of African descent. For two schools the percentages of nonblack enrollment and nonresident alien enrollment were not available (N/A).

Alabama

Alabama A&M University
Founded: 1875
Control: Public
Carnegie Classification: Doctoral/Research Universities—Intensive
Total Enrollment: 5,000-5,999
Nonblack Enrollment: 15 percent
Nonresident Alien Enrollment: 8 percent
City: Normal
Telephone: 256/851-5000
Website: http://www.aamu.edu/

Alabama State University
Founded: 1874
Control: Public
Carnegie Classification: Master's Colleges and Universities I
Total Enrollment: 5,000-5,999
Nonblack Enrollment: 3 percent
Nonresident Alien Enrollment: 1 percent
City: Montgomery
Telephone: 334/229-4100
Website: http://www.alasu.edu/

Bishop State Community College
Founded: 1936
Control: Public
Carnegie Classification: Associate's Colleges
Total Enrollment: 4,000-4,999
Nonblack Enrollment: 47 percent
Nonresident Alien Enrollment: 0 percent
City: Mobile
Telephone: 251/690-6801
Website: http://www.bscc.al.us

Concordia College
Founded: 1922
Control: Private
Carnegie Classification: Baccalaureate/Associate's Colleges
Total Enrollment: 999 and below
Nonblack Enrollment: 10 percent
Nonresident Alien Enrollment: 3 percent
City: Selma
Telephone: 334/874-5700
Website: http://higher-ed.lcms.org.selma.htm

J. F. Drake State Technical College
Founded: 1961
Control: Public
Carnegie Classification: Associate's Colleges
Total Enrollment: 999 and below
Nonblack Enrollment: 55 percent
Nonresident Alien Enrollment: 2 percent
City: Huntsville
Telephone: 256/539-8161
Website: http://www.dstc.cc.al.us

Lawson State Community College
Founded: 1963
Control: Public
Carnegie Classification: Associate's Colleges
Total Enrollment: 2,000-2,999
Nonblack Enrollment: 3 percent
Nonresident Alien Enrollment: 0.3 percent
City: Birmingham
Telephone: 205/925-2515
Website: http://www.ls.cc.al.us/

Miles College
Founded: 1905
Control: Private
Carnegie Classification: Baccalaureate Colleges—General
Total Enrollment: 1,000-1,999
Nonblack Enrollment: 0.2 percent
Nonresident Alien Enrollment: 0 percent
City: Birmingham
Telephone: 205/929-1000
Website: http://www.miles.edu

Oakwood College
Founded: 1896
Control: Private
Carnegie Classification: Baccalaureate Colleges—General
Total Enrollment: 1,000-1,999
Nonblack Enrollment: 1 percent
Nonresident Alien Enrollment: 12 percent
City: Huntsville
Telephone: 256/726-7000
Website: http://www.oakwood.edu/

Selma University
Founded: 1878
Control: Private
Carnegie Classification: N/I (offers baccalaureate degree)
Total Enrollment: 999 and below
Nonblack Enrollment: 0.4 percent
Nonresident Alien Enrollment: 0 percent
City: Selma
Telephone: 205/872-2533

Stillman College
Founded: 1876
Control: Private
Carnegie Classification: Baccalaureate Colleges—General
Total Enrollment: 1,000-1,999
Nonblack Enrollment: 2 percent
Nonresident Alien Enrollment: 0 percent
City: Tuscaloosa
Telephone: 800/841-5722 or 205/349-4240
Website: http://www.stillman.edu

Talladega College
Founded: 1867
Control: Private
Carnegie Classification: Baccalaureate Colleges—Liberal Arts
Total Enrollment: 1,000-1,999
Nonblack Enrollment: 4 percent
Nonresident Alien Enrollment: 0 percent
City: Talladega
Telephone: 205/761-0206
Website: http://www.talladega.edu

Trenholm State Technical College
Founded: 1966
Control: Public
Carnegie Classification: Associate's Colleges
Total Enrollment: 999 and below
Nonblack Enrollment: 22 percent
Nonresident Alien Enrollment: 0 percent
City: Montgomery
Telephone: 334/832-9000
Website: http://www/tstc.cc.al.us

Tuskegee University
Founded: 1881
Control: Private
Carnegie Classification: Master's Colleges and Universities I
Total Enrollment: 3,000-3,999
Nonblack Enrollment: 7 percent
Nonresident Alien Enrollment: 1 percent
City: Tuskegee
Telephone: 800/622-6531 or 334/727-8496
Website: http://www.tusk.edu/

Arkansas

Arkansas Baptist College
Founded: 1901
Control: Private
Carnegie Classification: Baccalaureate Colleges—Liberal Arts
Total Enrollment: 999 and below
Nonblack Enrollment: 1 percent
Nonresident Alien Enrollment: 0 percent
City: Little Rock
Telephone: 501/374-7856

Philander Smith College
Founded: 1877
Control: Private
Carnegie Classification: Baccalaureate Colleges—General
Total Enrollment: 999 and below
Nonblack Enrollment: 7 percent
Nonresident Alien Enrollment: 0.3 percent
City: Little Rock
Telephone: 501/370-5215
Website: http://www.philander.edu

Shorter College
Founded: 1886
Control: Private
Carnegie Classification: N/I (offers associate's degree)
Total Enrollment: 999 and below
Nonblack Enrollment: 0 percent
Nonresident Alien Enrollment: 27 percent
City: North Little Rock
Telephone: 501/374-6305

University of Arkansas, Pine Bluff
(Formerly Arkansas AM&N College)
Founded: 1873
Control: Public
Carnegie Classification: Baccalaureate Colleges—General
Total Enrollment: 2,000-2,999
Nonblack Enrollment: 14 percent
Nonresident Alien Enrollment: 0.4 percent
City: Pine Bluff
Telephone: 870/543-8000
Website: http://www.uapb.edu/

Delaware

Delaware State University
Founded: 1891
Control: Public
Carnegie Classification: Master's Colleges and Universities I
Total Enrollment: 3,000-3,999
Nonblack Enrollment: 32 percent
Nonresident Alien Enrollment: 1 percent
City: Dover
Telephone: 302/739-4917
Website: http://www/dsc/edu/

District of Columbia

Howard University
Founded: 1867
Control: Private
Carnegie Classification: Doctoral/Research Universities—Extensive
Total Enrollment: 9,000 and above
Nonblack Enrollment: 5 percent
Nonresident Alien Enrollment: 7 percent
City: Washington, DC
Telephone: 202/806-6100
Website: http://howard.edu/

University of the District of Columbia
Founded: 1977
Control: Public
Carnegie Classification: Master's Colleges and Universities I
Total Enrollment: 9,000 and above
Nonblack Enrollment: 8 percent
Nonresident Alien Enrollment: 7 percent
City: Washington, DC
Telephone: 202/274-5000
Website: http://udc2.org/index-b.htm

Florida

Bethune-Cookman College
Founded: 1931
Control: Private
Carnegie Classification: Baccalaureate Colleges—General
Total Enrollment: 2,000-2,999
Nonblack Enrollment: 1 percent
Nonresident Alien Enrollment: 4 percent
City: Daytona Beach
Telephone: 904/255-1401
Website: http://www.bethune.cookman.edu/

Edward Waters College
Founded: 1866
Control: Private
Carnegie Classification: Baccalaureate Colleges—General
Total Enrollment: 999 and below
Nonblack Enrollment: 0.1 percent
Nonresident Alien Enrollment: 5 percent
City: Jacksonville

Telephone: 904/355-3030
Website: http://www/ewc.edu/

Florida A&M University
Founded: 1877
Control: Public
Carnegie Classification: Master's Colleges and Universities I
Total Enrollment: 9,000 and above
Nonblack Enrollment: 10 percent
Nonresident Alien Enrollment: 2 percent
City: Tallahassee
Telephone: 850/599-3000
Website: http://www.famu2.edu/

Florida Memorial College
Founded: 1879
Control: Private
Carnegie Classification: Baccalaureate Colleges—General
Total Enrollment: 1,000-1,999
Nonblack Enrollment: 8 percent
Nonresident Alien Enrollment: 5 percent
City: Miami
Telephone: 800/822-1362 or 305/626-3600
Website: http://www.fmc.edu/

Georgia

Albany State University
Founded: 1903
Control: Public
Carnegie Classification: Master's Colleges and Universities I
Total Enrollment: 3,000-3,999
Nonblack Enrollment: 12 percent
Nonresident Alien Enrollment: 0 percent
City: Albany
Telephone: 912/430-4600
Website: http://argus.asurams.edu/asu/default.asp

Clark Atlanta University
Founded: 1989 (Merged: Clark College, founded 1869, and Atlanta University, founded 1867)
Control: Private
Carnegie Classification: Doctoral/Research Universities—Intensive
Total Enrollment: 5,000-5,999
Nonblack Enrollment: 2 percent

Nonresident Alien Enrollment: 2 percent
City: Atlanta
Telephone: 404/880-8000
Website: http://www.cau.edu/

Fort Valley State University
Founded: 1869
Control: Public
Carnegie Classification: Master's Colleges and Universities I
Total Enrollment: 3,000-3,999
Nonblack Enrollment: 6 percent
Nonresident Alien Enrollment: 0.5 percent
City: Fort Valley
Telephone: 912/825-6211
Website: http://www.fvsc.peachnet.edu

Interdenominational Theological Center
Founded: 1958
Control: Private
Carnegie Classification: Specialized Institutions—Theological Seminary
Total Enrollment: 999 and below
Nonblack Enrollment: 4 percent
Nonresident Alien Enrollment: 4 percent
City: Atlanta
Telephone: 404/527-7700
Website: http://www.itc.edu

Morehouse College (male only)
Founded: 1867
Control: Private
Carnegie Classification: Baccalaureate Colleges—Liberal Arts
Total Enrollment: 3,000-3,999
Nonblack Enrollment: 0.5 percent
Nonresident Alien Enrollment: 0.1 percent
City: Atlanta
Telephone: 404/215-2632
Website: http://www.morehouse.acu.edu/

Morehouse School of Medicine
Founded: 1975 (as part of Morehouse College)
Control: Private
Carnegie Classification: Specialized Institutions—Medical Schools and Medical Centers
Total Enrollment: 999 and below
Nonblack Enrollment: 2 percent

Nonresident Alien Enrollment: 0 percent
City: Atlanta
Telephone: 404/752-4500
Website: http://www.msm.edu/

Morris Brown College
Founded: 1881
Control: Private
Carnegie Classification: Baccalaureate Colleges—General
Total Enrollment: 2,000-2,999
Nonblack Enrollment: 0.2 percent
Nonresident Alien Enrollment: 2 percent
City: Atlanta
Telephone: 404/220-0270
Website: http://www.morrisbrown.edu

Paine College
Founded: 1882
Control: Private
Carnegie Classification: Baccalaureate Colleges—Liberal Arts
Total Enrollment: 999 and below
Nonblack Enrollment: 1 percent
Nonresident Alien Enrollment: 1 percent
City: Augusta
Telephone: 706/821-8200
Website: http://www.paine.edu/homeus4.htm/

Savannah State University
Founded: 1890
Control: Public
Carnegie Classification: Master's Colleges and Universities II
Total Enrollment: 3,000-3,999
Nonblack Enrollment: 7 percent
Nonresident Alien Enrollment: 2 percent
City: Savannah
Telephone: 800/788-0478
Website: http://www.savstate.edu

Spelman College (female only)
Founded: 1881
Control: Private
Carnegie Classification: Baccalaureate Colleges—Liberal Arts
Total Enrollment: 2,000-2,999
Nonblack Enrollment: 0.1 percent
Nonresident Alien Enrollment: 2 percent

City: Atlanta
Telephone: 800/982-2411
Website: http://www.spelman.edu

Kentucky

Kentucky State University
Founded: 1866
Control: Public
Carnegie Classification: Master's Colleges and Universities II
Total Enrollment: 2,000-2,999
Nonblack Enrollment: 50 percent
Nonresident Alien Enrollment: 1 percent
City: Frankfort
Telephone: 502/227-6000
Website: http://www.state.ky.us/ksu

Simmons University Bible College
Founded: 1873
Control: Private
Carnegie Classification: N/I (offers baccalaureate degree)
Total Enrollment: 999 and below
Nonblack Enrollment: N/A
Nonresident Alien Enrollment: N/A
City: Louisville
Telephone: 502/776-1443

Louisiana

Dillard University
Founded: 1869
Control: Private
Carnegie Classification: Baccalaureate Colleges—General
Total Enrollment: 1,000-1,999
Nonblack Enrollment: 0.7 percent
Nonresident Alien Enrollment: 0 percent
City: New Orleans
Telephone: 504/283-8822
Website: http://www.dillard.edu/

Grambling State University
Founded: 1901
Control: Public
Carnegie Classification: Master's Colleges and Universities I

Total Enrollment: 7,000-7,999
Nonblack Enrollment: 4 percent
Nonresident Alien Enrollment: 0.5 percent
City: Grambling
Telephone: 318/274-3395
Website: http://www.gram.edu

Southern University and A&M College
Founded: 1880
Control: Public
Carnegie Classification: Master's Colleges and Universities I
Total Enrollment: 9,000 and above
Nonblack Enrollment: 6 percent
Nonresident Alien Enrollment: 0 percent
City: Baton Rouge
Telephone: 225/771-4500
Website: http://www.subr.edu/

Southern University at New Orleans
Founded: 1959
Control: Public
Carnegie Classification: Master's Colleges and Universities II
Total Enrollment: 4,000-4,999
Nonblack Enrollment: 5 percent
Nonresident Alien Enrollment: 1 percent
City: New Orleans
Telephone: 504/286-5000
Website: http://suno.edu

Southern University at Shreveport
Founded: 1967
Control: Public
Carnegie Classification: Associate's Colleges
Total Enrollment: 1,000-1,999
Nonblack Enrollment: 7 percent
Nonresident Alien Enrollment: 0.4 percent
City: Shreveport
Telephone: 800/458-1472
Website: http://www.susbo.edu

Xavier University of Louisiana
Founded: 1915
Control: Private
Carnegie Classification: Master's Colleges and Universities I
Total Enrollment: 3,000-3,999

Nonblack Enrollment: 8 percent
Nonresident Alien Enrollment: 2 percent
City: New Orleans
Telephone: 504/486-7411
Website: http://www/xula.edu

Maryland

Bowie State University
Founded: 1865
Control: Public
Carnegie Classification: Master's Colleges and Universities I
Total Enrollment: 4,000-4,999
Nonblack Enrollment: 26 percent
Nonresident Alien Enrollment: 2 percent
City: Bowie
Telephone: 301/464-3000
Website: http://bsu.umd.edu/

Coppin State College
Founded: 1900
Control: Public
Carnegie Classification: Master's Colleges and Universities I
Total Enrollment: 3,000-3,999
Nonblack Enrollment: 6 percent
Nonresident Alien Enrollment: 2 percent
City: Baltimore
Telephone: 410/383-5400
Website: http://www.coppin.umd.edu/

Morgan State University
Founded: 1867
Control: Public
Carnegie Classification: Master's Colleges and Universities I
Total Enrollment: 6,000-6,999
Nonblack Enrollment: 4 percent
Nonresident Alien Enrollment: 2 percent
City: Baltimore
Telephone: 443/885-3333
Website: http://www.morgan.edu

University of Maryland-Eastern Shore
Founded: 1886
Control: Public
Carnegie Classification: Master's Colleges and Universities I

Total Enrollment: 3,000-3,999
Nonblack Enrollment: 24 percent
Nonresident Alien Enrollment: 6 percent
City: Princess Anne
Telephone: 410/651-2200
Website: http://www.umes.umd.edu

Michigan

Lewis College of Business
Founded: 1930
Control: Private
Carnegie Classification: Associate's Colleges
Total Enrollment: 999 and below
Nonblack Enrollment: 0 percent
Nonresident Alien Enrollment: 0 percent
City: Detroit
Telephone: 205/925-2515
Website: http://207.91.252.4/lewis/

Mississippi

Alcorn State University
Founded: 1871
Control: Public
Carnegie Classification: Master's Colleges and Universities I
Total Enrollment: 2,000-2,999
Nonblack Enrollment: 6 percent
Nonresident Alien Enrollment: .3 percent
City: Lorman
Telephone: 601/877-6100
Website: http://www.alcorn.edu/

Coahoma Community College
Founded: 1949
Control: Public
Carnegie Classification: Associate's Colleges
Total Enrollment: 1,000-1,999
Nonblack Enrollment: 2 percent
Nonresident Alien Enrollment: 0 percent
City: Clarksdale
Telephone: 662/627-2571
Website: http://www.ccc.cc.ms.us/

Hinds Community College-Utica Campus
Founded: 1903
Control: Public
Carnegie Classification: Associate's Colleges
Total Enrollment: 999 and below
Nonblack Enrollment: 7 percent
Nonresident Alien Enrollment: 0 percent
City: Utica
Telephone: 601/354-2327
Website: http://www.hinds.cc.ms.us/

Jackson State University
Founded: 1877
Control: Public
Carnegie Classification: Doctoral/Research Universities—Intensive
Total Enrollment: 6,000-6,999
Nonblack Enrollment: 4 percent
Nonresident Alien Enrollment: 2 percent
City: Jackson
Telephone: 800/848-6817
Website: http://www.jsums.edu/

Mary Holmes College
Founded: 1892
Control: Private
Carnegie Classification: Associate's Colleges
Total Enrollment: 999 and below
Nonblack Enrollment: 0.3 percent
Nonresident Alien Enrollment: 3 percent
City: West Point
Telephone: 622/494-6820
Website: http://maryholmes.edu/index.shtml

Mississippi Valley State University
Founded: 1946
Control: Public
Carnegie Classification: Baccalaureate Colleges—General
Total Enrollment: 2,000-2,999
Nonblack Enrollment: 0.7 percent
Nonresident Alien Enrollment: 0 percent
City: Itta Bena
Telephone: 601/254-3344
Website: http://mvsu.edu/

Rust College
Founded: 1866
Control: Private
Carnegie Classification: Baccalaureate Colleges—General
Total Enrollment: 1,000-1,999
Nonblack Enrollment: 3 percent
Nonresident Alien Enrollment: 3 percent
City: Holly Spring
Telephone: 601/252-8000
Website: http://www.rustcollege.edu

Tougaloo College
Founded: 1869
Control: Private
Carnegie Classification: Baccalaureate Colleges—Liberal Arts
Total Enrollment: 1,000-1,999
Nonblack Enrollment: 0 percent
Nonresident Alien Enrollment: 0 percent
City: Tougaloo
Telephone: 888/424-2566 or 601/977-7700
Website: http://www.tougallo.edu/

Missouri

Harris-Stowe State College
Founded: 1857
Control: Public
Carnegie Classification: Specialized Institutions—Teachers Colleges
Total Enrollment: 1,000-1,999
Nonblack Enrollment: 24 percent
Nonresident Alien Enrollment: 1 percent
City: St. Louis
Telephone: 314/340-3366
Website: http://www.hssc.edu

Lincoln University
Founded: 1866
Control: Public
Carnegie Classification: Master's Colleges and Universities I
Total Enrollment: 3,000-3,999
Nonblack Enrollment: 72 percent
Nonresident Alien Enrollment: 2 percent
City: Jefferson City
Telephone: 573/681-5000
Website: http://www.lincolnu.edu/

North Carolina

Barber-Scotia College
Founded: 1867
Control: Private
Carnegie Classification: Baccalaureate Colleges—Liberal Arts
Total Enrollment: 999 and below
Nonblack Enrollment: 0.4 percent
Nonresident Alien Enrollment: 0 percent
City: Concord
Telephone: 704/789-2900
Website: http://www.barber-scotia.edu

Bennett College (female only)
Founded: 1873
Control: Private
Carnegie Classification: Baccalaureate Colleges—Liberal Arts
Total Enrollment: 999 and below
Nonblack Enrollment: 0.3 percent
Nonresident Alien Enrollment: 1 percent
City: Greensboro
Telephone: 910/370-8624
Website: www.bennett.edu/

Elizabeth City State University
Founded: 1891
Control: Public
Carnegie Classification: Baccalaureate Colleges—General
Total Enrollment: 1,000-1,999
Nonblack Enrollment: 25 percent
Nonresident Alien Enrollment: 0.3 percent
City: Elizabeth City
Telephone: 252/335-3400
Website: http://www.ecsu.edu/

Fayetteville State University
Founded: 1867
Control: Public
Carnegie Classification: Master's Colleges and Universities I
Total Enrollment: 4,000-4,999
Nonblack Enrollment: 36 percent
Nonresident Alien Enrollment: .1 percent
City: Fayetteville
Telephone: 910/486-1371
Website: http://www.fsufay.edu/

Johnson C. Smith University
Founded: 1867
Control: Private
Carnegie Classification: Baccalaureate Colleges—General
Total Enrollment: 1,000-1,999
Nonblack Enrollment: 0.3 percent
Nonresident Alien Enrollment: 0 percent
City: Charlotte
Telephone: 704/378-1010
Website: http://www/jcsu.edu/

Livingstone College
Founded: 1879
Control: Private
Carnegie Classification: Baccalaureate Colleges—General
Total Enrollment: 999 and below
Nonblack Enrollment: 0.1 percent
Nonresident Alien Enrollment: 0 percent
City: Salisbury
Telephone: 704/797-1000
Website: http://livingstone.edu

North Carolina A&T State University
Founded: 1891
Control: Public
Carnegie Classification: Master's Colleges and Universities I
Total Enrollment: 7,000-7,999
Nonblack Enrollment: 12 percent
Nonresident Alien Enrollment: 1 percent
City: Greensboro
Telephone: 910/334-7500
Website: http://www.ncat.edu/

North Carolina Central University
Founded: 1910
Control: Public
Carnegie Classification: Master's Colleges and Universities I
Total Enrollment: 5,000-5,999
Nonblack Enrollment: 15 percent
Nonresident Alien Enrollment: 1 percent
City: Durham
Telephone: 919/560-6100
Website: http://www.nccu.edu

Saint Augustine's College
Founded: 1867
Control: Private
Carnegie Classification: Baccalaureate Colleges—Liberal Arts
Total Enrollment: 1,000-1,999
Nonblack Enrollment: 0.6 percent
Nonresident Alien Enrollment: 0.5 percent
City: Raleigh
Telephone: 919/516-4000
Website: http://www/st-aug.edu

Shaw University
Founded: 1865
Control: Private
Carnegie Classification: Baccalaureate Colleges—General
Total Enrollment: 2,000-2,999
Nonblack Enrollment: 5 percent
Nonresident Alien Enrollment: 4 percent
City: Raleigh
Telephone: 919/546-8200
Website: http://www.shawuniversity.edu

Winston-Salem State University
Founded: 1892
Control: Public
Carnegie Classification: Baccalaureate Colleges—General
Total Enrollment: 2,000-2,999
Nonblack Enrollment: 24 percent
Nonresident Alien Enrollment: 0.6 percent
City: Winston-Salem
Telephone: 800/257-4052
Website: http://www.wssu.edu

Ohio

Central State University
Founded: 1887
Control: Public
Carnegie Classification: Baccalaureate Colleges—General
Total Enrollment: 3,000-3,999
Nonblack Enrollment: 5 percent
Nonresident Alien Enrollment: 4 percent
City: Wilberforce
Telephone: 937/376-6348
Website: http://www/centralstate.edu/

Wilberforce University
Founded: 1856
Control: Private
Carnegie Classification: Baccalaureate Colleges—General
Total Enrollment: 999 and below
Nonblack Enrollment: 3 percent
Nonresident Alien Enrollment: 0 percent
City: Wilberforce
Telephone: 937/376-2911
Website: http://www.wilberforce.edu

Oklahoma

Langston University
Founded: 1897
Control: Public
Carnegie Classification: Baccalaureate Colleges—General
Total Enrollment: 4,000-4,999
Nonblack Enrollment: 44 percent
Nonresident Alien Enrollment: 1 percent
City: Langston
Telephone: 405/466-4000
Website: http://www.lunet.edu/

Pennsylvania

Cheyney University of Pennsylvania
Founded: 1837
Control: Public
Carnegie Classification: Master's Colleges and Universities I
Total Enrollment: 1,000-1,999
Nonblack Enrollment: 5 percent
Nonresident Alien Enrollment: 0.1 percent
City: Cheyney
Telephone: 610/399-2000
Website: http://www.cheyney.edu

Lincoln University
Founded: 1854
Control: Public
Carnegie Classification: Master's Colleges and Universities I
Total Enrollment: 1,000-1,999
Nonblack Enrollment: 7 percent
Nonresident Alien Enrollment: 3 percent

City: Lincoln
Telephone: 610/932-8300
Website: http://www.lincoln.edu

South Carolina

Allen University
Founded: 1870
Control: Private
Carnegie Classification: Baccalaureate Colleges—General
Total Enrollment: 999 and below
Nonblack Enrollment: 0 percent
Nonresident Alien Enrollment: 0 percent
City: Columbia
Telephone: 803/376-5735
Website: http://ww.scicu.org/allen/auhome.htm

Benedict College
Founded: 1870
Control: Private
Carnegie Classification: Baccalaureate Colleges—General
Total Enrollment: 2,000-2,999
Nonblack Enrollment: .1 percent
Nonresident Alien Enrollment: 2 percent
City: Columbia
Telephone: 803/256-4220
Website: http://bchome.benedict.edu

Claflin College
Founded: 1869
Control: Private
Carnegie Classification: Baccalaureate Colleges—General
Total Enrollment: 999 and below
Nonblack Enrollment: .2 percent
Nonresident Alien Enrollment: 2 percent
City: Orangeburg
Telephone: 803/535-5349
Website: http://www.claflin.edu

Clinton Junior College:
Founded: 1894
Control: Private
Carnegie Classification: N/I (offers associate's degree)
Total Enrollment: 999 and below

Nonblack Enrollment: N/A
Nonresident Alien Enrollment: N/A
City: Rock Hill
Telephone: 803/327-7402
Website: http://clintonjrcollege.org/

Denmark Technical College
Founded: 1947
Control: Public
Carnegie Classification: Associate's Colleges
Total Enrollment: 999 and below
Nonblack Enrollment: 6 percent
Nonresident Alien Enrollment: 0 percent
City: Denmark
Telephone: 803/793-5176
Website: http://www.den.tec.sc.us/

Morris College
Founded: 1908
Control: Private
Carnegie Classification: Baccalaureate Colleges—General
Total Enrollment: 999 and below
Nonblack Enrollment: 0.3 percent
Nonresident Alien Enrollment: 0 percent
City: Sumter
Telephone: 803/934-3200
Website: http://www/scicu.org/morris/mchome.htm

South Carolina State University
Founded: 1896
Control: Public
Carnegie Classification: Doctoral/Research Universities—Intensive
Total Enrollment: 4,000-4,999
Nonblack Enrollment: 6 percent
Nonresident Alien Enrollment: 0.1 percent
City: Orangeburg
Telephone: 803/536-7000
Website: http://www.scsu.edu/

Voorhees College
Founded: 1897
Control: Private
Carnegie Classification: Baccalaureate Colleges—General
Total Enrollment: 999 and below

Nonblack Enrollment: 2 percent
Nonresident Alien Enrollment: 0 percent
City: Denmark
Telephone: 804/524-5000
Website: http://www.voorhees.edu

Tennessee

Fisk University
Founded: 1867
Control: Private
Carnegie Classification: Baccalaureate Colleges—Liberal Arts
Total Enrollment: 999 and below
Nonblack Enrollment: 0 percent
Nonresident Alien Enrollment: 0.3 percent
City: Nashville
Telephone: 615/329-8500
Website: http://www.fisk.edu/

Knoxville College
Founded: 1875
Control: Private
Carnegie Classification: Baccalaureate Colleges—Liberal Arts
Total Enrollment: 999 and below
Nonblack Enrollment: 2 percent
Nonresident Alien Enrollment: 0 percent
City: Knoxville
Telephone: 800/743-5669

Lane College
Founded: 1882
Control: Private
Carnegie Classification: Baccalaureate Colleges—Liberal Arts
Total Enrollment: 999 and below
Nonblack Enrollment: 0 percent
Nonresident Alien Enrollment: 0 percent
City: Jackson
Telephone: 901/426-7500
Website: http://www.lanecollege.edu

LeMoyne-Owen College
Founded: 1871
Control: Private
Carnegie Classification: Baccalaureate Colleges—General
Total Enrollment: 1,000-1,999

Nonblack Enrollment: 0.4 percent
Nonresident Alien Enrollment: 0 percent
City: Memphis
Telephone: 901/774-9090
Website: http://mecca.org/LOC/page/LOC.html

Meharry Medical College
Founded: 1876
Control: Private
Carnegie Classification: Specialized Institutions—Medical Schools and Medical
    Centers
Total Enrollment: 999 and below
Nonblack Enrollment: 13 percent
Nonresident Alien Enrollment: 5 percent
City: Nashville
Telephone: 615/372-6000
Website: http://www.mmc.edu/

Tennessee State University
Founded: 1912
Control: Public
Carnegie Classification: Doctoral/Research Universities—Intensive
Total Enrollment: 8,000-8,999
Nonblack Enrollment: 36 percent
Nonresident Alien Enrollment: 0 percent
City: Nashville
Telephone: 615/963-5000
Website: http://tnstate.edu/

Texas

Huston-Tillotson College
Founded: 1876
Control: Private
Carnegie Classification: Baccalaureate Colleges—General
Total Enrollment: 999 and below
Nonblack Enrollment: 15 percent
Nonresident Alien Enrollment: 8 percent
City: Austin
Telephone: 512/505-3027
Website: http://www.htc.edu

Jarvis Christian College
Founded: 1912
Control: Private

Carnegie Classification: Baccalaureate Colleges—General
Total Enrollment: 999 and below
Nonblack Enrollment: 1 percent
Nonresident Alien Enrollment: 0 percent
City: Hawkins
Telephone: 903/769-5700
Website: http://168.44.172.2

Paul Quinn College
Founded: 1872
Control: Private
Carnegie Classification: Baccalaureate Colleges—General
Total Enrollment: 999 and below
Nonblack Enrollment: 3 percent
Nonresident Alien Enrollment: 0 percent
City: Dallas
Telephone: 214/302-3250
Website: http://www.pqc.edu

Prairie View A&M University
Founded: 1876
Control: Public
Carnegie Classification: Master's Colleges and Universities I
Total Enrollment: 6,000-6,999
Nonblack Enrollment: 12 percent
Nonresident Alien Enrollment: 2 percent
City: Prairie View
Telephone: 409/857-2626
Website: http://www.pvamu.edu/index.html

Southwestern Christian College
Founded: 1949
Control: Private
Carnegie Classification: Specialized Institutions—Faith-Related Institutions
Total Enrollment: 999 and below
Nonblack Enrollment: 4 percent
Nonresident Alien Enrollment: 9 percent
City: Terrell
Telephone: 972/524-3341
Website: http://www.swcc.edu/

Texas College
Founded: 1894
Control: Private

Carnegie Classification: Baccalaureate Colleges—Liberal Arts
Total Enrollment: 999 and below
Nonblack Enrollment: 2 percent
Nonresident Alien Enrollment: 0.8 percent
City: Tyler
Telephone: 903/593-8311
Website: http://www.texascollege.edu

Texas Southern University
Founded: 1947
Control: Public
Carnegie Classification: Doctoral/Research Universities—Intensive
Total Enrollment: 9,000 and above
Nonblack Enrollment: 8 percent
Nonresident Alien Enrollment: 10 percent
City: Houston
Telephone: 713/313-7011
Website: http://www.tsu.edu/

Wiley College
Founded: 1873
Control: Private
Carnegie Classification: Baccalaureate Colleges—General
Total Enrollment: 999 and below
Nonblack Enrollment: 2 percent
Nonresident Alien Enrollment: 4 percent
City: Marshall
Telephone: 800/658-6889
Website: http://199.171.201.14/college

Virgin Islands

University of the Virgin Islands
Founded: 1962
Control: Public (territory)
Carnegie Classification: Master's Colleges and Universities II
Total Enrollment: 3,000-3,999
Nonblack Enrollment: 11 percent
Nonresident Alien Enrollment: 7 percent
City: St. Thomas
Telephone: 340/776-9200
Website: http://www.uvi.edu/

Virginia

Hampton University
Founded: 1868
Control: Private
Carnegie Classification: Master's Colleges and Universities I
Total Enrollment: 5,000-5,999
Nonblack Enrollment: 11 percent
Nonresident Alien Enrollment: 24 percent
City: Hampton
Telephone: 757/727-5000
Website: http://www.hamptonu.edu/

Norfolk State University
Founded: 1935
Control: Public
Carnegie Classification: Master's Colleges and Universities I
Total Enrollment: 8,000-8,999
Nonblack Enrollment: 19 percent
Nonresident Alien Enrollment: 1 percent
City: Norfolk
Telephone: 757/683-8600
Website: http://www.nsu.edu/

Saint Paul's College
Founded: 1888
Control: Private
Carnegie Classification: Baccalaureate Colleges—General
Total Enrollment: 999 and below
Nonblack Enrollment: 6 percent
Nonresident Alien Enrollment: 0.4 percent
City: Lawrenceville
Telephone: 804/848-3111
Website: http://www.utoledo.eud/~wfraker.stpaul.html

Virginia State University
Founded: 1882
Control: Public
Carnegie Classification: Master's Colleges and Universities I
Total Enrollment: 4,000-4,999
Nonblack Enrollment: 9 percent
Nonresident Alien Enrollment: 0.8 percent
City: Petersburg
Telephone: 804/524-5000
Website: http://vsu.edu/

Virginia Union University
Founded: 1865
Control: Private
Carnegie Classification: Baccalaureate Colleges—Liberal Arts
Total Enrollment: 1,000-1,999
Nonblack Enrollment: 1 percent
Nonresident Alien Enrollment: 1 percent
City: Richmond
Telephone: 800/368-3227
Website: http://www.vuu.edu

West Virginia

Bluefield State College
Founded: 1895
Control: Public
Carnegie Classification: Baccalaureate Colleges—General
Total Enrollment: 2,000-2,999
Nonblack Enrollment: 92 percent
Nonresident Alien Enrollment: 0 percent
City: Bluefield
Telephone: 304/327-4000
Website: http://www.bluefield.wvnet.edu/

West Virginia State College
Founded: 1891
Control: Public
Carnegie Classification: Baccalaureate Colleges—General
Total Enrollment: 4,000-4,999
Nonblack Enrollment: 87 percent
Nonresident Alien Enrollment: 0 percent
City: Institute
Telephone: 304/766-3000
Website: http://www.wvsc.edu

Appendix 2: Selected Graduates of Historically Black Colleges and Universities

Every day in the United States and around the world, graduates of historically black colleges and universities influence the lives of others in significant ways. In this appendix the authors endeavor to list selected HBCU graduates to illustrate their span of influence. Many of the graduates are readily recognized, nationally and internationally. Others might be recognized only by blacks, and some may not be recognized at all. Together they illustrate the varying arenas in which HBCUs graduates can be found.

Those noted are contemporary persons who held the positions listed between 1950 and 2002.

The name of the HBCU they attended for baccalaureate study and their achievements are included. The current name of the HBCU is used. Because no systematic listing of HBCU graduates and their accomplishments exists, the information was in part gathered through conversations. Every attempt was made to be as specific as possible about the achievements of each person listed.

Eula L. Adams, Morris Brown University (Ga.), executive vice president of First Data, a major credit card business

Clara Adams-Ender, North Carolina A&T State University, first woman to earn the masters of Military Arts and Science degree at the U.S. Army Command and Staff College in Leavenworth, Kansas, U.S. Army Nurses Corps general

Ronald B. Adrine, Fisk University (Tenn.), judge, founder and past president of the Norman S. Minor Bar Association, the largest association of black attorneys

Elreta M. Alexander, North Carolina A&T State University, first black female to graduate from the Columbia University Law School, first black woman to practice law in North Carolina, first black female judge elected in the United States

Debbie Allen, Howard University (D.C.), dancer, actress, choreographer, director, producer, author

James H. Ammons, Florida A&M University, served as chairman of the accreditation committee for the Commission on Colleges of the Southern Association of Colleges and Schools, president of North Carolina Central University

Bernard Anderson, Livingston College (N.C.), U.S. assistant secretary, Employment Standards Administration

Richard Arrington Jr., Miles College (Ala.), mayor of Birmingham, Alabama

Nnamdi Azikiwe, Lincoln University–Pennsylvania, first president of Nigeria

Sondra Johnson Bailey, Southern University (La.), electrical engineer, researcher, inventor, member of the design team that developed IBM's prototype for the Scalable Parallel Processor that is the base machine for "Deep Blue," IBM's world renowned chess machine; holds ten patents

Ella Baker, Shaw University (N.C.), civil rights activist

Charles R. Baquet III, Xavier University (La.), deputy director of the U.S. Peace Corps

Imamu Amiri Baraka (Leroi Jones), Howard University (D.C.), playwright, poet, political activist

Claude Albert Barnett, Tuskegee University (Ala.), businessman, founded the Associated Negro Press (ANP)

Julius W. Becton Jr., Prairie View A&M University (Tex.), U.S. Army general

Robert Benham, Tuskegee University (Ala.), lawyer, elected to Georgia Supreme Court

Mary Frances Berry, Howard University (D.C.), chair, U.S. Commission on Civil Rights

John T. Biggers, Hampton University (Va.), artist

Rufus L. Billups, Tuskegee University (Ala.), U.S. Air Force general

*Sanford Bishop, Morehouse College (Ga.), U.S. Representative for Georgia. Committee membership: Agriculture, Veterans' Affairs, Intelligence

John W. Blassingame, Fort Valley State University (Ga.), historian

Daniel T. Blue Jr., North Carolina Central University, North Carolina Speaker of the House

Frances Bonner, Bennett College (N.C.), medical researcher

Frederick Oliver Boone, Morgan State University (Md.), Delta Air Lines pilot

Ed Bradley, Cheyney University of Pennsylvania, coeditor, cohost, and correspondent of CBS *60 Minutes* news program for twenty-one years

Pamela E. Bridgewater, Virginia State University, twenty-year career Foreign Service officer in Belgium, Jamaica, the Bahamas, and South Africa; ambassador to the Republic of Benin in West Africa

Randolph W. Bromerg, Howard University (D.C.), geologist and geophysicist, one of the Tuskegee Airmen

Edward W. Brooke, Howard University (D.C.), won a Bronze Star for bravery during World War II, first black to be elected to the U.S. Senate from Massachusetts since Reconstruction

*Corrine Brown, Florida A&M University, U.S. Representative for Florida. Committee membership: Transportation and Infrastructure, Veterans' Affairs

Dorothy Lavinia Brown, Bennett College (N.C.), first black female surgeon in the Southeast

Robert L. Brown Jr., Tuskegee University (Ala.), architect, served as president of R. L. Brown & Associates, an architectural and construction management company located in Georgia

Tarlee Brown, Tuskegee University (Ala.), architect

Marjorie L. Browne, Howard University (D.C.), mathematician, second black woman to earn a Ph.D. degree in mathematics, taught at North Carolina Central University, made North Carolina Central University the first HBCU to receive a National Science Foundation Institute award for secondary teachers of mathematics

Calvin Butts, Morehouse College (Ga.), senior pastor of Abyssinian Baptist Church in New York City

Sherian Grace Cadoria, Southern University (La.), first black woman director for the Joint Chiefs of Staff, first woman to attend the army's top colleges—Command and General Staff College and the U.S. Army War College—received the Distinguished Service Medal, Defense Superior Service Medal, and Legion of Merit

Shirley Caesar, Shaw University (N.C.), pastor, international gospel recording artist, second black woman to receive the Grammy Award, elected councilwoman for Durham, North Carolina

Ralph Campbell Jr., Saint Augustine's College (N.C.), first black elected as North Carolina State Auditor

Hattie Carwell, Bennett College (N.C.), research scientist, author

Julius L. Chambers, North Carolina Central University, first black to be editor-in-chief of the law review of University of North Carolina–Chapel Hill, director of the Counsel of the NAACP Legal Defense and Education Fund, former chancellor of North Carolina Central University

Spencer Christian, Hampton University (Va.), weather forecaster for twelve years on ABC's *Good Morning America*

*Eva Clayton, Johnson C. Smith University (N.C.), first woman elected from North Carolina as U.S. Representative. Committee membership: Agriculture, Budget

*James Clyburn, South Carolina State University, U.S. Representative for South Carolina. Committee membership: Appropriations

Alice Coachman, Tuskegee University (Ala.), first black to win an Olympic gold medal in the high jump

Elizabeth Bias Cofield, Hampton University (Va.), educator, elected to the Waked County (N.C.) Board of Education and Wake County Commissioner, served as National Vice President of National Association of Counties

Rodney Coleman, Howard University (D.C.), U.S. assistant secretary, Manpower Affairs, Department of the Air Force

Karyne Jones Conley, Clark Atlanta University (Ga.), educator, elected to Texas State Legislature

Eugene R. Cromartie, Florida A&M University, U.S. Army general

*Elijah Cummings, Howard University (D.C.), U.S. Representative for Maryland. Committee membership: Transportation and Infrastructure, Government Reform

Christine Darden, Virginia State University, aerospace engineer, one of the lead researchers on sonic boom and its effects on supersonic and hypersonic aircraft

Jannette L. Dates, Coppin State College (Md.), author, educator, renowned expert on blacks in the media, coeditor of *Split Image: African Americans in the Mass Media,* coauthor of the resource guide for the play "Having Our Say: The Delaney Sisters' First 100 Years"

*Danny K. Davis, University of Arkansas at Pine Bluff, U.S. Representative for Illinois. Committee membership: Small Business, Government Reform

Ossie Davis, Howard University (D.C.), actor, activist

Russell C. Davis, Tuskegee University (Ala.), first black Air National Guard general

Yvonne V. Delk, Norfolk State University (Va.), first ordained black woman for the United Church of Christ (UCC) and the first black woman ordained in a mainstream Protestant denomination, executive director of Community Renewal Society of the UCC in Chicago

David Dinkins, Howard University (D.C.), mayor of New York City

Henry Doctor Jr., South Carolina State University, U.S. Army general

Joe L. Dudley Sr., North Carolina A&T University, founder and CEO of Dudley Products Inc. hair care and beauty products

Allyson K. Duncan, Hampton University (Va.), first black woman appointed to the North Carolina state court of appeals, first black woman appointed to the North Carolina Utilities Commission

Julian M. Earls, Norfolk State University (Va.), deputy director for Operations at the National Aeronautics Space Administration Lewis Research Center in Ohio

Marian Wright Edelman, Spelman College (Ga.), founder of the Children's Defense Fund, first black female admitted to the Mississippi Bar, received the Presidential Medal of Freedom (the nation's highest civilian award), author

M. Joycelyn Elders, Philander Smith College (Ark.), first black surgeon general of the United States

Medgar Wiley Evers, Alcorn State University (Miss.), civil rights leader

Etta Z. Falconer, Fisk University (Tenn.), mathematician, catalyst for and first director of the National Aeronautics and Space Administration Women in Science and Engineering Scholars at Spelman College (Ga.), recipient of the Association of Women in Mathematics Louise Hay Award for outstanding achievements in mathematics education

James Farmer, Wiley College (Tex.), civil rights leader, founder and director of the Congress of Racial Equality, received the Presidential Medal of Freedom in 1998, U.S. assistant secretary for the Department of Health, Education, and Welfare

Evelyn J. Fields, Norfolk State College (Va.), first black and first woman to become director of the National Oceanic and Atmospheric Administration; Commissioned Officers Corps, the nation's seventh uniformed service, nominated by President William Clinton

Milton F. Fitch Jr., North Carolina Central University, first black in North Carolina to preside over the House of Representatives, first black elected to House majority leader

Roberta Flack, Howard University (D.C.), singer, composer, musician

Floyd H. Flake, Wilberforce University (Ohio), pastor, U.S. Representative for New York, president of Wilberforce University

John Hope Franklin, Fisk University (Tenn.), historian, author, received the Presidential Medal of Freedom presented by President William Clinton

Shirley Clarke Franklin, Howard University (D.C.), first female appointed chief administrative officer in Atlanta, Georgia; first female mayor of Atlanta

Algeania W. Freeman, Fayetteville State University (N.C.), educator, first female president of Livingston College (N.C.)

Henry Frye, North Carolina A&T State University, North Carolina Supreme Court justice

Mary H. Futrell, Virginia State University, three-term president of the National Education Association

Willie E. Gary, Shaw University (N.C.), attorney, businessman, philanthropist

James Gavin, Livingston College (N.C.), physician, researcher, educator, senior scientific officer at Howard Hughes Medical Institute (HHMI), director of the HHMI–National Institutes of Health Research Scholars Program, president of Morehouse School of Medicine (Ga.)

Althea Gibson, Florida A&M University, professional tennis player and golfer who was the first black athlete to play in the United States Lawn Tennis Association tournament, to win a Wimbledon singles title, to play and win a U.S. Open, to play in the French Open, and to earn a Ladies Professional Golf Association membership.

Paula Giddings, Howard University (D.C.), author

Gloria Gilmer, Morgan State University (Md.), mathematician, president of Math-Tech, a corporation that translates research findings into programs for mathematics education, especially for people of color and women

Vanessa Gilmore, Hampton University (Va.), federal judge

Nikki Giovanni, Fisk University (Tenn.), world-renowned poet

Gabrielle Glass, Hampton University (Va.), pilot, only black female pilot employed by Mesaba Airlines, a Northwest Airlines link, as a first officer

Wilson W. Goode, Morgan State University (Md.), mayor of Philadelphia, recognized as being largely responsible for ensuring the public protection of citizens while continuing the uninterrupted flow of power during the investigation into the disaster at Three Mile Island nuclear generating station

Samuel Graveley, Virginia Union University, first black to serve as a U.S. Navy midshipman, to be commissioned an ensign in World War II, to command a U.S. Navy warship, and to become a rear admiral.

Earl Graves, Morgan State University (Md.), founder and publisher of *Black Enterprise* magazine

Darrell Green, Saint Paul's College (Va.), professional athlete, founder of the Darrell Green Youth Life Foundation in Washington, D.C.

Archibald Henry Grimke, Lincoln University–Pennsylvania, lawyer, writer, civil rights leader

Beverly Guy-Sheftall, Spelman College (Ga.), educator, writer, editor

Harriett N. Haith, Shaw University (N.C.), science educator, first woman chair of the Asheville, North Carolina, city school board

Alex Haley, Alcorn State University (Miss.), author

Titus Hall, Tuskegee University (Ala.), U.S. Air Force general

James F. Hamlet, Tuskegee University (Ala.), U.S. Air Force general

Barbara Hamm, Bennett College (N.C.), first black female television news director in the United States

Edward L. Hamm Jr., Hampton University (Va.), president of E. L. Hamm and Associates, a management and engineering consulting firm

Andrea L. Harris, Bennett College (N.C.), social activist, president of the North Carolina Institute of Minority Economic Development, a nonprofit corporation

James Harris, Houston-Tillotson College (Tex.), nuclear chemist, member of the research team that discovered two elements, Rutherfordian and Hahnium

Jean L. Harris, Virginia Union University, physician, politician, established the J. L. Harris Scholarship for minority students in the sciences at Virginia Union.

Patricia R. Harris, Howard University (D.C.), first black women cabinet member as secretary of the U.S. Department of Health, Education, and Welfare, which was changed to the Department of Health and Human Services during her tenure

*Alcee Hastings, Fisk University (Tenn.), U.S. Representative for Florida. Committee membership: International Relations, Rules

J. C. Hayward, Howard University (D.C.), journalist, award-winning broadcaster, including the Emmy Award and the Ted Yates Award (the highest award given by the National Academy of Television Arts and Sciences), first woman to anchor a television newscast in the Washington, D.C., region I.

Patricia Henry, Bennett College (N.C.), first black and first woman master brewer in the country

Willie Herenton, LeMoyne Owens College (Tenn.), mayor of Memphis

Alexis M. Herman, Xavier University (La.), secretary of the U.S. Department of Labor

Gloria Hewitt, Fisk University (Tenn.), mathematician, fourth black woman to receive a Ph.D. degree in mathematics, leader and part of team to develop Advance Placement calculus examinations, member of the board of governors of the Mathematics Association of America, chair of the Mathematics Department at the University of Montana

Juanita Hicks, Bennett College (N.C.), elected clerk of the Fulton County Superior Court in Atlanta, Georgia

Michael Hightower, Clark Atlanta University (Ga.), first black elected to the College Park, Maryland, City Council

Patrice A Hinnant, Spelman College (Ga.), district court judge

Beverly Wade Hogan, Tougaloo College (Miss.), educator, first woman president of Tougaloo College

Edward Honor, Southern University (La.), U.S. Army general

Alice H. Howard, Johnson C. Smith University (N.C.), educator, administrator, first black public school superintendent in the Fredericksburg, Virginia, area

Frederick S. Humphries, Florida A&M University, scientist, educator, first alumnus to be president of Florida A&M University, CEO of the National Association for Equal Opportunity in Higher Education

Deborah Hyde, Tougaloo College (Miss.), physician, founded the Beacon of Hope Scholarship Foundation in 1991.

Jesse Jackson, North Carolina State A&T University, civil rights leader, founded the Rainbow Coalition, first black to campaign for president of the United States

*Jesse Jackson Jr., North Carolina State A&T University, U.S. Representative for Illinois. Committee membership: Appropriations

Maynard Jackson, Morehouse College (Ga.), first black mayor of a major southern city (Atlanta, Georgia), National Development chair for the Democratic National Committee

Samuel L. Jackson, Morehouse College (Ga.), actor

William S. Jackson, West Virginia State College, founded the first adoption agency for children of color in New York City, dean of the School of Social Work at Atlanta University (during his office the school became the first HBCU School of Social Work to be accredited by the Council of Social Work Education), first black Social Security Insurance executive administrator for the Social Security Administration in the Southeast

Daniel "Chappie" James, Tuskegee University (Ala.), first black four-star U.S. Army general

*William Jefferson, Southern University (La.), U.S. Representative for Louisiana. Committee membership: Ways and Means

Renaldo M. Jensen, Howard University (D.C.), engineer, educator

Charles B. Jiggetts, Tuskegee University (Ala.), U.S. Air Force general

Alberta Helyn Johnson, Talladega College (Ala.), first black woman elected to public office in Wyoming

Charles Spurgeon Johnson, Virginia Union University, first black president of Fisk University (Tenn.)

*Eddie Bernice Johnson, Texas Christian College, U.S. Representative for Texas and chair of the Congressional Black Caucus. Committee membership: Transportation and Infrastructure, Science

Lonnie Johnson, Tuskegee University (Ala.), engineer, inventor, founder of Johnson Research and Development, which holds over sixty patents including one of the biggest selling toys, the Super Soaker Squirt Gun, sales of which have topped $200 million

Paula T. Johnson, Bowie State University (Md.), sixteen-year veteran of the Baltimore (Md.) City Police Department, first black female to become a major in the department

Marian Johnson-Thompson, Howard University (D.C.), microbiologist, educator

Elaine R. Jones, Howard University (D.C.), first woman to be appointed president and director-counsel of the NAACP Legal Defense and Educational Fund

Barbara C. Jordan, Texas Southern University (Tex.), first black elected to the Texas State Senate since 1883, elected to the U.S. House of Representatives, keynote speaker at Democratic National Conventions of 1976 and 1992

Kim Jordan, Howard University (D.C.), musician, producer, composer-arranger, vocalist; her publishing company (Kimberlyn Music) received the ASCAP Music Award for writing and producing "We Must Be In Love"

Tom Joyner, Tuskegee University (Ala.), national radio personality and founder of the Tom Joyner Foundation

Vivian Davis Kendricks, Fort Valley State University (Ga.), first black elected to serve two terms as director of the Southeast Region Chapters of Kappa Delta Epsilon Honorary Professional Education Fraternity, an interracial organization formed in 1923

Sharon Pratt Kelly, Howard University (D.C.), first black woman to be elected mayor of Washington, D.C.

Leon G. Kerry, Norfolk State University (Va.), commissioner of the Central Intercollegiate Athletic Association

Darnita R. Killian, Spelman College (Ga.), executive director for A Better Chance, a thirty-eight-year-old national organization that identifies and recruits academically talented students of color and guides them toward various educational opportunities, including private college preparatory schools

Martin Luther King, Jr., Morehouse College (Ga.), minister, civil rights activitst

James R. Klugh, South Carolina State University, U.S. Army general

Elizabeth Duncan Koontz, Livingston College (N.C.), educator, diplomat, served as president of the National Education Association, U.S. deputy assistant secretary of Employment Standards, director of the Woman's Bureau of the U.S. Department of Labor

Samuel Lee Kountz, University of Arkansas at Pine Bluff, member of the team to do the first kidney transplant on the West Coast of the United States, developed the technique to detect and treat kidney transplant rejections

George M. Langford, Fayetteville State University (N.C.), scientist

Andrea Lawrence, Spelman College (Ga.), first black to receive the Ph. D. degree in computer science from Georgia Tech University, chair of Computer Science Department at Spelman College

Shelton Jackson (Spike) Lee, Morehouse College (Ga.), film producer, director, actor

George Lewis, Hampton University (Va.), retired president and CEO of Philip Morris Capital Corporation

*John Lewis, Fisk University (Tenn.), U.S. Representative for Georgia. Committee membership: Ways and Means

Reginald F. Lewis, Virginia State University, lawyer, entrepreneur, philanthropist, established the Reginald F. Lewis Foundation in 1987

Clarence E. Lightner, North Carolina Central University, businessman, politician, first black to serve as mayor of a major city (Raleigh) in North Carolina

Earl Lloyd, West Virginia State College, first black to sign a contract with the National Basketball Association (NBA)

Michael L. Lomax, Morehouse College (Ga.), chair of the Fulton County Commissions in Atlanta, Georgia; president of Dillard University (La.)

Calvin W. Lowe, North Carolina A&T State University, scientist, educator, president of Bowie State University (Md.)

Yvonne Maddox, Virginia Union University, acting deputy director of the National Institutes of Health

Charles Malone, North Carolina Central University, only black to serve as acting head of the National Institutes of Health

Vernon Malone, Shaw University (N.C.), educator, politician, North Carolina senator

Vivienne Malone-Mayes, Fisk University (Tenn.), mathematician, fifth black woman to receive a Ph.D. in mathematics, first black faculty member at Baylor University (Tex.)

Audrey Forbes Manley, Spelman College (Ga.), physician, U.S. deputy assistant secretary for the Department of Health and Human Services, first alumna to be president of Spelman College

Marion Mann, Tuskegee University (Ala.), medical corps general

Bradford Marsalis, Southern University (La.), musician

Henry L. Marsh III, Virginia Union University, civil rights lawyer, first black mayor of Richmond, Virginia, Virginia State senator

Thurgood Marshall, Lincoln University–Pennsylvania, civil rights lawyer, U.S. Supreme Court justice

Harold L. Martin Sr., North Carolina A&T State University, engineer, educator, president of Winston-Salem State University (N.C.)

Walter E. Massey, Morehouse College (Ga.), physicist, president of Morehouse College, director of the National Science Foundation

Georgia B. McCallum, North Carolina Central University, health educator, left over $200,000 to NCCU to establish an endowed scholarship to students pursuing careers in health education and music

Floyd B. McKissick, Morehouse College (Ga.), first black to study law at North Carolina Law School, director of the Congress of Racial Equality, created Soul City, a black rural town in North Carolina

Gwendolyn Williams McMullins, Fort Valley State University (Ga.), science educator

Ronald McNair, North Carolina State A&T University, astronaut

*Carrie Meek, Florida A&M University, U.S. Representative for Florida. Committee membership: Appropriations

*Gregory Meeks, Howard University (D.C.), U.S. Representative for New York. Committee membership: Financial Services, International Relations

Samuel Metters, Prairie View A&M University (Tex.), engineer, businessman, founder and CEO of Metters Industries Inc., a technology company

Tonya Miller, Hampton University (Va.), first black to receive a Ph.D. degree in industrial/organizational psychology from Old Dominion University in Virginia

Yvonne Bond Miller, Virginia State University, first black woman elected to the Virginia House of Delegates and, later, the Senate

Parren J. Mitchell, Morgan State University (Md.), elected Maryland's first black congressman

Earl "The Pearl" Monroe, Winston-Salem State University (N.C.), professional athlete, first CIAA player to lead the nation in scoring 41.4 points per game

Lee Monroe, Shaw University (N.C.), senior education adviser to the governor of North Carolina, special assistant to the assistant secretary of management for the U.S. Department of Education, president of Voorhees College (S.C.)

Ernest N. Morial, Xavier University (La.), first black graduate from Louisiana State University Law School and first black elected mayor of New Orleans

Chloe Anthony (Toni) Morrison, Howard University (D.C.), author, recipient of the Nobel Prize for Literature

Azie Taylor Morton, Huston-Tillotson College (Tex.), U.S. Treasurer

Samuel Nabrit, Morehouse College (Ga.), member of the Atomic Energy Commission

Kwame Nkrumah, Lincoln University–Pennsylvania, first prime minister and first president of Ghana

Jessye Norman, Howard University (D.C.), opera singer

Kenneth Olden, Knoxville College (Tenn.), cell biologist, biochemist, first black director of the National Institute of Environmental Health Sciences (one of the eighteen institutes of the National Institutes of Health)

Hazel O'Leary, Fisk University (Tenn.), secretary of the U.S. Department of Energy

*Major Owens, Morehouse College (Ga.), U.S. Representative for New York. Committee membership: Education and the Workforce, Government Reform

Roderick Paige, Jackson State University (Miss.), first black secretary of the U.S. Department of Education

Roderick Pettigrew, Morehouse College (Ga.), physician, researcher, first director of the National Institute on Biomedical Imaging and Bioengineering at the National Institutes of Health

William Lawrence Pollard, Shaw University (N.C.), dean and founder of the Syracuse University College of Human Services and Health Professions, dean and founder of Grambling State University School of Social Work, president of the University of the District of Columbia

Susie Powell, Bennett College (N.C.), attorney, businesswoman

George Price, South Carolina State University, U.S. Army general

Leontyne Price, Central State College (Ohio), opera singer

Stephanie Ready, Coppin State College (Md.), first female to coach a men's professional basketball team as the assistant coach of the National Basketball Developmental League's Greenville, South Carolina, team

Eddie Reed, Philander Smith College (Ark.), cancer research scientist

Orien Reid, Clark Atlanta University (Ga.), broadcaster, first black elected to serve as chairman of the Alzheimer's Association national board of directors

Tim Reid, Norfolk State University (Va.), actor, producer, director, established with his wife, actress Daphne Maxwell Reid, the first full-service film studio in Petersburg, Virginia, New Millennium Studios

Louis W. Roberts, Fisk University (Tenn.), physicist, mathematician, electronic specialist

Carl Rowan, Tennessee State University, journalist

Wilma Rudolph, Tennessee State University, athlete, first woman to win three gold medals in a single Olympics

John Ruffin, Dillard University (La.), associate director for Research on Minority Health, National Institutes of Health

Jayne Burrows Sargent, Tougaloo College (Miss.), educator, first black to serve as superintendent of Jackson Public School System, the largest school system in the state of Mississippi

David Satcher, Morehouse College (Ga.), surgeon general of the United States

Lottie H. Shackelford, Philander Smith College (Ark.), businesswoman, elected mayor of Little Rock, Arkansas

John W. Shannon, Central State University (Ohio), served as undersecretary of the U.S. Army

Robert E. Shurney, Tennessee State University, aeronautical engineer, test conductor for NASA, designed the tires for the moon buggy

Ruth J. Simmons, Dillard University (La.), educator, administrator, scholar of romance languages and literature, president of Brown University in Rhode Island, where she became the first black to serve as president of an Ivy League institution

Fatima Sokera, Clark Atlanta University (Ga.), science researcher, businesswoman

Leonard Spearman, Florida A&M University, executive director of the White House Initiative for HBCUs

Louis W. Sullivan, Morehouse College (Ga.), secretary of the U.S. Department of Health and Human Services

Lucius Theus, Tuskegee University (Ala.), U.S. Air Force general

Elaine F. Thomas, Tuskegee University (Ala.), accomplished artist, researcher, served as curator and director of the George Washington Carver Museum in Tuskegee

Lydia Thomas, Howard University (D.C.), president and CEO of Mitretek Systems

*Bennie Thompson, Tougaloo College (Miss.), U.S. Representative for Mississippi. Committee membership: Agriculture, Budget

John Thompson, Florida A&M University, CEO of Symantec, a software and Internet security company

Sharmon Paschal Thornton, Central State University (Ohio), U.S. Air Force deputy for equal opportunity in the Office of the Assistant Secretary of the Air Force for Manpower, Reserve Affairs, Installations, and Environment

Edgar A. Toppin, Howard University (D.C.), educator, historian, author

Edolphus Towns, North Carolina A&T State University, U.S. Representative for New York. Committee membership: Energy and Commerce, Government Reform

Guthrie L. Turner, Shaw University (N.C.), U.S. Army general

Teresa Vincent, North Carolina Central University, district court judge

Alice Walker, Spelman College (Ga.), author

Leroy T. Walker, Benedict College (S.C.), educator, internationally renowned track coach and Olympic administrator, president of North Carolina Central University

Charles D. Walton, Shaw University (N.C.), educator, Rhode Island state senator

Craige Anthony Washington, Prairie View A&M University (Tex.), criminal lawyer served in the Texas State Senate and the U.S. House of Representatives

Sonja M. Watts, Norfolk State University (Va.), founder of Watts Works Communications, a public relations company

Gladys White, Hampton University (Va.), educator, raised over $3 million for Hampton University

L. Douglas Wilder, Virginia Union University, first black elected governor of a state, Virginia

George Williams, Saint Augustine's College (N.C.), legendary track and field coach for Olympics and college programs

Vickie Lynn Wilson, Knoxville College (Tenn.), poet

Oprah Winfrey, Tennessee State University, journalist, actor, author, first black woman to own her own television and film production company

Dorothy C. Yancey, Johnson C. Smith University (N.C.), educator, first female president of Johnson C. Smith University, first black to be tenured as a full professor at Georgia Tech, first woman to be president of the Central Intercollegiate Athletic Association

Andrew Young, Howard University (D.C.), civil rights activist, mayor of Atlanta, Georgia; U.S. ambassador to the United Nations

Mary Cummings-Young, Savannah State University (Ga.), lawyer, politician, state representative to the Georgia House of General Assembly

---

* as of June 2002

⋆⋆ Glossary

Access—The availability of needed and desired services and resources without prejudice.

Accreditation—The process used to determine if specified educational standards are met and the nature of educational programs that can be offered by education institutions.

Affirmative action—The programs and policies that are designed to redress past discrimination and prevent current discrimination based on race, color, religion, gender, or national origin.

African American—People of African decent who are born in the United States and who have ancestral lineage in the United States system of slavery. Also refers to people of African descent who live in the United States and its territories.

Afrocentric curriculum—Subject matter covered in a class or course of study that is grounded in the history, experiences, traditions, contributions, and thought of people of African descent.

Appropriations—Funds designated by the federal or state governments to be used by specific institutions.

Black—*See* African American. For the purposes of this book, the terms are used interchangeably.

Culture—The shared perceptions, experiences, beliefs, knowledge, values, norms, and social forms of a group of people.

Curriculum—A course of study for a grade level or discipline.

De facto segregation—Separation of people by race through practices and traditions without the support of laws.

De jure segregation—Separation of people by race that is sanctioned by laws.

Desegregation—The plans and processes developed and implemented to eliminate racial separation in education, housing, or public facilities.

Discrimination—The practices and traditions of an organization or society that unequally or unfairly limit the opportunities and participation of an individual or group.

Distance education—Instruction where the majority of instruction occurs when the learner and instructor are not in the same place and are often separated by time. Instructional methods can include computers and other types of dissemination of information.

Dominant group—People of a racial or ethnic group in a society whose knowledge, beliefs, art, and customs, to name a few, govern the structure of a culture.

Dominated group—People of a racial or ethnic group in a society whose knowledge, beliefs, art, and customs, to name a few, are considered a subculture secondary to the dominant group's culture.

Endowment—Institutional funds owned and invested by education institutions to support school operations.

Eurocentric curriculum—Subject matter covered in a class or course of study that is grounded in the history, experiences, traditions, contributions, and thought of people of European descent.

Financial need—The cost of attending a school less the anticipated financial contributions of the family.

Free Blacks—People of African ancestry in the United States who were not born into slavery prior to 1865.

Freed Blacks—People of African ancestry in the United States who were born into slavery.

Governance—Federal and state governmental authorities as well as institutional bodies that establish the policies, procedures, and guidelines for the operations of postsecondary institutions.

Higher education—Education beyond high school.

Historically black colleges and universities (HBCUs)—Postsecondary institutions established specifically to educate African Americans.

Historically white colleges and universities—Postsecondary institutions established specifically to educate Americans of European descent.

Institutional climate—An intangible sense of human interactions in the school.

Institutional culture—The behaviors, values, and assumptions that people make about each other and their roles in the school.

Institutional environment—The internal and external forces, practices, and procedures in which education occurs.

Land-grant institutions—Land given by the federal government through the Morrill Acts of 1862 and 1890 for the purpose of state agricultural or mechanical colleges.

Liberal arts—Academic fields of study that include the humanities, sciences, and social studies. Liberal arts are distinct from technical and professional education.

Minority—People of racial and ethnic groups that are not of European descent. They are part of the dominated group.

Multicultural curriculum—The focus of subject matter covered in a class or course of study that is grounded in the history, experiences, traditions, thoughts, and contributions of all racial and ethnic groups present.

Pell Grant—A federal grant that provides funds to students based on financial need.

People of color—*See* Minority.

Quality in education—Standards used to determine that the highest levels of instructional staff, instructional resources, and achievement are acquired and attained.

Racism——The power of one racial group to exclude individuals or other racial groups from societal rights. Exercise of the power is based solely on race.

Regional accreditation—Approval by one of the six regional accrediting agencies that education institutions have met predetermined standards. These agencies are the closest entity in the United States to national quality control of education. They appraise the quality of education offered at the elementary, secondary, and postsecondary levels. The six agencies are recognized by the U.S. Department of Education.

Two-year colleges—Community and junior college education that usually culminates in an associate's degree.

Segregation—Separation of people based on race.

Slaves—People of African ancestry who were considered property of whites. They were denied the tenets of life, liberty, and the pursuit of happiness as stated in the U.S. Constitution. They were prohibited, the majority of time by state law, an education.

Title IV Loans—Program established through the Higher Education Act of 1965 that developed student loan programs called the Federal Family Education Loan Program (FFELP).

Transcript—An official education institution document of a student's academic program and performance.

Western curriculum—*See* Eurocentric curriculum.

Whites—People of European descent.

Index

❦ About the Authors

Cynthia L. Jackson is a faculty member at the Union Institute in Cincinnati, OH. She is the author of ABC-CLIO's *African American Education*.

Eleanor F. Nunn is director of the Historically Minority Universities Biotechnology Center at the North Carolina Biotechnology Center in Research Triangle Park, NC.